Strategy + Structure = Performance

STRATEGY + STRUCTURE = PERFORMANCE

The Strategic Planning Imperative

Edited by

HANS B. THORELLI

E. W. Kelley Professor of Business Administration

 INDIANA UNIVERSITY PRESS
Bloomington & London

Published in Canada by Fitzhenry & Whiteside Limited, Don Mills, Ontario

Manufactured in the United States of America

Library of Congress Cataloging in Publication Data

Main entry under title:
Strategy + structure = performance.
    Essays and comments from a conference arranged
under the auspices of the Graduate School of
Business of Indiana University in Nov. 1975.
    Bibliography
    Includes index.
    1. Corporate planning—Congresses. 2. Indus-
trial management—Congresses. I. Thorelli, Hans
Birger, 1921–   II. Indiana. University.
Graduate School of Business.
HD30.28.S74 1977   658.4'01   76-26413
ISBN 0-253-35495-1   1 2 3 4 5 81 80 79 78 77

CONTENTS

Foreword

E. W. KELLEY

The key challenge of managers is to achieve a match between the capabilities of their organizations and the opportunities of the marketplace. This is basic to optimal attainment of objectives. The crucial factor in this perennial game of wits is strategy.

These ideas are not new. Thus it is all the more surprising that so little is known about which strategy will generate the desired performance under which structural conditions. One gets the impression that "a lot more has been written about this subject than is known about it." Entrepreneurs and executives typically have been too busy with practical problems to take the time to draw useful generalizations from their own experience.

The urgency of the subject and the conviction that a coalescence of disparate efforts is a prerequisite to new insight stimulated the conference on Structure-Strategy-Performance relationships reported in this volume. The conference was arranged by the E. W. Kelley Chair under the auspices of the Graduate School of Business of Indiana University in November 1975. It was clear from the outset that representatives of such classic subjects as economics and the sociology of organizations should be participants.

It was equally natural to turn to the business disciplines of marketing, accounting, and finance. The market is "where the action is"—whether we are concerned with business or nonprofit organizations. Accounting is needed in order to build the kinds of information systems required for a better understanding of structure-strategy-performance relations. Conventional financial data do not of themselves say very much about the likely future of a company. However, when related to strategy and structure, financial management will acquire a new dimension, as suggested by the pioneering empirical research effort named Profit Impact of Market Strategies (PIMS). The PIMS project also indicates that progress in this area depends on a more intimate and continuous dialogue between business and academia than there has been in the past. The select group of executives attending the conference contributed markedly to the discussions.

The resulting collection of essays on a common, albeit wide-ranging, theme is directed to practicing managers and students of business alike.

Twelve of the fourteen essays plus the comments of a handful of especially invited discussants are published here for the first time. Professor Hans B. Thorelli, initiator and general chairman of the conference, joins me in a profound note of thanks to all those contributors who made this a successful venture. Special thanks are due to Professors Louis F. Biagioni, Irvin M. Grossack, David D. Martin, and Donald L. Tuttle of Indiana University, who chaired individual sessions.

E. W. KELLEY
President and Chief Executive Officer
Fairmont Foods Company

PART ONE

Overview

1

Introduction of a Theme

HANS B. THORELLI

Purpose of This Book

Strategy + Structure = Performance. Whatever we want from that bundle of resources that constitutes a business, its performance is essentially a derivative of the interaction between it and the environment in which it operates. This proposition constitutes the theme of this book.[1]

A prime purpose of this book, and the conference on which it reports, is to take stock of our progress in developing a theory of corporate strategy and strategic planning with a closer reality fit than the classic theory of the firm, industrial organization theory, and classic organization and management theory. Another is to present empirical data of relevance in this context drawn from current and recent research and business experience. A third and equally important purpose is to bring together in one volume contributions from a variety of disciplines. The contributors found this a highly stimulating venture, and we hope that our work will encourage renewed effort. Several papers have been enriched by the comments of executives who attended the conference.

In this introduction an attempt will be made to synthesize a Strategy-Structure-Performance (SSP) paradigm from the Preston (chapter 2 of this volume) and Thorelli (1968, and chapter 14 of this volume) essays. This will be done with a broad brush; for flavor and detail and, sometimes, for a difference in slant, the reader is referred to the originals. We shall then make clear how individual contributions relate to the SSP paradigm; in the process we shall point out some areas in special need of further re-

3

search and development. Finally, we shall comment briefly on the significance of each chapter from the viewpoint of the central theme.

First it is necessary to clear at least a temporary path through the conceptual jungle around our subject.

Strategy-Structure-Performance: Semantics

If industrial organization theory (a branch of economics) is the father of the SSP paradigm, organization and management theory is its mother. Marketing theory is another close relative. The conceptual apparatus developed by these disciplines are similar in some respects and different in others, making for semantic confusion. For instance, "structure" to the industrial organization or marketing theorist typically refers to the market or environment in which an industry (or company) operates, while "structure" in organization and management language generally means hierarchical arrangements, resource mix, and other characteristics of individual organizations. Thus, in part the confusion is rooted in the fact that economists have been mainly concerned with factors external to the individual organization, while organization theorists have focused on matters internal to it. (Marketing has made modest attempts to bridge the gap.) In part the conceptual derangement appears to result from a striking difference in the unit of analysis: industrial organization economists have more often dealt with entire industries than with single firms, while both organization and marketing theorists have in the past tended to concentrate on individual firms (organizations) or even their subunits.

We make no pretense of bringing total clarity. However, since this book is interdisciplinary and also directed to managers, it does seem desirable to define some key notions at least operationally. This will facilitate the presentation of our paradigm and, more importantly, help establish the context of individual contributions to follow. A few concepts will be further developed and reinterpreted in various essays.

MISSION, SCOPE, OBJECTIVES, AND PERFORMANCE

Some of these terms may not figure in a simplistic representation of the SSP paradigm. Yet it must be understood that they are an integral part of it. In our parlance, the mission of the firm comprises both its scope and its objectives.

The scope of a business is its extension along five critical dimensions: product (services) or "offer," clientele, territory, functions performed, and time. In effect, its scope defines the business.[2] For instance, "Jeans, Inc., founded in 1972, manufactures and distributes breeches for teenagers in the Middle West." These dimensions are critical in that they define *all* avenues of expansion (or contraction) of the firm. We note in passing that Ansoff's pioneer "growth vector" grid was confined to the two dimensions, product and clientele.[3] To be complete, it should have been five-dimensional.

The scope defines the business. The primary objectives of the business are those achievements (outputs) considered necessary or desirable to assure its sustained viability (the "ultimate" objective of most organizations), or to meet its moral obligations to stakeholders. These overall objectives form the cluster of ends at the top of the ends-means hierarchy. One objective may well be to change the scope of the business. Perhaps the most pleasing definition of an objective is that it is an anticipated performance. Objectives may be couched in terms so broad—"we wish to satisfy consumers, stockholders, employees, and the community alike"—as to be meaningless as guides to action. At the other extreme they may be so narrowly defined as to hamstring the operation. Experience shows that objectives should be made fairly specific if they are to serve in a planning and evaluation context.

In the final analysis, objectives express a set of values; objectives are subjective. A set of objectives can be at least semiobjectively evaluated in terms of such characteristics as ambition, specificity, consistency, realizability, and even creativity.

Although they may be poorly articulated, objectives represent the preferences and intentions of management. Thus it is that while an objective is an anticipated performance, the latter term is broader than the former. There may be aspects of performance ("outcomes") never even contemplated by management, such as air pollution or the generation of unexploited patents.

STRUCTURE

Because of the mixed, interdisciplinary parentage of ssp, we are obliged to use the term *structure* in two widely different senses, i.e., the structure of the organization (henceforth: O-structure) and the structure of the environment in which it operates (E-structure). Since the relationships between the organization and its environment are the subject of ssp analysis, it is imperative that these two structures be distinguished. Starbuck has brilliantly demonstrated that in any given case the boundary between the two may be far from obvious.[4] To the extent that the environment is analyzed essentially in terms of the perceptions of organization executives it may even be viewed as a somewhat arbitrary artifact.[5]

Nonetheless, some important generalizations can be made. O-structure variables frequently dealt with by organization theorists include leadership (skill, style), size (employees, sales, etc.), and such aspects of organization design as departmentalization and degree of centralization. Some theorists have added the technology employed (unit, batch, continuous flow) and functions performed.[6] It may well be that one should also include all elements of capability of the organization. Certainly the

mix of fixed and liquid assets is a key determinant of flexibility and strategic discretion. The degrees of diversification and vertical integration may
also belong here. The specific variables to be included in any given study
(or executive decision) will depend on the purpose at hand. Summarizing,
we may say that O-structure is the configuration of design and resources of
the organization.

The E-structure may fruitfully be viewed as a collage of interrelated
supplier and buyer *markets*. Conventionally, these would include the
capital, labor, vendor, and customer markets. It hardly needs saying that
the most important of these is the customer market (no sale, no organization). Beyond these markets are the general social, economic, political,
legal, and cultural factors that constitute the framework around organized
activity. Adopting Preston's happy adjective we may label this the societal
market. Quite a few—though far from all—of the numerous issues of social responsibility now so widely discussed are emerging in this area. In
each market the nature of the product(s) or service(s) as the object of
transactions, and the number, size distribution, geographical dispersion,
and values of buyers, sellers, distributors, competitors and regulators constitute perhaps the most salient features of structure.[7]

Implicit in the concept of structure (both O and E) is the assumption of
some degree of permanence, that is, stability over a period of time, however limited.

STRATEGY

In principle, strategy is the primary means of reaching the focal objective. The focal objective is whatever objective is in mind at the moment.
Strictly speaking, it is literally meaningless to talk about strategy without
having an objective in mind.[8] Viewed in this context, strategy becomes an
integral part of the ends-means hierarchy. While the president may have a
strategy of mergers, the typist has one for filing correspondence efficiently.
(Because of the difference in perspective, the typist's strategy would be
regarded by the president as a matter of tactics, at most.) The organization
will have a strategy in all relevant markets—e.g., financial, labor relations,
and sourcing (supply) strategies. Most important will be the one in
the customer market, i.e., its "marketing strategy." In this volume, when
the term is not qualified, strategy will refer to the customer market or
"industry" in which a business is active.

Common to the markets in the E-structure is that to survive the business
organization must engage in *transactions* in all of them. The strategy of
generating transactions suitable to fulfilling business objectives becomes
critical in each market. What are the elements of strategies aimed at generating transactions? Though the problem is common to several functions
and disciplines, it would appear that it has been most clearly recognized

from an SSP point of view by the practitioners and theorists of marketing. The textbooks list these strategic variables: the offer (product, service), price, promotion and intelligence (communications), distribution, and after-sales service. To these "universal" market strategy variables we have added trust (Thorelli in chapter 14 of this volume) and now wish to add politics. "Politics" in this connotation means the use of influence other than that flowing directly from the inherent merits of the offer (including price). Such influence may be based on friendship, "clout," or bargaining power stemming from less than perfectly competitive conditions. Sometimes the exercise of such influence is considered undue (bribing foreign officials to obtain airplane sales, taking advantage of minors, etc.); frequently it is recognized as quite legitimate (in collective bargaining, for instance). Some expressions of the use of politics as conceived here are strikes and boycotts, exclusive-dealing contracts, tying arrangements, reciprocity, refusal to deal, and lobbying. A modest form of politicking is making a point of belonging to the same club as a potential transaction partner; another is playing golf with him. Less innocent, perhaps, is inviting him to serve on one's board. Trade associations, pressure groups, and cartels are all "political" instruments. In some cases politicking really involves no more than building a relationship of trust and credibility. Important to the understanding of buyer-seller (and, often, intercompetitor) relationships in many customer markets, politics is apparently an indispensable element in labor and financial markets and in most markets in which nonprofit organizations operate.

Strategy is planned or, at least, purposeful behavior. Strategy emerges from decision centers. (Nature has no strategy, Murphy's Law notwithstanding.) Though the environment as such has no strategy, customers, competitors, and distributors do. So may the government in any one or several of its roles as buyer, seller, distributor, tax-collector, mediator, lawmaker, and law enforcer. But, to the extent that governmental measures apply uniformly to all in all markets, they are hardly to be viewed as strategies: such measures are like the weather or other aspects of nature from the vantage point of the individual business. Similarly, the business has to adjust to such developments as an aging population, women's liberation, the energy crisis. These may be viewed as *stimuli* calling for some sort of response—but they are not strategies. However, the response may well be an "energy conservation strategy," an "affirmative action strategy," and so on.

Similarly, the business organization itself is not confined to giving off strategic stimuli. Because of unintended malfunction at the plant level, a batch of deficient products may hit the market. The use of routine contracts forms with standard conditions of sale may be an unexamined, routine practice rather than an element of strategy. Surely polluting air or water is not done deliberately to provoke the ire of the environment. Again, decision centers in the environment may react to these inadvertent stimuli with strategic response.

We find that an *interaction* process takes place between the business organization and its environment. Strategy encompasses crucial elements in this process. However, important parts of the interaction are represented by response (strategic or otherwise) to nonstrategic stimuli.

The fact that we are dealing with an interaction process was largely ignored by the classic school of industrial organization of Edward S. Mason and his followers. The tremendous contribution of that school was its insistence that differences in market (industry) structure are associated with differences in performance via the mechanism of *conduct*. But Mason tacitly postulated a one-way causality from structure to performance. With such an assumption, conduct could easily become mere conduit. Mason would surely not subscribe to this interpretation; indeed, like Thurman Arnold and Corwin D. Edwards, he stressed the fact that under imperfect competition the firm has a range of discretion, a choice of strategies. Nevertheless, conduct was in an uncomfortable in-between position, which may help explain its relative underdevelopment in the writings of the school.

We prefer the term *strategy* to *conduct,* as the focus of strategy unmistakably is planned or, at least, purposeful interaction. Strategy is also a widely used term in recent organization, business policy, and marketing literature, which now seems to be contributing as much to the field as industrial organization economics. It is true, however, that strategy is associated with individual firms or decision centers. Thus, Preston's suggestion that the term *conduct* be reserved for behavior at the industry level seems eminently sensible. Some papers in this volume (e.g., Arndt, Bucklin) are indeed using the concept in this sense.

Strategy-Structure-Performance: Dynamics

BUSINESS AS A GAME

As an introduction to the SSP paradigm it may be instructive to look upon business (or management in general) as a game. There is nothing farfetched about this; it is no accident that strategy simulation exercises are called business games, war games, urban planning games, and so on. If we use a ball game as our metaphor, the organization is the home team; the court, the rules, the visiting team, etc., make up the environment; and the score, number of fouls and free-throws, and so on, are performance. The play would correspond to the general interaction between organization and environment, and the stance and ploys of the home team to the part of total interaction we label strategy. One might contend that the court and rules stay relatively constant in a ball game, while the E-structure of a business is constantly changing. Although there may be a difference in degree here, it is not one in kind. There are subtle yet important differences in courts; referees may differ in their interpretations of rules; the quality and strategies of adversary teams vary, as do weather conditions and audience reactions. On the other hand, even in the E-structure of business, some things tend to be fairly permanent, such as the laws of contract or the availability of advertising media.

From the viewpoint of the individual business Structure is the House of Parameters,[9] while Strategy is the House of Variables. The E-structure, of course, tends to present the business with more "givens" than does the O-structure, which, at least in principle, may be changed by managerial fiat. Yet any business—no matter how small—is able to "reset" *some* parameters in the E-structure by means of strategic action. Generally speaking, however, strategy is more likely to be a derivative of the E-structure than vice versa. Naturally, managerial philosophy and the resources of the business (O-structure) also play (or should play) a major role in shaping strategy—again as in the game situation.

Another suitable analogy is that with biological ecosystems (Thorelli in chapter 14 of this volume, see also in chapter 2 Preston's term *interpenetrating systems*). The focus here is on the adaptation of an organism (or population) to its habitat, although even biology increasingly deals with two-way impact. As ecology tends to become synonymous simply with "environmental interaction," it is felt that the term *ecosystem* is highly appropriate to depict the dynamics of strategy-structure-performance relations.

THE SSP ECOSYSTEM

The paradigm of SSP is illustrated in figure 1–1. Its makeup should offer no surprise. Similar diagrams are presented in chapter 2 (Preston) and chapter 14 (Thorelli). The paradigm is intended to reflect continuous relationships. The strategy variables identified are those believed relevant to the factor and customer markets of a going concern. We are assuming that the entrepreneurial decisions on scope of the business have already been made, *because they largely define the relevant environment*. No claim is made that the paradigm is pertinent to such cataclysmic events as large-scale mergers, recapitalization, or wholesale transformation of a business from one mission to another.

A convenient starting-point for examining the diagram is performance. Following Preston we distinguish between performance of the organization (O-performance) and of the environment (E-performance). A major part of O-performance and at least some part of E-performance is the result of strategic interaction between O-structure and E-structure. (If the focal organization is small, E-performance may not be affected greatly.)

Performance may in turn feed back into strategy changes via revised objectives. Changes in O-structure may also change O-performance, e.g., a productivity increase due to internal cost reductions. On the other hand, changes in E-structure will generally affect O-performance only through interaction between the O and E structures. Similarly, the effect of changes in O-structure on E-performance would tend to be indirect.

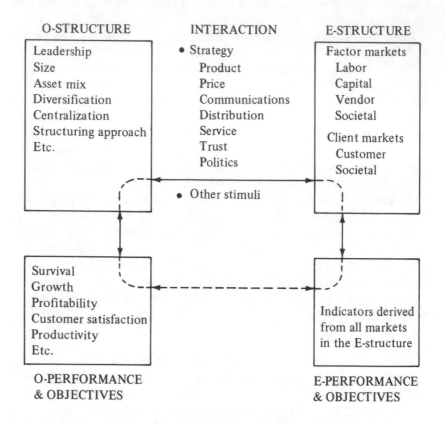

O-STRUCTURE	INTERACTION	E-STRUCTURE
Leadership	• Strategy	Factor markets
Size	Product	Labor
Asset mix	Price	Capital
Diversification	Communications	Vendor
Centralization	Distribution	Societal
Structuring approach	Service	
Etc.	Trust	Client markets
	Politics	Customer
		Societal
	• Other stimuli	

O-PERFORMANCE & OBJECTIVES	E-PERFORMANCE & OBJECTIVES
Survival	
Growth	
Profitability	
Customer satisfaction	Indicators derived
Productivity	from all markets
Etc.	in the E-structure

Note: The societal market typically has both factor and client aspects.

Figure 1–1
Structure-Strategy-Performance Ecosystem

Performance may also affect structure and strategy. This is most evident in the performance audit that constitutes an integral part of strategic planning. It is also illustrated by the fact that, depending on the purpose at hand, a given indicator may be associated with either structure or performance. Sales volume and market share are frequently taken as performance measures. Clearly, they may also serve as indicators of absolute and relative organization size. It may be that such measures should be regarded mainly as indicators of size, while in the performance context attention would more often focus on *change* in their magnitude during a given time period.

The figure also suggests interaction between O- and E-performance. Because the organization is itself a part of its environment, O-performance is indeed part of E-performance (as is O-structure of E-structure). Conversely, if E-performance in the shape of gross national product is increasing rapidly, chances are that O-performance is also improving. Many a company forecast has been built on this easy assumption. One may doubt, however, that such a result stems from direct "interaction" between the two types of performance. It would seem more natural to trace such relationships through the structure-strategy interaction mechanism. Certainly, this is the only way of establishing the underlying causal forces.

Perhaps it should be emphasized that there are varying degrees of interaction between the variables *inside* each set suggested in the paradigm. This is especially significant in the E-structure set. Not only does one customer or supplier market interact with the next, one labor market with another (e.g., steel and auto workers), and so on, but also, especially important from a strategic planning viewpoint, there is a fair amount of interaction between customer, capital, labor, supplier, and societal markets. The last part of chapter 2 discusses interaction between the societal and customer markets.

LEVELS OF ANALYSIS

Preston, Pennings, and Bass et al. (as well as the Scherer comment) stress the importance of levels of analysis and aggregation. They remind us that the ssp paradigm must be modular. The focus in the O-structure may be on the corporation or, because organizations are like Chinese boxes, the focus may also be on the individual businesses within the corporation. We may choose to examine the trade organization or industry of which the corporation is a member, or even a nation struggling in the world arena. Or, we may study an entire vertical system from manufacturer to consumer, as Bucklin and McCammon have done. Interorganizational relations of the type discussed by Pennings may be incorporated by adding one or more O-structures (and attendant strategies and performances). As one organization always constitutes a more or less relevant part of the environment of the other, one might also substitute another O-structure for the E-structure in cases where the mutual interactions of organizations seem more important than their interrelations with the environment.

It is not possible to examine all things at the same time, however desirable this might be. Yet rigid confinement to one level (unit) of analysis may artificially exclude from the view important interrelations between levels (units). To engage in strategic planning for the Chevrolet Division without reference to General Motors as a whole or to the Pontiac Division would indeed be hazardous. Similarly, if a trade association has established standard package sizes, an individual member organization can no longer vary its package sizes as an element of its strategy. In effect, the trade association constitutes an important part of the E-structure of that organization.

It is clear that to each O-level corresponds a specific E-level (or "slice" of the environment). It is also helpful to note that each O-level tends to have an "opposite number" in the hierarchy of ends and means. Thus, what constitutes strategy (means) to the marketing vice-president—such as the launching of a promotional campaign—would typically be in the realm of objectives (ends) from the viewpoint of his manager of advertising.

RELEVANCE

A legitimate criticism of the SSP paradigm is its very generality. It seems to suggest that everything relates to everything else. What then is the criterion of relevance? We submit that it is defined in any given case by the purpose at hand. The set of variables relevant to strategic planning is apt to differ from that needed for an analysis of productivity, which, in turn, would be different from the set used in a study of how varying degrees of environmental volatility affect organizational design. In each case, the paradigm facilitates the search for the relevant set. In due time, academic research and management experience will establish a growing body of empirical regularities in various areas of the paradigm, enabling us to derive normative rules for strategic planning in business (and other) organizations as well as sensible approaches to public regulation. The essays in this collection are grappling with the issues of relevance. In several of them fascinating relationships between SSP variables are demonstrated or indicated.

This collection is based on the notion that the several contributions not only represent a fair sample of current SSP research but also improve our understanding of it. To this end, *the scope of the subject matter is confined to business organizations, marketing strategies, market (industry) structures, and to economic performance.* The rationale is simple: there is every reason to believe that in no other context will SSP relationships manifest themselves more clearly than in open markets.

Goodness of Fit of Contributors

The diversified portfolio of contributors to this volume was not selected at random. They are, of course, well known in their fields of expertise. Their work is often synergetic; in many cases the essays directly supplement or reinforce each other, e.g., the Buzzell-Farris, Cox, and Schoeffler essays on strategy-performance relationships at the firm level; and the Arndt, Bucklin, and McCammon-Bates essays on determinants of performance at various levels in distribution systems. Other essays provide new insights by critical evaluation of conventional wisdom, e.g., the Bass et al. reexamination of the use of concentration ratios and advertising/sales ratios in industrial organization studies and Pennings's review of major aspects of environmental organization theory and research. Ansoff is pushing his pioneering work on strategic planning a big step further, while Starbuck-Hedberg and Patterson account for major case studies at the firm and industry levels. Preston effectively reminds us that beyond the economic concerns on which the other papers are deliberately focused are equally important societal ones, still awaiting analyses of equal incisiveness. Most significant from the vantage point of this work as a whole is the fit of the contributions with the ssP paradigm—and, indeed, vice versa.

The mesh of essays and paradigm may be demonstrated most effectively by diagram (see figure 1–2). The principal elements of the ssP paradigm occur as independent ("input") variables along the rows and as dependent ("output") variables at the head of the columns. As there are varying degrees of mutual interaction between dependent and independent variables at all times, the reader is cautioned against the oversimplification attendant to any diagram of this kind. In the studies represented in this volume, the variables viewed as primarily dependent all relate to the focal organization (at firm or, occasionally, industry levels). The structural variables viewed as primarily independent in these studies all pertain to a broader environment (the industry or the societal, or both). Strategy and performance as independent variables in the Ansoff and Starbuck-Hedberg essays essentially pertain to the focal organization.

The most pungent observation we offer about figure 1–2 is that all bases of the ssP paradigm are in some measure covered by our contributors as far as dependent variables at the firm and industry levels are concerned. That is, all cells in the upper right-hand half of the matrix are represented by at least one essay. In this sense the collection is both diverse and comprehensive. The figure serves to place the contributions in relation to one another as well as to the paradigm itself. (Deliberately, authors have not been invited to comment on their classification.)

Several essays summarize or evaluate the state of the art in various parts of the field, notably those by Preston; Bass, Cattin, and Wittink; and Pennings. A majority of them are empirical studies (Buzzell-Farris; McCammon-Bates; Schoeffler) or based on government data (Arndt, Bucklin). Studies of industry are well represented (Bass et al., Buzzell-Farris, Cox, Schoeffler, Starbuck-Hedberg) and we were fortunate in obtaining several studies of distribution (Arndt, Bucklin, McCammon-Bates). Patterson examines the gasoline business from well to consumer, while Pennings has investigated brokerage services.

| | STRUCTURE | | | STRATEGY OF FIRM | PERFORMANCE | |
	SOCIETAL	INDUSTRY	FIRM		FIRM	INDUSTRY
SOCIETAL		(Pennings)	(Bucklin)	Ansoff (Patterson)	(Patterson)	Bucklin
INDUSTRY			Pennings	Cox Patterson (Schoeffler)	Bass (Cox) (Schoeffler)	Arndt
FIRM				(Schoeffler)	(Buzzell)	(Bucklin)
STRATEGY OF FIRM			Ansoff		Buzzell Cox McCammon Schoeffler	(Bass)
PERFORMANCE OF FIRM			Starbuck			

(Left axis label: **STRUCTURE** spanning SOCIETAL, INDUSTRY, FIRM rows)

NOTE: Parentheses indicate what seemed to be a secondary focus of a contributor. Strategy and performance refers to the focal organization (firm) except in the last column.

Figure 1–2
The Contributors and the SSP Paradigm

INDEPENDENT
VARIABLES

Methodologically, the contributions show a great variety, from case studies of firms or industries (Starbuck-Hedberg, Patterson) to large-scale statistical surveys such as the PIMS project reported by Schoeffler and Buzzell-Farris. After all, the field is just opening. We need to search for theory, for salient variables and measures. We need case studies catching the holistic flavor and effect of entire market strategies as much as—or perhaps more than—studies of price or advertising or any other isolated subelement of strategy. We need to learn to derive the advantages of combining research methods without simply incurring the disadvantages of each.[10]

Action, reaction, and interaction of organizations is largely what the SSP paradigm is about. Although most contributions are essentially analytical in character, it is only natural that they should have normative overtones (Cox, Buzzell-Farris, McCammon-Bates, Schoeffler, Starbuck-Hedberg). Ansoff's essay is deliberately normative, being a guide to strategic planning in response to weak signals from the environment. But then we know—or think we know—a good deal more about the process of strategy formation than about its content.

Outline of Book

There are several ways in which the book might be organized in terms of coherent clusters of essays. We have chosen to focus on a set of groupings derived in a natural way from the SSP paradigm. The parts of the book are:

Part I   Overview
Part II   The Corporation in Strategic Interaction
Part III Industry Structure, Strategy, and Performance
Part IV   Organization and Interorganization Structure, Strategy, and Performance

After the introductory overview of the SSP area, Part II focuses on strategic interaction at the level of the corporation or its separate businesses. The interest here is on strategic, environmental, and performance variables. Part III is primarily concerned with SSP at the industry level, although the essays also include some micro elements. The contributions in the last part, though more disparate, have in common their greater emphasis on organization structure variables.

The first part gives an overview of the SSP field and consists of this introduction and the Preston essay. In introducing the theme of the book we have drawn extensively on Preston's ideas, which have been indispensable; however, Lee Preston is in no way personally responsible for the form this introduction has taken.

Preston (chapter 2). Lee Preston clearly feels that the strategy-structure-performance area needs some structure—and he sets out to provide it. In the process of developing his framework for organization-environment analysis he makes a fascinating tour of the hinterland. He sees the "contingency approach" of recent fashion in organization theory as essentially an environmentalist approach combining organizational action with environmental attributes (and, sometimes, processes) to yield organizational performance. Largely missing, however, is *interaction* between organizational and environmental forces. In his survey of legal-social-political literature Preston rightly points out that only a few works treat the development of legislation and law enforcement as a societal strategy. To the treatises cited this writer will immodestly add his own on the origins of the federal antitrust policy of the United States, a piece of research based on the notion that law does not originate in a vacuum but is essentially a derivative of the societal structure in which it operates, and as such requires an integrated social science treatment.[11]

Many will find Preston's particular distinctions between units of analysis and variables of great value. Organization and environment are seen as units of analysis; strategy, structure, and performance as variables. This differentiation is a useful one. It does, for instance, point up that strategy and performance (and not merely structure) may be features of the environment. However, one might ask if on occasion strategy itself might not be the unit of analysis. (E.g., under what environmental and/or organizational circumstances would one expect Strategy X to be a typical one?) An analogous case might be made for performance at the societal, market, or organization levels as constituting a plausible unit of analysis. While undoubtedly of didactic value, the distinction between units of analysis and variables may partly be one of semantics.

Part II deals with the corporation in strategic interaction. It comprises the contributions by Ansoff, Cox, Schoeffler, Buzzell-Farris, and McCammon-Bates.

Ansoff (3). Strategic planning—the process of strategy formation— is the subject of Igor Ansoff's essay. We were fortunate in securing this contribution in that Ansoff more than other writers successfully combines the analysis of planning with that of its object, that is, strategy itself. In this paper he develops a planning approach designed to improve the firm's responsiveness to strategic discontinuities and to help it avoid surprises. The approach relies on the recognition and use of "weak signals"— early warning information about impending discontinuities. Citing recent examples of such discontinuities with shock-like impact on business, Ansoff predicts that such surprise events will become increasingly common in the next decade.

As a first step, he develops a taxonomy of states of ignorance—the degree of ignorance decreases progressively as a strategic discontinuity matures. The concern here is with identifying how much information the firm can reasonably expect to find in the early warning signals. The second step is to define "weak" and "strong" responses feasible at different states of ignorance.

The dynamic interaction of threat and response is next explored to provide the concept of *graduated* strategic preparedness for planning and action. This is translated into a practical planning approach called Strategic Issue Analysis (SIA). Several examples are used to show that responses and initiatives in SIA are less precise and less focused than in conventional strategic planning. However, current strategic planning often assumes a more highly structured situation and a much higher degree of (perceived) informedness about likely futures than is really the case. By its flexibility, SIA gains the advantage of earlier and more effective response to fast-developing discontinuities.

At the conference Ansoff pointed out that a future of strategic discontinuities may call for much greater flexibility in organizational design, in effect an emphasis on "mobile warfare" rather than "Maginot Line" defenses. In fact, de novo redesign of organizations may well become fairly commonplace. We might add that the Strategic Business Units now evolving in such companies as General Electric and Union Carbide—in effect separating strategic from operational planning—in an era of environmental turbulence may well be more effective response mechanisms than the several component operating businesses served by each such unit.

Cox (4). This chapter makes use of both interesting concepts and empirical applications in the SSP area. A few illustrations are at the industry level. More important, several are at the firm level. We say "more important" because microeconomics has been rather short on empirical illustrations used with any degree of rigor. Several essays in Part II are helping to fill this void.

Cox suggests that there is a specific mathematical relationship between firm size, as measured by market share for specified time periods, and the firm's market share rank in an industry in which all important firms (i.e., those with significant market shares) are identified. He draws on unpublished research with Ernest F. Cooke to indicate the relevant "proportionality constants" in ten industries ranging from air transport to cigarettes, from beer to steel. The values of these constants may then be used to calculate an "equilibrium" distribution of market shares towards which each industry might be expected to move under certain assumptions.

One of the key findings of the PIMS project (Schoeffler) is the strong positive correlation between market share and profitability. An antitrust-oriented economist would say that this relationship is mainly due to the concentration of power (and/or ease of collusion) in markets under imperfect competition. No one could seriously doubt that this is a factor. Findings of both PIMS and the Boston Consulting Group (BCG)—with which Cox has had a working relationship—suggest, however, that we are dealing with something more than an issue of power, that the market share-profitability picture is indeed a complex one. The BCG "experience curve" analysis suggests, for instance, that total unit costs for a product will tend to decline by a fairly consistent percentage as output increases. Thus, the competitor with the largest accumulated output will tend to have the largest market share and the lowest unit cost. That there are economies of scale (and learning experience) within each management function has long been evident. However, we may not have made enough of the fact that as sales grow the firm may reach new plateaus of such economies in production, marketing, finance, and general management sequentially. Interfunctional synergy effects (e.g., as regards inventory/sales/production ratios) have not been given enough attention, nor has sufficient study been made of the role of basic management and entrepreneurial (innovative) skills in the growth and success of corporations.

Perhaps the most important part of Cox's essay is his analysis of product portfolio strategy in the breakfast cereal industry, singling out Kellogg and General Foods for special examination. He has successfully combined in-depth case study with statistical analysis at the aggregate industry level. Empirical examination of strategy—still a relative rarity—and its relationship to structure is the key in this analysis.

The formal discussant of this essay was Joseph C. Miller.

Schoeffler (5). The Profit Impact of Market Strategies (PIMS) program is the most significant development in the SSP area thus far. From the time of its inception at General Electric in the late fifties through its affiliation with the Marketing Science Institute to its current independent operation within the Strategic Planning Institute, the common denominator of the program has been its originator, Sidney Schoeffler. PIMS's major methodological premise is that to develop valid generalizations about structure, strategy, and performance it is crucial to access data at the individual business and market-structure levels. The project is focused not on the approximately 60 participating corporations but on the more than 600 businesses in which they are active. Hundreds of data are collected annually from each business on a longitudinal basis. As might be expected, data requirements go considerably beyond conventional accounting systems.

Thus far, data analysis has been essentially cross-sectional. As the accumulation of longitudinal data proceeds, an especially exciting prospect is large-scale and broad-gauge examination of empirical SSP patterns in the course of the product life cycle. Although Schoeffler, Buzzell, and other PIMS workers would emphasize that the analytical effort at this time has only just begun, a significant number of empirical regularities have already been established. Not unnaturally, the initial focus has been the explanation of variation in return on investment (ROI). In the aggregate, about 80 percent of the cross-sectional variances in observed ROI has been accounted for. It is to be hoped that participating companies will soon permit the publication of the basic equations. In the meantime, Schoeffler does present the relationships between several pairs and triads of variables. Although the total number of data points in the project is almost staggering, a listing of the subset of variables that have proven important in accounting for variations in ROI may be instructive. Presented here in the context of the SSP paradigm, they are listed in a somewhat different arrangement in the appendix to the Schoeffler essay.

E-Structure	*O-Structure*
market growth long-term	market share
market growth short-term	size of parent company
percent industry exports	diversification of parent
industry concentration ratio	vertical integration
customer concentration ratio	relative salary level
industrial vs consumer goods	value added/sales
	sales/employee
	relative salary level

Strategy	*Performance*
relative price	ROI
relative product quality	change in market share
marketing expense/sales	change in relative price
R & D cost/sales	change in product quality
new product introductions	change in capacity

The relationship between market share and profitability was commented on in the introduction of Cox's essay. It may be noted that PIMS also finds market share even more important in explaining ROI for industrial than for consumer-product businesses. One might hypothesize that bargaining power enters here. Greater market share in an industrial market would tend to generate a better bargaining position relative to customers. Individual customers (as opposed to consumers in general) are relatively "powerless" in consumer goods markets regardless of the seller's market share, and this "power slack" may often be reflected at intermediary stages of distribution (though this is far from being always the case). Schoeffler demonstrates that capital investment intensity—especially if the cost of capital is explicitly taken into consideration—tends to be an obstacle to sustained high rates of ROI. One is reminded of J. M. Clark's classic examination of the role of overhead costs, now supplemented with substantial empirical experience.

In commenting on the PIMS project we are "accentuating the positive." Naturally any large-scale pioneering effort will have its weaknesses. Some of these are mentioned by the authors and others will surely be discussed at length in the academic and business communities as the project unfolds. It is regrettable that in the interest of discretion reporting businesses are asked to classify their markets as merely industry or consumer goods rather than by the five-digit SIC code, and that in some sensitive areas data may be masked by multiplication by some constant. PIMS's data base might also be improved by the incorporation of organizational design variables—a group of SSP variables now almost excluded from representation. In fine, PIMS merits an encore for the continuing dialog between executives and academics it has stimulated and for its capacity to combine basic and applied research. In the latter area normative conclusions can be drawn by any business. More than that, thanks to the systematic feedback of different forecasts of future performance based on their past PIMS data and varying assumptions about the future environment and changes in company policies, subscribing concerns have at their disposal a top management information system literally akin to a Strategic Laboratory.

Buzzell and Farris (6). Also relying on PIMS data, Robert Buzzell and Paul Farris contribute a pioneer analysis of variables associated with marketing cost as a percentage of sales at the micro level, that is, for individual product categories of consumer goods companies. Most of the independent variables pertain to E-structure, such as customer and product characteristics, stage in product life cycle, and the combined market share of the three largest competitors. O-structure variables include trading margin and capacity utilization. Marketing costs—and their distribution over marketing subfunctions—may be viewed as an embodiment of strategy.

No less than 75 percent of the variations in marketing cost/sales ratios can be explained by multiple regression analysis. Several relationships turn out to be more complex than has been conventionally understood, notably those involving the role of product-specific characteristics in affecting marketing costs. The view that such costs as a percent of sales tend to decrease in the latter stages of the life cycle is affirmed (although it should be noted that the definition of marketing costs does not include costs of quality or style change and changes in the reseller discount structure). Regional marketers tend to have higher total marketing expenditures in relation to sales than do national marketers. Marketing costs of most kinds seem to be a lower proportion of sales for durable goods than for nondurables. The analysis suggests that a firm that has pioneered in a market can maintain a strong market position and still spend less on marketing relative to sales than its competition.

The interrelations between marketing costs/sales as well as some subsets thereof with return on investment and return on sales were also examined. The correlation coefficients between marketing costs/sales, sales force expenditure/sales and advertising plus promotion/sales on one hand and the two performance measures on the other are all zero or negative.

Of marketing costs isolated in the study only advertising media cost/sales showed a slight positive correlation with profitability. It will be remembered that these are micro-level findings. They need not necessarily contradict industry-level findings suggesting a stronger relationship between media advertising and profitability. They do, however, emphasize the dangers of drawing simplistic conclusions in this area. Chapter 8 of this volume (Bass et al.) raises further questions concerning past studies of advertising effects on profitability.

In general, the Buzzell-Farris essay demonstrates how little we still really know about marketing efficiency and effectiveness. There is indeed a challenge here for accounting, finance, and marketing experts in business and academia to join hands in the effort to increase our understanding of marketing performance. No doubt future analyses based on the PIMS project will also become more refined. It would, for instance, be instructive to know the relationship between perceived product quality and the market cost-sales ratio.

McCammon and Bates (7). This essay is a pioneering presentation of strategic vs financial profiles in the area of distribution. The data base is groupings of multiple case studies. The work of Bert McCammon and Albert Bates does show that conventional financial statements may be useful in analyzing the structure-strategy relationship, an idea about which others have had strong reservations. Although the study includes only successful firms, it does appear to demonstrate the importance of a strategy of "nichemanship" in distribution.

In retailing the McCammon-Bates data re-emphasize the importance of such classic relationships as sales per square foot of selling area and inventory turnover to return on assets. In recent years high-performance strategies in retailing include the adoption of supermarket retailing in such trades as furniture, home improvements, and sporting goods; store positioning for particular market segments (deluxe foods, electronics enthusiasts, the "under 35" market, etc.); and, perhaps most important, nonstore retailing in various forms (mail order, buying clubs, etc.). Specialization by product category also gained distinct headway as a successful retailing strategy, although Europeans will never cease to wonder about the low degree of specialization in the huge U.S. market.

In wholesaling there appears to have been a stronger trend towards somewhat polarized market niches based on strong product or clientele specialization on one hand and the single-source-of-supply-for-all-needs concept on the other. At the latter end of the spectrum some "total-capability" wholesalers were even basing their strategy on furnishing not only the requisite products but also any and all related services. A number of wholesalers integrated forwards towards consumer markets or backwards towards manufacturing. Though changes in the degree of integration at the wholesale level have long been with us, there were some distinctly novel developments, such as large-scale warehouse furniture retailing by wholesalers.

For each retail and wholesale success strategy identified by McCammon-Bates, case examples are given, including liquidity and growth potential ratios as well as the ratios of the now classic "strategic profit model" of distributive firms and compound annual sales and profit growth rates. Store positioning appears to have been an eminently successful retailer strategy in recent years. It seems difficult to go much further in generalizing about the different strategy-performance patterns of successful distributors owing to considerable intra-group variations (with two to five cases in each group) and some paucity of information as to the base points at which the dynamics reported originated. The reader is referred to the detailed appendix. We may note, however, that the study does lend support to the notion that a fair number of different strategies may be viable (or even successful) in any given general market environment at any given time. There may be a single optimum strategy for a given firm (although even this is a subject of controversy), but that particular strategy is certainly not going to be optimal for all the other firms in the market—if, indeed, for any of them.

Part III deals with structure, strategy, and performance at the industry level. It comprises the contributions by Bass-Cattin-Wittink, Patterson, Bucklin, and Arndt.

Bass, Cattin, and Wittink (8). "There is good reason to question the validity of conclusions that have been developed from a very large body of literature on industrial organization." This dramatic quote is from the essay by Frank Bass, P. J. Cattin, and D. R. Wittink. Relationships between profit performance and market structure variables like concentration or strategy variables such as advertising/sales (A/S) ratios are often sought through multiple regression analysis of data from a cross-section of firms. Indeed, most past FTC as well as academic research of profit-concentration relations have been done in this manner. But, ask Bass et al., are the findings valid and meaningful? Is it appropriate to pool data from a sample of firms from different industries in estimating the long-run relationships? As indicated by the quote, these authors do not think so.

The authors take us several steps further on the basis of time-series (1957, 1963, and 1970) as well as cross-sectional analysis of 63 corporations broadly classified into ten industries. In addition to profitability, variables brought into play include four-firm concentration ratio, firm market share, A/S ratios and diversification ratios. As in the Cox and PIMS papers, Bass and his colleagues found a positive and significant relationship between market share and profitability both in two subsets and in data pooled over all observations. Thus, this conclusion does not seem to depend on the data base or the level of aggregation. On the other hand, the findings about the influence of other variables—and notably the A/S ratio—do appear to depend critically on the data base and pooling scheme.

The formal discussant of this essay was F. M. Scherer.

Patterson (9). James Patterson studies the gasoline industry, using a wealth of SSP variables and moving deftly back and forth between macro and micro levels. We are presented with a blend of good old political economy, industrial organization, institutional economics, and marketing —if this cocktail can be imagined. More than any other contribution this essay illustrates Preston's point that in the end structure-strategy analysis cannot be isolated from public policy and societal issues. Patterson outlines the pivotal role of public regulatory measures in the gasoline industry all the way from the early days of the Standard Oil Trust through depletion allowances and prorationing to import controls, OPEC, supply allocation, and stand-by rationing schemes. Willard H. Burnap, vice-chairman and director of Continental Oil Company, as formal discussant of the paper predicts that in the future political forces, to an even greater extent than before, will be the most important determinants of industry and company structure and strategy.

Patterson makes clear the cardinal role of vertical integration in the SSP drama of the gasoline industry. To achieve (and maintain) vertical integration has been a key strategy of major oil companies since the days of John D. Rockefeller. The principal motivating factor seems to have been the resultant synergy of managerial discretion at all market levels from crude through transportation, refining, and bulk marketing to retailing. Thus, within fairly wide limits it became possible to shift the points at which profits were derived in the vertical system to the levels where competition was the least or where taxation, allocation, and other regulatory measures were most favorable. Naturally, once integration had been attained—and thus became a feature of company *structure*—it, in turn, became a powerful influence on later strategy. Patterson's analysis of past, present, and likely future strategies of the major oil companies in retail distribution is particularly instructive.

The formation of OPEC along with government price fixing and output regulation and, frequently, nationalization at the crude level has inevitably shifted the strategic planning focus of the majors towards diversification. The current trend to shift company organization from a regional to a functional structure would appear to be one strategic response to the changing environment.[12] The diversification impulse principally has been directed towards other forms of energy. In view of the energy crisis this may be a natural development from the perspective of the companies, even though there seem to be few dramatic synergy opportunities. Whether the possibly resulting concentration of economic power in the entire energy market is desirable from a public policy point of view is indeed debatable. If conglomeration there must be, Mobil's acquisition of a majority interest in MARCOR may be preferable from this vantage point to the vast purchases of coal and uranium reserves by some other majors.

Bucklin (10). SSP relationships in the distributive trades are the concern of Louis Bucklin and Johan Arndt. Their level of analysis is essentially the industry rather than the firm, as in the McCammon-Bates essay. Bucklin's main thrust is cross-sectional, while Arndt's is longitudinal. A principal component of performance in both essays is productivity, variously defined.

Bucklin finds that the economic and social environments in Japan and the United States engender substantial but different effects upon the productivity of retailing in the two countries. An especially interesting observation is that although Japan seemingly offers much greater opportunities for economies of scale in retail establishments than the United States (where most of these economies may already be exhausted), the extraordinary population density and urban congestion of the island nation may actually militate against the exploitation of such economies. Generally speaking, differences in the stage of economic development, consumer purchasing patterns, market growth, and rationalization of facilities by way of capital investment appear to be the most important determinants of retail productivity. Local market conditions and variations in managerial skill give evidence of swamping the impact of vertical control. The modest role indicated as regards the latter factor is somewhat surprising in view of the oft-touted merits of vertical control systems in distribution.[13]

Arndt (11). The dynamics of retailing in Norway is the focus of this essay. Johan Arndt assumes that market structure (as measured by the degree of concentration of retail establishments) via the different types of conduct (strategy) for concentrated vs nonconcentrated trades postulated by classic industrial organization theory will manifest itself in different performance patterns. Other things being equal, concentrated trades would be expected to have a higher percentage gross margin—the only profit measure available in census data—and lower labor productivity than unconcentrated trades. Over a period of time such conditions would be expected to result in a relative increase (decrease) of stores in the concentrated (unconcentrated) trades. Owing to the lack of guidelines in the international literature as well as shortcomings in census data, the criterion for a "concentrated" trade is defined in a manner as ingenious as it is artful and heroic.

It was found in line with the model that the average gross margin for the low-concentration trades was lower than for high-concentration groups. Similarly, while the number of retail stores has decreased generally in Norway as in other developed countries, the decline between the 1963 and the 1968 census of distribution was markedly greater for the low-concentration trades. In the area of productivity as measured by relative increase in sales per employee in 1963–68 the results are more ambiguous.

There was a marked increase in labor productivity in groceries (unconcentrated), presumably due to the supermarket revolution. Generally, however, labor productivity rose as fast in concentrated as in unconcentrated trades—or even somewhat faster.

Arndt's essay brings to the fore several methodological problems in macro studies of distribution. They are brought into sharp relief in the data on regulated trades, i.e., retail industries owned and/or tightly regulated by the government, notably liquor stores and pharmacies. Although this is a "concentrated" group, the stores had an even smaller gross margin than the unconcentrated stores in 1963. But this may be due to government control of margins or simply inefficient operation. Labor productivity increased fastest in the regulated trades between 1963 and 1968—but the waiting lines in the liquor stores remained. Similarly, in the pharmacies the emphasis shifted from preparing medicaments on the spot to dispensing factory-made preparations. In effect, customer service was not the same as for unregulated stores, and a major function was shifted to manufacturers during the period examined. These kinds of complications become especially relevant when one is trying to evaluate performance at any point in a vertical system from a total-system or societal perspective.

Part IV deals with organization and interorganization strategy, structure, and performance, with some emphasis on the role of O-structure variables. It comprises the contributions by Starbuck and Hedberg, Pennings, and Thorelli (1968).

Starbuck and Hedberg (12). In at least one major respect this essay compliments Ansoff's (chapter 3). Starbuck and Hedberg point out that very successful organizations tend to become "programmed" in their "success rut," and increasingly indifferent to signs of change—Ansoff's "weak signals"—in the environment. In effect, the more successful a business is, the more inertia it is apt to build up. Three recent classic examples quoted in the discussion are A & P in the United States, Volkswagen in Germany, and Facit AB in Sweden.

The principal problem attacked by Starbuck and Hedberg is this: how can a formerly highly successful organization that finds itself in a stagnating (or even declining) environment be saved? Clearly this topic will be one of increasing currency in an age emphasizing ZEG, ZPG and ZSG (zero sum games). Starbuck and Hedberg seem to base their research on three propositions: 1) the organization and its environment are intertwined, 2) the hitherto successful organization frequently will not face up to environmental stagnation when it sets in, and 3) the only effective means of emancipating such an organization may well be to replace its leadership. There is an element of Greek tragedy in the fact that often it is really the organization rather than its environment which is manifesting stagnation.

Starbuck and his Swedish colleague studied the Facit AB case intensively. In the mid-1960s this was still an eminently successful maker of hand-cranked and electric calculators and office furniture, active in all important export markets of the world. The company may have seen the electronic calculator revolution coming, but management was simply unable to face up to the implications. One reason an "inert" organization does not change is that it cannot accomplish the unlearning necessary for change. Clearly, there was no good reason to believe that strategies that worked in the old environment would work just as well in the new. Several managers were replaced and consulting firms turned the company inside out, but nothing helped. Ultimately Facit AB was sold to Electrolux, another Swedish concern. After drastic surgery and reorientation Facit has again become a viable organization as a subsidiary of Electrolux. The case would indeed seem to illustrate the initial propositions.

Stagnation may affect the organization precisely because it mistakenly perceives the environment as stagnating. In the last several years academics have been lamenting a seemingly stagnating environment surrounding the universities; yet, one may legitimately ask whether the stagnation is in the environment or in the universities themselves. Or, if in both, what are the universities doing to break the vicious circle? In his comment on this chapter Paul Gordon stresses that replacement of management in formerly successful organizations facing stagnating environments may be a necessary but not sufficient antidote. New management must also be capable of seeing the nature of environmental change and its strategic implications, and it must have the courage to reshape organizational structure and strategy in the face of inertia and vested interests.

Pennings (13). Like Starbuck and Hedberg, Johannes Pennings is concerned with O-structure correlates of E-structure characteristics. Within the O-structure he is more interested in organizational design than in the resource mix. He has an eye for performance as comprising a set of intermediary variables, but he is relatively unconcerned with strategy.

Pennings makes the important observation that most research in the contingency theory area has examined the organization-environment interface from the perspective of the focal organization; only rarely has inquiry moved to the next higher level of organization to examine how the environment as a *population* of organizations (competing or otherwise) affects its components. He suggests that the interaction mechanism comprising a single organization and its environment may not qualify as a system at all; for a contrary view the reader is referred to chapter 2 (Preston) and earlier parts of this chapter. He also suggests, as a special merit of studying organizations as members of populations of organizations, that systems at this higher level of aggregation may be seen as political economies, a view that presumably allows an ssp researcher to draw at once from organization theory, the theory of industrial organization, the theory of pluralism in political science, and so on. Elsewhere this writer has observed that an individual organization may indeed also be viewed as a political economy in microcosm.[14] This is in no way to deny the value of research at higher levels of aggregation.

After surveying a number of studies of the organizational correlates of environment, Pennings is led to the conclusion that there is fairly scant evidence that environmental factors exercise a strong influence on O-structure. Maybe the support is not overwhelming, although one may refer to such well-known studies as those of William R. Dill and Joan Woodward as positive evidence. More elementarily, we may observe that the post office in Chicago is bigger than that of Kokomo, as the former city is bigger than the latter. And surely it is not by accident that a number of multinational companies are organized geographically rather than by function or product. A number of similar, everyday examples are given in Thorelli (1968). Perhaps the problem is that Pennings expects too much at this early stage of organizational ecology; it may be that his own study of brokerage offices failed to yield any interesting organizational correlates of environment simply because the objectives, strategies, and activities of these offices were so standardized from the center that the differences between offices were too subtle to be caught in his net. It is also possible that local variations in O-structure were not amenable to the particular set of variables chosen by Pennings. In any case, his study does not exclude the obvious possibility that there may be significant differences in O-structure between a brokerage office and a community hospital in the same town—or even between a chain-store office of the type studied by Pennings and a locally owned brokerage office in the same community.

The preceding paragraphs in no way deny that Pennings has rendered a valuable contribution. His preliminary finding that on the focal organization level O-structure is a powerful predictor of performance and that on the industry/market level E-structure is a strong predictor of performance is an extremely important one. This ties in with Preston's plea that more attention be given to E-performance. Important, too, is Pennings's admonition that interorganizational research be given a more prominent place next to intraorganizational. Further, the fact that such an insightful observer would question the rather basic notion in SSP theory that different environments tend to have different O-structure correlates should serve as a call to researchers in the field to redouble their efforts.

Thorelli (1968) (14). With this essay we have in a sense come full circle, in that it is closely linked to Preston's as well as to the early parts of this introduction. It does develop a number of topics—such as the origination of organizational objectives—in greater detail than we have been able to do here. It also poses a number of specific hypotheses as to organizational correlates of different environments. In this respect the paper may be viewed as a reinforcement of the call for further research emanating from Johannes Pennings's essay.

NOTES AND REFERENCES

1. Individual contributors to the volume may or may not agree with this and other propositions in the introductory essay.

2. "Scope" seems a more expressive term than "domain," used in Thorelli (1968, and chapter 14 of this volume).

3. Ansoff, H. Igor. *Corporate Strategy.* New York: McGraw-Hill, 1965, p.109.

4. Starbuck, William H. *Organizations and Their Environments.* Berlin: International Institute of Management, 1973.

5. This is a source of possible weakness in the PIMS project (Schoeffler and Buzzell essays). The problem is twofold: by asking respondents to categorize the environment in terms of his variables, the researcher may impose a framework alien to the thinking of the organization, and even if he merely asks executives to identify those aspects of the environment they consider most relevant, he may not get an adequate picture. Indeed, misjudging the environment has been the downfall of many an organization (and the mainspring of success of some).

6. Woodward, Joan. *Industrial Organization: Theory and Practice.* London: Oxford University Press, 1965.

7. It requires but little stretch of the imagination to see that the strategies pursued by actors in the marketplace other than the focal organization are a feature of the E-structure.

8. Thus, we cannot agree with several writers of Harvard affiliation who include objectives within strategy. According to Chandler, for instance, "strategy can be defined as the determination of the basic long-term goals and objectives of an enterprise, and the adoption of courses of action and the allocation of resources necessary for carrying out these goals." Chandler, Alfred D., Jr. *Strategy and Structure.* Cambridge, Mass.: MIT Press, paperback ed., 1969, p.13. We are well aware that the fashionable notion of *strategic planning* (heir apparent to long-range planning?) does indeed include a consideration of (changes in) scope and overall objectives. See, for instance, Ansoff's essay, chapter 3 of this volume.

9. Two proverbial statements are relevant here: "in the long run all givens are variables"; on the other hand, "in the long run we are all dead."

10. A somewhat successful merger of case study and quantitative modeling approaches is represented by Hatten, K. J. *Strategic Models in the Brewing Industry.* Unpublished doctoral thesis, Purdue University, 1974.

11. Thorelli, Hans B. *The Federal Antitrust Policy—Origination of an American Tradition.* Baltimore: The Johns Hopkins University Press, 1954.

12. Hamilton, Adrian. "Reorganization by Oil Companies: What Does It Mean?" *Oil Daily*, September 15, 1975, pp.5, 10.

13. As a point of semantics, this writer would see the existence of vertical control as a characteristic of structure rather than, with Bucklin, as a feature of conduct (strategy).

14. Thorelli, Hans B. "The Political Economy of the Firm—Basis for a New Theory of Competition," *Schweizerische Zeitschrift für Volkswirtschaft und Statistik*, Vol. 101, 1965, pp.248–62.

2

Strategy-Structure-Performance: A Framework for Organization/Environment Analysis

LEE E. PRESTON

> Some things you miss because they're so tiny you overlook them, but some things you don't see because they're so *huge*. We were both looking at the same thing, seeing the same thing, talking about the same thing, thinking about the same thing, except he was looking, seeing, talking and thinking from a completely different *dimension*. . . . What we have here is a conflict of *visions of reality*.
>
> ROBERT M. PIRSIG
> *Zen and the Art of Motorcycle Maintenance*

Introduction

This paper begins with a confession, although not with an apology. When I volunteered to take this particular role in the conference, I thought that I already had in mind a comprehensive integrated framework that would draw together a number of diverse strands in the literature and, most important, would demonstrate their underlying consistency. However, in preparing the paper I have found the conceptual elements in the literature more diverse and less amenable to synthesis than I had realized. I find the same words—such words as *strategy, structure,* and *performance*—used in quite different senses in different branches of the literature. And, correspondingly, the same empirical phenomena and research results are described in quite different terminology, and variously interpreted as benign and malign, in the work of different major analysts.

In seeking an explanation for this situation, I have identified two major conceptual questions that seem to account for the diversity in the literature and to prohibit an easy synthesis. The fact that these two questions are not, so far as I can discover, specifically discussed in much of the literature may seem surprising. The reason for this, I think, is that they are "so *huge*" that most analysts begin with some implicit answer to them already in mind, and therefore leave the questions themselves unexamined. The two fundamental conceptual questions, as I now see them, are as follows:

I. What are the units of analysis (i.e., organization and/or environment) to which the attributes *strategy, structure,* and *performance* pertain?

II. What are the basic causal model(s) underlying organization-environment relationships?

The three main branches of the organization-environment literature appear to be based on different implicit answers to these two questions, and thus on differing choices of research agendas and methodologies. The three branches of the literature, as I see them, are these:[1]

1. The *micro-organizational literature* arising out of traditional organization theory and extended to include environmental interactions in, for example, the original study of Lawrence and Lorsch (25). Many related analyses at the Harvard Business School (2,41), Carnegie-Mellon (14), Indiana (48), and elsewhere can be included in this category, as can the work of Oliver Williamson, which, however, ranges into the next category as well (51,52).

2. The conventional *economics and marketing literature,* particularly the field of industrial organization as pioneered by Mason and Bain, recently codified by Scherer (42) and Shepherd (43), and further developed in marketing by Grether (22), Bucklin (6), and many others.[2]

3. The *legal-social-political literature,* particularly those contributions emphasizing the connection between individual organizations and these aspects of their larger environments. Salient examples include Hurst (23) and Lindsay (26) on the legal side; Truman (50), Olson (28), Solo (45), and Bauer et al. (4) on the political side; and the eclectic collection of papers assembled and edited by Marris (27). Two particularly important recent contributions to this general literature, the Fels Lectures of Arrow (3) and Coleman (12), will be discussed in more detail.

In order to examine the diverse conceptual foundations underlying these literatures, let us consider the two major units of analysis (organization and environment) and the three analytical variables (strategy, structure, performance) in brief detail.

Elements of Analysis: Units and Variables

ORGANIZATION

The meaning of the term *organization* does not seem to be much in dispute, although there are significant differences between open-systems and closed-systems modes of analysis—a point strongly emphasized by Thompson (48). A short definition that will suffice for our immediate purposes is the following:

> An organization is a means of coordinating the activities of a number of people for the achievement of a common purpose or goal. Organizations generally involve both internal specialization—so that some people perform one activity while others perform another—and a hierarchy of authority and responsibility through which the various specialized activities are coordinated and directed toward the common purpose. (40, pp.5–6)

ENVIRONMENT

The concept of *environment* presents somewhat greater difficulty. In the simplest terms, everything that is not *inside* a particular organization is inevitably *outside* it, and therefore part of its *environment*. The difficulty lies in specifying which dimensions of the larger environment are relevant to the analysis of the behavior and performance of an organization.

A significant portion of the total literature deals only with the *market* environment of the firm. This is not only the traditional focus of the economics and marketing literature; it is also the principal theme of the "contingency" theory of organization behavior as exemplified by the work of Lawrence and Lorsch, who focus on three critical environmental variables: (1) the "strategic competitive issue," including both market trends and technological change; (2) the degree of environmental stability, and therefore, the "certainty" with which the organization views its environment; and (3) the "diversity" or multi-dimensionality of the environment, as perceived by the organization (25, see chapter 2). Although the fundamental Lawrence and Lorsch theory can be extended to encompass nonmarket aspects of the environment, their original empirical study and most of the follow-up literature focus on market aspects only.

This focus on the *market* environment of the firm, although by no means narrow, is, at least in principle, bounded. By contrast there is now in the literature—and certainly in the management curriculum—a very strong emphasis on environmental considerations extending well beyond specific market contacts. Much of this literature emphasizes nonmarket aspects exclusively. Several more recent contributions have attempted to link market and nonmarket aspects of the environment, and to provide some criteria for distinguishing those environmental features (market and nonmarket) that are relevant to analysis and management in a particular organization from those that are irrelevant (24, 40, 46).

For purposes of this discussion, I have chosen the word *societal* to mean all legal, social, political, and economic aspects of an organization's environment *except* those that are involved directly in its market activities. *Societal structure* therefore refers to the structure of the nonmarket environment in all relevant dimensions. The word *social* cannot be used in this sense, because *social structure* has sometimes been given a more precise and narrower meaning. The term *nonmarket* seems scarcely descriptive, and repetition of the full list—social, economic, and political—would be tiresome and possibly fail to convey the comprehensiveness intended. The Preston-Post analysis (40) identifies the *relevant* dimensions of the organizational environments as (1) primary involvement (i.e., market contact) areas; and (2) secondary involvement (i.e., societal contact) areas. The distinction between these two levels of organizational involvement and other environmental features that, although present, are irrelevant is not important in the overall framework for analysis presented there.

We shall return to the conceptual problems involved in defining the relevant dimensions of the organizational environment. Let us now consider the variables—strategy, structure, and performance—and see how each is (or is not) related to the two units of analysis: organization and environment. This discussion is summarized in figure 2–1.

Figure 2–1
Elements of Analysis in Three Literatures

Literatures	Units of Analysis and Variables	
	Organization	Environment
Organizational Behavior	Strategy	. . . .
	Structure	Structure
	Performance	. . . .
Economics and Marketing	Strategy	. . . .
	Structure	Structure
	Performance	Performance
Legal-Societal	Strategy	(Public Policy?)
	*	Structure
	Performance	*

*The societal literature dealing with organization-environment relationships places very little emphasis on the internal structure of organizations and on performance evaluation in the larger environment. On the contrary, it might be said that the organization pursues a strategy of its own, within the structure of the environment, in order to achieve its own performance goals, which are not subjected to evaluation in the larger environmental context. The Bauer et al. study (4) is generally considered the classic of this literature, and certainly illustrates this particular analytical approach.

STRATEGY

The concept of *strategy* is clearly related to the concept of *organization*. We hypothesize that the organization develops a strategy in order to accomplish its functions and achieve its goals. Indeed, the greater part of "management" literature deals specifically with corporate strategy and its implementation through organizational structure, procedures, tactics, etc.

There remains, however, the question of whether the concept of strategy is in any way associated with the environment. Certainly the individuals and organizations composing the environment of any particular organization (i.e., the "focal organization," to use Pennings's term) will have their own goals and strategies. However, it is not generally suggested in the literature that the larger environment possesses a strategy of its own in any specific sense. It may be useful in some cases to refer to public policy as the "strategy" of the larger society; such usage would be entirely consistent with the Preston-Post analysis (40). However, as directions of change and policy goals become more sharply defined in the larger society, they tend to become the responsibilities of specific organizations, which then develop strategies to accomplish them.

STRUCTURE

Both an organization and its environment exhibit characteristics that can be broadly described as *structure;* and Thorelli has suggested the E-structure/O-structure code to indicate the appropriate distinction. The hierarchical, functional, and size dimensions of organizational structure have been exhaustively discussed in the standard literature. More recent analysis has emphasized that such intraorganizational features as differentiation, integration, goal-conflict, and communications are key structural attributes as well.

Similarly, the environment of organizations is generally described in terms that are either explicitly or implicitly structural. This is most clearly illustrated in economic analysis, especially in the fields of industrial organization and marketing, where the emphasis on market structure has produced a wide range of well-defined categories: i.e., perfect competition, monopolistic competition, oligopoly, and monopoly. The theoretical apparatus of economics offers explicit predictions about the behavior of imaginary "firms" in each of these market structures, and of the net result of such behavior by all such firms on prices, sales volumes, profits, etc., in such hypothetical markets.

In the other two main branches of the literature—micro-organizational studies and legal-societal studies—features of the environment of organizations are often identified without any specific emphasis on their *structural* character. Nevertheless, many of the environmental features selected for emphasis are evidently structural (e.g., Lawrence and Lorsch's concept of environmental "diversity"), and some of them explicitly so (e.g., the prevailing legal and political systems within which the organization operates). Hence, the concept of *structure* applies to both the organization and its environment, regardless of the particular concept of *environment* under analysis. Moreover, the notion that a critical aspect of *organizational strategy* is the development of an appropriate *organizational structure* in relation to the functional demands and opportunities presented by the external environment is a dominant theme throughout most of the literature.

PERFORMANCE

But what about *performance?* Are performance variables identified with both the organization and its environment, or only with one of them, and if so, which? (I note with some surprise that Thorelli did *not* suggest an E-performance/O-performance code for use at this conference.) On this issue the three main branches of the literature diverge sharply. In the main body of economics and marketing literature, performance variables are identified both for the organization and for the market environment; and, if there is any difference in emphasis between the two, the *latter* receives the greater attention. In particular, the traditional industrial organization analysis of structure-conduct-performance (SCP) places primary emphasis on the market group or industry (i.e., the "environment" of any particular organization); and the key performance variables of price-cost relationships, profitability, market growth, and technological change are associated exclusively with the market as a whole (i.e., the environment) and not with any individual firm. An individual firm ("focal organization") becomes important in the analysis only if it appears to account for some particular performance feature of the entire market, as in the case of a monopoly.[3]

The strong emphasis on the performance characteristics of environmental entities (e.g., industries and markets) in the economics and marketing literature contrasts sharply with both of the other main branches. In most of the organizational behavior analysis, performance variables are associated exclusively with the individual organization itself. These performance measures may be limited to economic and financial considerations—profitability, sales, etc.—or may include such broader considerations as organizational stability and growth. In this enormous and important branch of the literature, I find only one analyst—Oliver Williamson, who after all stands with one foot in each camp—who combines a strong emphasis on organizational performance variables with a recognition of environmental performance features as well.

In the societal or macro-analysis literature, which deals almost exclusively with the environment and not with the individual organization at all, the notion is that the environment has characteristics, trends, and evolutionary processes rather than *performance* attributes in the usual sense. When the micro-organization is related to this environment—as in the discussion of "corporate social responsibility"—the tendency is once again to evaluate the "performance" of the micro-unit only. As the title of one of the leading articles suggests, the emphasis is on "How Companies Respond to Social Demands" (1), not on how the performance features of the larger environment are either reflected in or influenced by the structure and performance of the micro-units.

Causal Models

It is now time to turn to our second fundamental question: What are the basic causal models underlying organization-environment relationships? It seems to me that three quite distinct conceptions may be found in the literature. Two of these—which I shall refer to as *stimulus-response* and *contingency* models—are well recognized and highly articulated; the third has made its explicit appearance only recently, and is intended to embrace both of the previous models and many others as well.[4] In addition to these three clearly differentiated conceptions, there appears to be a fourth approach to organization-environment studies that is essentially descriptive and pre-scientific in character. This descriptive emphasis may reflect a belief that it is too early to rely upon or test a causal model, and that additional observations and evidence are required in order to develop a basis for theoretical analysis.

STIMULUS-RESPONSE MODELS

The classic conception of both economic and organization theory has been that the organization (firm) responds to conditions and stimuli existing in and arising from its host environment. Economists from Adam Smith to Paul Samuelson have treated the environment of the firm—the market, the micro-economy, and the larger society—as essentially "out there" and independent of any action that the organization itself may or may not choose to take. Similarly, throughout the evolution of organization theory from the mechanical "task" approach (searching for the one best method) through the human relations or "organic" phase to the modern contingency approach, the external environment has been treated as a "given." Whether that environment is defined narrowly, as for example by Chamberlain (7) or Lawrence and Lorsch (25), or very broadly, as by Cole (11) and Steiner (46), it nevertheless remains essentially impervious to the behavior of the individual organization. The organization "adapts" to conditions encountered or stimuli generated by the environment, but apparently does not cause the environment to be other than it would have been in the absence of the organization and its adaptation.

The stimulus-response model may also be utilized with the causal initiatives reversed. That is, it may be hypothesized that the environment itself is shaped and changed by the behavior of individual organizations within it. This is, of course, a common idea in history, sociology, and political science. In economics it is associated with the names of Marx and Weber, and with the theory of monopoly from Adam Smith (or maybe Aristotle) right down to the present day. The notion of organizational dominance over the society was dramatized by Galbraith in the concept of "the technostructure," the cadre of professional managers who control the large organizations of modern society and, through them, the society itself (19). Hence, we have referred to this particular conception as a *technostructure model* of the organization-society relationship. Galbraith originally presented this model as neutral or even benign in its implications; and his more recent critical interpretation—including suggested ways in which a democratic polity can shake off the rule of the technocrats (18)— should not blind us to the neutrality of the basic idea, as, for example, in its earlier presentation by Boulding (5).

CONTINGENCY MODELS

Since the pioneering work of Lawrence and Lorsch (25), the organization and management literature has become characterized by the "contingency" approach. In its simplest form, the analysis deals with (a) an initial set of decisions and actions by the "focal organization" that combine with (b) a set of environmental attributes and processes (not always investigated in detail), to yield (c) organizational performance results. This basic analytical model can be investigated by both economic and behavioral research techniques, and at many different levels of detail and aggregation.

INTERPENETRATING OR ECOSYSTEMS MODELS

Although both of the previous types of models have a considerable amount of descriptive validity and analytical usefulness, many contemporary analysts seem to feel that neither of them offers a sufficiently comprehensive or flexible conception of organization-environment relationships. Thorelli has suggested an ecological approach to this problem, and has offered the term *ecosystem,* "comprising the organization and its relevant environment," as the appropriate analytical unit (49). Attention is confined to the *market* aspects of the ecosystem, although he suggests in passing that the ecological conception "may hold the key to the seemingly endless debate about 'social responsibility' " (49, p.78).

Our own work has focused on the combination of nonmarket and

market considerations relevant to organizational management, and has
used the term *interpenetrating systems,* originally enunciated by Parsons
(29, p.16). Our argument, briefly stated, is that there are important areas
of organization-society interaction that are not readily explained either as
exchange transactions or as the result of dominance on the part of either
party. Rather, there is a single process under analysis that involves the
independent action and the interaction of both the organization and its
environment. Cohen and Cyert have described the basic conception quite
accurately in the following passage:

> The organization and the environment are parts of a complex interactive
> system. The actions taken by the organization can have important effects
> on the environment, and, conversely, the outcomes of the actions of the
> organization are partially determined by events in the environment. These
> outcomes and the events that contribute to them have a major impact on
> the organization. Even if the organization does not respond to these
> events, significant changes in the organizational participants' goals and
> roles can occur. (10, p.352)

Most of the business history literature reflects what I would call an
interpenetrating systems approach, as do many of the industry studies
that make up a large portion of the industrial organization literature.
Again, however, I would emphasize that interpenetrating systems analysis
is in its infancy, and many specific analytical features and variants undoubtedly will be developed in the future.

A Synthetic Framework

Having gone to this length to describe the great diversity of analytical
elements and variables, conceptual models, and subject matter of the
organization-environment literature, I am naturally hesitant to put forward the promised comprehensive synthetic framework for analysis; and
what I have to offer is a good deal messier than I anticipated when I so
enthusiastically committed myself to this task some months ago. Nevertheless, I have made an attempt to sort out the situation as I see it, and have
tried to summarize the results in figure 2–2 and a few brief remarks. In
offering these comments and this rather complicated picture, I do not by
any means intend to disparage any of the simpler, narrower, and partial
pieces of analysis that can be found in the literature and in the other conference papers. Quite the contrary, it seems to me very important that
simple and partial models be utilized wherever possible in order to see
how far they will go in explaining observed phenomena, and in specifying
exactly what remaining aspects of the situation require further investiga-

tion. In addition, rigorous partial analysis is a valuable defense against holistic conceptions in which everything depends upon everything else, but in unspecified and unpredictable ways.

With these introductory comments out of the way, let us turn directly to figure 2–2. On the left side we have the organization and its three analytical variables: strategy, structure, and performance. Strategy and structure are linked because of their mutual dependence on intraorganizational decision making, and the direction of the arrow reflects the widely accepted Chandler thesis that strategy gives rise to structure, rather than the other way around (8). (Thorelli and other institutional critics have noted, of course, that established structures also give rise to strategies. However, most analysts appear to agree that strategy dominates structure in the explanation of organizational *change*.)

The simple half-loop (*a-a*) from strategy/structure out through the environmental variables and back to organizational performance describes the analytical framework of a very large part of the organization-environment literature. Analysts working with either stimulus-response or contingency models may begin by identifying the environmental variables, then analyze the strategy and structure developed by the organization in adaptation to these variables, and then trace the effects of these adaptive responses back through the environment in order to explain organizational performance. High profits and rapid growth indicate "success"; "failure" is obvious. This conception dominates not only the organizational behavior literature but also most of the "social responsibility" literature as well. In the latter, a broader set of environmental variables is included, but the success of the organization is nevertheless appraised in terms of its ability to adapt to (accept or fend off) the "demands" arising from its environment.

The two other main elements of the literature, however, explore the environmental side of this relationship in considerably more detail. As previously noted, the industrial organization and marketing literature stresses the concept of *market* structure—which involves the action and interaction of multiple organizations, as well as environmental influences —and conducts an analysis on this level in order to explain *market* performance (the *a-b* links, in figure 2-2). It is an apparent paradox in the literature—and a perpetual red herring in the antitrust courts—that high profitability is taken as evidence of favorable performance on the organization side of the line and unfavorable on the environment side. The truth, of course, is that there is no paradox at all. Rather, the argument is that successful performance by a single organization (as reflected, for example, in high profits) should lead to imitation and competitive pressures by others, and thus to improved *market* performance in the form of greater output and lower prices. *Market* performance is thus clearly connected

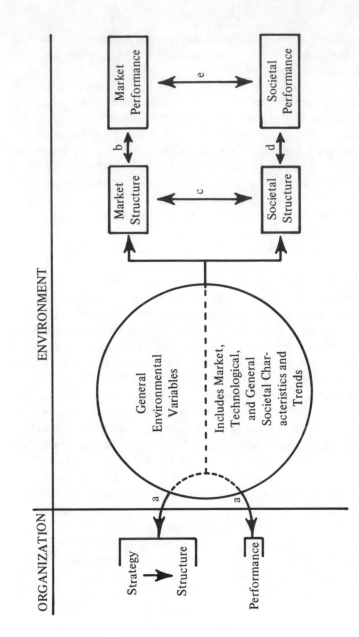

Figure 2–2

Synthetic Framework for Organization-Environment Analysis

with *organizational* performance, but the two are by no means the same thing.

A similar analysis may be suggested with respect to the organization and the societal environment (the *a-d* links in figure 2–2). It is obvious that most organizations are shaped by, indeed, are creatures of, their social milieu. However, the Marx-Weber thesis that organizations shape their environment has been around for more than a century. Continuing scholarly research, such as Chatov's analysis of the relationship between the accounting profession and the SEC (9), as well as more dramatic post-Watergate revelations strongly suggest its continued relevance. Galbraith has clearly been the most prominent recent analyst of this set of relationships; but his contributions may have been less influential (although perhaps more popular) than they might otherwise have been for at least two critical reasons: (a) a general lack of rigor in the analysis, which makes it difficult to replicate, or sometimes even to follow in any serious way; and (b) his essentially conflicting appraisals of societal performance as being broadly satisfactory in *American Capitalism* (17) and *The New Industrial State* (19), and broadly unsatisfactory in *The Affluent Society* (16) and *Economics and the Public Purpose* (18). I think it is therefore useful to draw attention in the next section to more recent work by several authors that has to do with societal structure and performance.

Organization/Management/Society:
Some Examples of Interaction

The purpose of this final section is to give some substance to the right-hand side of the framework for analysis suggested in figure 2–2 and, in particular, to offset slightly the heavy emphasis on organization/*market*-environment relationships which characterizes most of the papers to be presented at this conference. I was warned in advance by our chairman that an attempt to include all aspects of social interaction in this program would be entirely hopeless, and I quite agree with him. On the other hand, I think it is important to illustrate the idea of *societal* structure and performance with some specific examples, and also to dramatize the point that these features of the larger environment may be closely linked to features of the *market* environment and to the organization itself. The examples selected are drawn from the current literature and illustrate some of the most important types of analytical variables and interaction patterns that require consideration.

COMANOR AND SMILEY

William Comanor is primarily known as an economist concerned with market structure-performance relationships, i.e., the *a-b* links, and particularly the *b* link, of the chain of analysis in figure 2–2. However, in a recent study (13), he and Robert H. Smiley have opened a whole new field of analysis of the c link, by investigating the impact of monopoly (market structure) on the distribution of wealth (social structure) in the United States since 1890. Their conclusion is "that past and current monopoly has had a major impact on the current degree of inequality" in the wealth distribution, accounting for perhaps two-thirds of the wealth of households whose net worth exceeded a half-million dollars at the end of 1962. (These households, 0.27 percent of the total, accounted for 18.5 percent of all household wealth.) These conclusions are hedged about with qualifications, and a number of alternative assumptions and results are presented. There is no need to analyze or defend their particular conclusions here. My purpose is simply to draw attention to this important study as an attempt at rigorous analysis of a subject cheapened by irresponsible rhetoric and neglected in most of the organization-environment literature.

GINTIS AND PARSONS (AND PARETO)

In a brilliant article and subsequent discussion (20, 21) Herbert Gintis has presented a neo-Marxian analysis of the contemporary economy and society of the United States. Gintis develops a "dialectical theory of the firm" based on the familiar two-dimensional Marxian organizational model—exploiters (owners and managers) and exploited (workers)—and then argues that all other major features of our society arise from this basic organizational structure, and from the interaction of units with similar structures in market and nonmarket relationships. The specific societal features singled out by Gintis for special analysis are work, technology, education, and the role of the consumer. The essential conception is that the capitalist organization, through its internal structure and the decisions of those who control it, determines the development of the individual's capacities, and therefore all aspects of the structure and performance of society.

Gintis's analysis has been severely criticized by Parsons (30), who shares Gintis's concern with broad patterns of social and economic interaction, but strongly challenges his argument with respect to the unidirectional flow of cause and effect (i.e., his extreme version of the techno-structure model). Parsons stresses professions and professionalism as an important addition to the exploiters/exploited dichotomy and, more generally, emphasizes the importance of the overall occupational structure in determining both social structure and societal performance. Parsons also stresses the multi-dimensional character of organization-environment interaction, implying (but not mentioning) the general concept of inter-penetrating systems.[5] His comments on the relationship between capitalist organizations and higher education are of particular interest:

It is quite correct to say that one of its [the university's] functions is to establish capacities that are prerequisite to effective occupational performance, including performance in business organizations. That this is true, however, is in no sense incompatible with the view that it has other functions that are essentially independent of this, including . . . advancement of knowledge . . . general education . . . and . . . the ideological definition of the situation through the role of what I have been calling . . . 'intellectuals' . . . [including] radical intellectuals of the type with whom Gintis identifies himself. Whereas Gintis speaks of the educational system as supportive of the capitalistic economy, it is equally· true to state the obverse, namely, the capitalist economy has been importantly supportive of the educational system, in particular that of higher education. (30, p.285)

Although we cannot deal here with these issues in further detail, the point is that the entire Gintis-Parsons debate, which is a continuation of the earlier Parsons-Mills debate (29, see chapter 6), deals with the *a-d* links of the analytical framework, and involves disagreement about both the flow of causal relationships and the specification and evaluation of societal performance results.

Parsons's comment on Gintis also draws attention to Pareto's fundamental distinction between economic welfare (referred to as ophelimity) and general social welfare (referred to as utility). This distinction parallels that between the market performance variables and the broader societal performance variables suggested in figure 2–2.

JOURNAL OF POLITICAL ECONOMY (AND MORE PARETO)

The August 1975 issue of the *Journal of Political Economy* is a gold mine of organization-environment analyses. Two papers deal with the measurement of actual (and estimation of optimal) societal performance, one with respect to automobile safety (31) and the other with respect to conservation-versus-destruction of a non-renewable resource, in this case prehistoric mammals (44).

In a third paper (33), Pincus examines the impact of business on international trade policy (the same topic investigated by Bauer et al. for the 1950s (4)) with respect to the U.S. Tariff of 1824. The model investigates the *a-c-d* links of our analytical framework. Pincus examines the impact of market structure on political structure (and therefore power), and hence on political performance, as reflected in the levying of tariffs. The analytical links are explicitly identified and investigated, and the conclusion is that market structure—particularly the geographic dispersion of firms—is positively associated with the firms' political power in the Congress, and hence with the presence and height of import duties. (Although Pincus finds location to be more important than market shares in explaining performance results, he seems unwilling to accept McPherson's conclusion that market concentration was negatively associated with tariff levels in the 1950s and 1960s.)

A fourth paper by Posner (34) emphasizes that the social costs of monopoly (market structure) include not only the familiar lump-sum welfare losses (market performance), but also the resources utilized to obtain monopolies and/or prevent or regulate them. In terms of our framework, Posner's analysis explores the *a-b-e* linkage, and includes a broad critique of many related investigations, including the Comanor and Smiley paper previously mentioned.

Finally, there are two shorter pieces related to the fundamental contributions of Pareto. Pareto-efficiency—i.e., a situation in which no unit under analysis can be made better off without making another worse off—has generally been accepted as a minimum criterion for desirable social and economic performance. In a brief mathematical note, Robert Dorfman (15) points out that although Pareto-efficient solutions to an allocation problem are often equated with maximizing solutions to a weighted-summation social welfare function in the welfare economics literature—a literature that accounts for a major portion of all serious analysis of societal performance—these two conditions are not identical. On the contrary, simple examples can be used to illustrate Pareto-efficient allocations that are not welfare-maximizing. In addition, in a review of Warren J. Samuels's *Pareto on Policy,* V. J. Tarascio (47) emphasizes that Pareto himself referred to the "social" optimum as one that maximizes the aggregate of individual "utilities" (including, as Parsons reminded us, both economic and noneconomic performance features) and therefore social welfare. The point here is that Pareto himself was concerned with final societal performance results, and not simply with a random or arbitrary choice among a wide array of Pareto-efficient outcomes.

ARROW AND COLEMAN

The two brief books by Arrow (3) and Coleman (12) have only recently become available; they contain the texts of lectures presented at the University of Pennsylvania in 1970–71 and 1971–72. Apart from this institutional connection, the two works have no other common origin or collaborative intent to my knowledge. They have, however, a great deal in common; and each supplements the other in important ways. Both stress the role of large organizations—particularly business organizations—in society, and the importance of intraorganizational relationships in defining that role and assessing its impact. Arrow focuses mainly on authority-responsibility relationships within the organization; while Coleman emphasizes the relationship between human individuals and the "corporate actor" (i.e., the organization itself). These latter relationships may, of course, be external as well as internal to the organization. Both authors stress the impact of organizations on their environments, in the inter-penetrating systems or ecosystems sense, as well as the important connec-tions between "close" environmental variables (e.g., market relationships or "primary involvements") and more distant or consequential effects (societal variables and "secondary involvements").

Coleman is concerned with a development of a theory of social *structure,* whereas Arrow deals primarily with a theory of social *performance.* In both cases, the lectures themselves barely suggest the depth and dimen-sions of the authors' analyses, and these brief comments can do little more than call attention to these publications, which focus on the *a-d* links of our analytical framework. Coleman's sketch of a theory of social structure includes individuals, "corporate actors" (organizations), and govern-ment. He notes that law serves to define the elements of social structure, and that the creation of "juristic" persons has lead to the separation of social power from its source. He identifies the restoration of social power to natural persons as our critical societal performance goal at the present time. Note that this performance goal is a structural characteristic of society, a proposition that reverses the more familiar flow of analytical relationships from structure to performance. This performance goal is simply one possible example of Arrow's more general societal perfor-mance criterion: "One situation, one system, or one allocation is better than another if every individual feels that it is better according to his own individual values" (3, p.19). In *Social Choice and Individual Values* (1951) Arrow demonstrated that such strong Pareto-efficient results can-not be attained by the maximization of individual utilities through the market mechanism. He now sees organizations as alternatives to the market, "means of achieving the benefits of collective action in situations in which the price system fails"; and in this discussion elaborates at some length the intraorganizational structures of authority and responsibility that may contribute to the achievement of Pareto-optimal results in so-ciety.

Concluding Remarks

I believe that our framework for analysis must include not only the strategy/structure/performance variables associated with the organiza-tion, and the E-structure/O-structure code suggested by our chairman, but also the following:

(1) An elaboration of the E-structure into its principal component parts—M(arket)-structure and S(ocietal)-structure, if you like;

(2) A recognition of performance characteristics associated with the environment—again, M-performance and S-performance, where appropriate; and,

(3) A strong emphasis on structure-performance and market-societal *interactions* on the environment side of the analysis.

My insistence on the importance of these additional analytical dimensions arises not simply from an academic preference for comprehensive conceptual schemes, but rather from the strong conviction that these environmental interactions (and perceptions about them) account for a great deal of intraorganizational behavior and encompass the principal roles and impacts of large managerial organizations in our society.

NOTES

1. This conception of the relevant literature has developed out of two recent survey articles of my own (37, 38), and out of my continuing collaboration with James E. Post (40). A much more extensive development and application of some of these concepts is contained in Post's forthcoming study of organization-environment relationships in the insurance industry (35). My present view of this entire situation has been strongly influenced by continuing contact with my colleague Professor Robert Chatov.

2. Much of my own previous work falls into this category, of course; for example (36, 39).

3. The question of whether there are, in fact, genuine "market" or "industry" performance features, or whether the evidence of such features is a statistical artifact imposed by the analyst and his particular models and methodology, is now a matter of considerable dispute. The counter-evidence has been provided both by empirical studies of organizational behavior and by sophisticated econometric analysis. This may also be an appropriate place to emphasize the point that the traditional industrial organization literature has focused on the "conduct" of groups of firms, both competitors and other related organizations, in the market environment, not on the "behavior" of individual firms alone, except as the latter was required to explain the former. This important distinction is brilliantly illustrated in Phillips's studies of organization-firm behavior (32).

4. In his forthcoming study (35), James E. Post describes the pattern of organizational behavior associated with each of these three models as "adaptation," "manipulation," and "responsiveness." His detailed analyses of specific examples involving a single industry and firm strongly support both the view that there are sharp distinctions separating these three conceptions and their associated behavior patterns and also the view that the familiar adaptive and manipulative approaches cannot explain a large and important portion of organization-environment interaction.

5. Among Parsons's many contributions to the organization-environment

literature, his 1960 treatise (29), particularly the technical-managerial-institutional model of organizations in chapter 2, has been the most useful in our own work.

REFERENCES

1. Ackerman, Robert W. "How Companies Respond to Social Demands," *Harvard Business Review,* Vol. 51, No. 4, July–August 1973, pp.88–98.
2. Andrews, Kenneth R. *The Concept of Corporate Strategy.* Homewood, Illinois: Dow Jones-Irwin, Inc., 1971.
3. Arrow, Kenneth J. *The Limits of Organization.* New York: W. W. Norton & Co., 1974. See also Arrow, "On the Agenda of Organizations," in (27).
4. Bauer, Raymond A.; de Sola Pool, Ithiel; and Dexter, Lewis Anthony. *American Business and Public Policy.* New York: Atherton Press, 1967.
5. Boulding, Kenneth E. *The Organizational Revolution.* New York: Harper & Brothers, Publishers, 1953.
6. Bucklin, Louis P. *Competition and Evolution in the Distributive Trades.* Englewood Cliffs, New Jersey: Prentice-Hall, Inc., 1972.
7. Chamberlain, Neil W. *Enterprise and Environment.* New York: McGraw-Hill Book Co., 1968.
8. Chandler, Alfred D., Jr. *Strategy and Structure: Chapters in the History of the American Industrial Enterprise.* Cambridge, Mass.: MIT Press, 1962.
9. Chatov, Robert. *Corporate Financial Reporting: Public or Private Control?* New York: The Free Press, A Division of Macmillan Publishing Co., Inc., 1975.
10. Cohen, Kalman J., and Cyert, Richard M. "Strategy: Formulation, Implementation, and Monitoring," *The Journal of Business,* Vol. 46, No. 3, July 1973, pp.349–67.
11. Cole, Arthur H. *Business Enterprise and Its Social Setting.* Cambridge, Mass.: Harvard University Press, 1959.
12. Coleman, James S. *Power and the Structure of Society.* New York: W. W. Norton and Co., 1974.
13. Comanor, William S., and Smiley, Robert H. "Monopoly and the Distribution of Wealth," *The Quarterly Journal of Economics,* Vol. 89, No. 2, May 1975, pp.177–94.
14. Cyert, Richard M., and March, James G. *A Behavioral Theory of the Firm.* Englewood Cliffs, New Jersey: Prentice-Hall, Inc., 1963.
15. Dorfman, Robert. "Note On a Common Mistake in Welfare Economics," *Journal of Political Economy,* Vol. 83, No. 4, August 1975, pp.863–64.
16. Galbraith, John Kenneth. *The Affluent Society.* Boston: Houghton Mifflin Co., 1958.
17. Galbraith, John Kenneth. *American Capitalism.* Boston: Houghton Mifflin Company, 1952.
18. Galbraith, John Kenneth. *Economics and The Public Purpose.* Boston: Houghton Mifflin Company, 1973.

19. Galbraith, John Kenneth. *The New Industrial State*. Boston: Houghton Mifflin Company, 1967.
20. Gintis, Herbert. "Welfare Economics and Individual Development," *Quarterly Journal of Economics*, Vol. 86, No. 4, November 1972, pp.572–99.
21. Gintis, Herbert. "Welfare Economics and Individual Development: Comment," *Quarterly Journal of Economics*, Vol. 89, No. 2, May 1975, pp.291–302.
22. Grether, E. T. *Marketing and Public Policy*. Englewood Cliffs, New Jersey: Prentice-Hall, Inc., 1966.
23. Hurst, James Willard. *Law and the Conditions of Freedom in the Nineteenth-Century United States*. Madison: University of Wisconsin Press, 1965.
24. Jacoby, Neil H. *Corporate Power and Social Responsibility*. New York: Macmillan Publishing Co., Inc., 1973.
25. Lawrence, Paul R., and Lorsch, Jay W. *Organization and Environment: Managing Differentiation and Integration*. Boston, Mass.: Division of Research, Graduate School of Business Administration, Harvard University, 1967.
26. Landsay, A. D. *The Modern Democratic State*. London: Oxford University Press, 1943; paperback, 1962.
27. Marris, Robin. *The Corporate Society*. New York: John Wiley & Sons, 1975.
28. Olson, Mancur. *The Logic of Collective Action*. Cambridge, Mass.: Harvard University Press, 1971.
29. Parsons, T. *Structure and Process in Modern Society*. Glencoe, Ill.: Free Press, 1960.
30. Parsons, T. "Commentary on Herbert Gintis, 'A Radical Analysis of Welfare Economics and Individual Development,'" *Quarterly Journal of Economics*, Vol. 89, No. 2, May 1975, pp.280–90.
31. Peltzman, Sam. "The Effects of Automobile Safety Regulation," *Journal of Political Economy*, Vol. 83, No. 4, August 1975, pp.677–726.
32. Phillips, Almarin. *Market Structure, Organization and Performance*. Cambridge, Mass.: Harvard University Press, 1962.
33. Pincus, J. J. "The Pressure Groups and the Pattern of Tariffs," *Journal of Political Economy*, Vol. 83, No. 4, August 1975, pp.757–58.
34. Posner, Richard A. "The Social Costs of Monopoly and Regulation," *Journal of Political Economy*, Vol. 83. No. 4, August 1975, pp.807–28.
35. Post, J. E. *Risk and Response: Management and Social Change in the American Insurance Industry*. Lexington, Mass.: Heath Lexington Books (forthcoming).
36. Preston, Lee E., and Collins, Norman R. *Concentration and Price-Cost Margins in Manufacturing Industries*. Berkeley, Cal.: University of California Press, 1968.
37. Preston, Lee E. "Corporation and Society: The Search For a Paradigm," *Journal of Economic Literature*, Vol. 13, No. 2, June 1975, pp.434–53.
38. Preston, Lee E. "Marketing, Competition, and Public Policy: A Commentary of the Work of E. T. Grether," The Ninth Paul D. Converse

Marketing Symposium *Proceedings,* The University of Illinois, May 16, 1975 (forthcoming).

39. Preston, Lee E. *Markets and Marketing: An Orientation.* Glenview, Ill.: Scott, Foresman & Co., 1970.

40. Preston, Lee E., and Post, James E. *Private Management and Public Policy.* Englewood Cliffs, New Jersey: Prentice-Hall, Inc., 1975.

41. Rumelt, Richard P. *Strategy, Structure, and Economic Performance.* Cambridge, Mass.: President and Fellows of Harvard College, 1974.

42. Scherer, Frederick M. *Industrial Market Structure and Economic Performance.* Chicago: Rand McNally & Co., 1970.

43. Shepherd, William G. *Market Power & Economic Welfare.* New York: Random House, Inc., 1970.

44. Smith, Vernon L. "The Primitive Hunter Culture, Pleistocene Extinction, and the Rise of Agriculture," *Journal of Political Economy,* Vol. 83, No. 4, August 1975, pp.727–56.

45. Solo, Robert A. *The Political Authority and the Market System.* Cincinnati: South-Western Publishing Co., 1974.

46. Steiner, George A. *Business and Society.* New York: Random House, 1971.

47. Tarascio, Vincent J. "Warren J. Samuels, Pareto on Policy," *Journal of Political Economy,* Vol. 83, No. 4, August 1975, pp.880–82.

48. Thompson, James D. *Organizations in Action.* New York: McGraw-Hill Book Company, 1967.

49. Thorelli, Hans B. "Organizational Theory: An Ecological View," Academy of Management *Proceedings,* 27th Annual Meeting, Washington, D.C., December 27–29, 1967, (1968) pp.66–84.

50. Truman, David B. *The Governmental Process: Political Interests and Public Opinion.* New York: Alfred A. Knopf, Inc., 1951.

51. Williamson, Oliver E. *Corporate Control and Business Behavior.* Englewood Cliffs, New Jersey: Prentice-Hall, Inc., 1970.

52. Williamson, Oliver E. *Markets and Hierarchies: Analysis and Antitrust Implications.* New York: The Free Press, 1975.

PART TWO

The Corporation in Strategic Interaction

3

Managing Surprise and Discontinuity: Strategic Response to Weak Signals

H. IGOR ANSOFF

Conceptual Framework

THE PROBLEM

The paradox of strategic military surprise has been a familiar phenomenon throughout recorded human history. From the Trojan Horse to Pearl Harbor to the Yom Kippur war, nations and armies have been confronted with sudden crises, in spite of ample information about enemy intentions.

The recent "petroleum crisis" was a comparable event in the industrial world: large and important firms were suddenly confronted with a major discontinuity, although advance forecasts of Arab action were not only publicly available, but on the day of the surprise were to be found on the desks of some of the surprised managers.

The petroleum crisis, because of its pervasive scope, highlighted the danger of strategic business surprises. But such surprises had overtaken numerous firms, one by one, since the early 1950s, enough of them to provide material for a *Fortune* book titled *"Corporations in Crisis."*

In the aftermath, it was argued that these corporations were caught unawares because they lacked modern forecasting and planning systems. But in the 1970s a majority of the firms caught by the petroleum crisis

Reprinted with kind permission from the original in *Schmalenbachs Zeitschrift für betriebswirtschaftliche Forschung,* March 1976, pp.130–53.

had such systems. In the mid-1960s, the management of one of the world's largest conglomerates proudly displayed its planning and control. A week after the public display, the same management made a red-faced admission of *two* multi-million dollar surprises: a major overrun in its office furniture division and another in its ship-building division.

The American automotive industry, a leader in modern planning and control, was certainly unprepared for the forceful Congressional position on automotive safety. And a bare four years later it was again "surprised" by the success of the small car.

Such events need little support from the voluminous literature on futurology to predict that discontinuities and surprises will occur with increasing frequency. If, as experience suggests, modern planning technology does not insure against surprises, the technology needs to be extended to provide such insurance. An exploration of such extension is the purpose of this paper.

THE NATURE OF STRATEGIC SURPRISE

Figure 3–1 plots, against time, the growth of a firm, which can be measured by any one of several common yardsticks, such as sales, profits, ROI. The middle line shows smooth extrapolation of past experience into the future. The two branching curves, a threat and an opportunity, show a

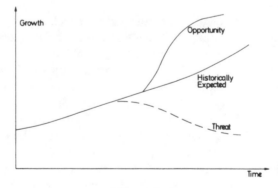

Figure 3–1
Impact of Threat/Opportunity

significant departure, a discontinuity from the past. In principle, such discontinuities can be anticipated by available forecasting techniques. Given enough warning, the firm should be able to avert the threat, or seize the opportunity.

In fact, firms often fail to anticipate and suddenly discover that a fleeting opportunity has been missed. Typically, at the "clear moment of truth," neither the causes nor the possible responses are clear and the firm confronts an unfamiliar and often threatening event. We shall call such events *strategic surprises*: sudden, urgent, unfamiliar changes in the firm's perspective which threaten either a major profit reversal or loss of a major opportunity.

A firm that wishes to prepare for strategic surprises has two options:

(1) To develop a capability for effective *crisis management:* fast and efficient, *after the fact* responsiveness to sudden discontinuities. A useful prototype is a fire-fighting company. Unable to predict or control occurrence of fires, it prepares itself, through repeated practice, to respond quickly and effectively to a whole range of different alarms.

(2) The second approach is to treat the problem *before the fact,* minimize the probability of strategic surprises: to prepare in such a way, that by the time it strikes, a strategic discontinuity has lost its suddenness, urgency, and unfamiliarity.

Both approaches deserve management attention: before-the-fact strategic preparedness because it is the more efficient approach; crisis preparedness because even the best advance efforts do not assure immunity from surprises. In a companion paper we have dealt with crisis preparedness.[1] In this paper we shall deal with before-the-fact strategic preparedness.

FOCUS ON RESPONSIVENESS

A common feature of strategic surprises is the failure of decision makers to act on information available in advance of the event. We need, therefore, to distinguish between the *available* and the *utilized* information. A way to do this is illustrated in figure 3–2, which suggests three levels

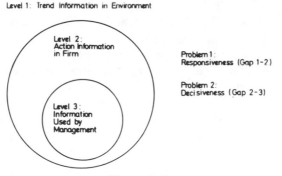

Figure 3–2
Information Levels in the "Surprise Problem"

of information. The first level is the "common knowledge" available in the environment of the firm through word of mouth, in publications, in intelligence analyses, in forecasts.

Level 2 is the information generally available within the firm. Part of it is in the same form as the outside information, but the bulk interprets this "raw" data into consequences for the firm: competitive analyses, threats and opportunities, sales and profits forecast, plans, program budgets. As the petroleum crisis has shown, typically, only historically familiar raw data find their way into the interpreted consequences. Reports on unfamiliar discontinuities, if they find their way into the firm, remain in raw form, because the methods and approaches for converting them into action typically do not exist.

Thus, as figure 3–2 suggests, there is a gap between the information available in the environment and actionable information available to managers. But there is also another gap between the latter and the information actually employed in managerial decision making and action. Again, it is the familiar, surprise-threatening information that is typically rejected by managers (until the moment of crisis) as "too abstract," unreliable, unrelated to past experience, and therefore irrelevant to the problems of the firm.

Thus avoiding of surprise involves closing two important *gaps*:

(1) The *responsiveness* gap between information available in the environment and action plans within the firm, and

(2) The *decisiveness* gap between the available plans and managerial use of plans.

Both need to be analyzed and reduced, if the firm is to avoid surprise. Since we have treated the latter in the companion paper referred to earlier, this paper focuses on the responsiveness gap.

LIMITATIONS OF ENVIRONMENTAL INFORMATION

There is now a well-developed technology, called *strategic planning,* for converting environmental information about threats and opportunities into concrete action plans, programs, and budgets. But to date strategic planning has had little success in dealing with surprises. One reason is the cumbersome, costly, and time-consuming process by which most firms prepare their plans. A potential surprise that surfaces suddenly needs to be of crisis proportions to justify interrupting the annual planning cycle. A majority of strategic discontinuities, unless they conveniently match the planning calendar, must wait for attention until the next cycle.

But lack of speed and responsiveness to environmental discontinuities is only one problem in treatment of surprises. Another, more fundamental problem is inherent limitation in the available information.

To be useful in strategic planning, information must satisfy two conditions. First, it must be forcastable far enough into the future to permit timely preparation and response to the threat/opportunity.

Second, the content of the forecast must be adequate for estimating the impact on the firm, for identifying specific responses, and for estimating the potential profit impact of these responses.

In both strategic planning literature and practice, an implicit assumption is made that both conditions can be satisfied; that the forecaster can meet the needs of the planner. This assumption turns out to be true when planning is concerned either with simple extrapolation of the past, or with "logical," incremental developments of historical trends. But when a potential surprise originates in an alien technology, or with a previously unknown competitor, or with a new political coalition, or with a new economic phenomenon—in all of these cases both the timeliness and the content requirements frequently cannot be met. The firm *can* have a longer time perspective, if it is willing to put up with increasing vagueness of content; or the firm can wait for originally vague information to become specific.

In the past, waiting has been the typical behavior. If by the time the information became specific, there was still enough time left for an orderly response, nothing was lost. But frequently the information arrived too late and the firm faced a crisis.

The ability of the firm to effect a timely response depends on two variables: the rapidity with which the threat/opportunity rises and decays, and the amount of time needed by the firm to plan and effect the response. Since the 1950s these two variables have been on a collision course: the rate of environmental change has accelerated, and the firm's response has been made slower by growing size and complexity.

Thus an apparent paradox: if the firm waits for information it will be increasingly surprised by a crisis; if it accepts vague information, the content will not be specific enough to estimate impact, alternatives, and consequences. A way out of this paradox is to change the planning approach: instead of deriving strategic information needs from a priori decisions on what responses are *desirable*, determine what responses are *feasible* in the light of available information. This implies that, early in the life of a threat, when the information is vague and its future course is unclear, the responses will be correspondingly unfocused, aimed at increasing flexibility. As the information becomes more precise, so will the firm's response, terminating eventually in a direct attack on the threat or an opportunity.

We might call this graduated response "amplification and response to weak signals"[2] in contrast to the conventional strategic planning, which depends on the existence of "strong signals." It is our purpose in this paper to develop a practical planning approach to such response. Our first task is to explore the range of "weak signals" that can be typically expected from a strategic discontinuity.

STATES OF IGNORANCE

Figure 3–3 illustrates the threat information typically required in strategic planning. The three curves at the left trace the alternative impact of a threat on the profits of the firm, the right side shows three possible responses to one of the impact curves. Without a detailed discussion of the mathematical notation, the multiplicity of probable paths gives the impression of information which is imperfect and uncertain. But a closer look at figure 3–3 shows that while uncertain, this is very *content-rich* information: the threat is well enough understood to compute the possible profit consequences, the responses are well enough developed to estimate both their costs and their countereffect on the threat.

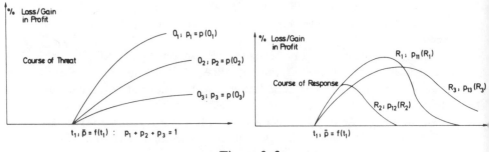

Figure 3–3
Example of Information Required for Threat
Analysis in Strategic Planning

It is reasonable to expect this much knowledge from a threat/opportunity that arises from a familiar prior experience. This will be the case when a competitor introduces a new marketing strategy, a new product, a new pricing strategy. But when the threat/opportunity is discontinuous (such as the impact of laser technology on land surveying, or of large-scale integration on electronic components), then, in the early stages, the nature, the impact, and the possible responses are unclear. Frequently, it is not even clear whether the discontinuity will develop into a threat or an opportunity.

Thus the information contained in figure 3–3, while desirable, is not to be arbitrarily expected from unfamiliar discontinuities. Initially, we must be prepared for very vague information which will progressively develop and improve with time. We shall characterize such progression by the successive *states of ignorance*. These are illustrated in figure 3–4, where State number five, the most information-rich state, contains exactly the same information as figure 3–3. As entries in the left-hand column indi-

States of Ignorance / Info Content	(1) Sense of Threat/ Opportunity	(2) Source of Threat/ Opportunity	(3) T/O Concrete	(4) Response Concrete	(5) Outcome Concrete
Conviction that discontinuities are impending	YES	YES	YES	YES	YES
Area or organization is identified which is the source of discontinuity	NO	YES	YES	YES	YES
Characteristics of threat, nature of impact, general gravity of impact, timing of impact	NO	NO	YES	YES	YES
Response identified: timing, action, programs, budgets	NO	NO	NO	YES	YES
Profit impact and consequences of responses are computable	NO	NO	NO	NO	YES

Figure 3–4
States of Ignorance under Discontinuity

cate, enough is known to compute both the probable profit impact of the discontinuity and the profit impact of the response.

At the other extreme, in column (1), is the vaguest state of information which can be of use to management. As the NOs show, all that is known is that *some* threats and opportunities will undoubtedly arise, but their shape and nature and source are not yet known. In today's "political and economic fog of uncertainty"[3] many firms find themselves in such a state of ignorance. Having witnessed and experienced shocks of change in recent past, managers are convinced that new discontinuities are coming, but they cannot identify the source.

States of ignorance on level two improve matters somewhat. For example, in the early 1940s, it was generally recognized by physicists that solid-state physics was pregnant with potential for the electronics industry. But the invention of the specific discontinuity, the transistor, was still several years off. The source of the threat was clear, but not the threat itself.

When the transistor was invented by Shockley and his team, the ignorance was reduced to State three; but at the outset, the ramifications of the inventions were unclear, as were the defensive and the aggressive responses which different firms were eventually to make.

When the firms developed and made the initial responses, the ignorance was reduced to State four, the eventual investments and the profits were not yet visible. Pioneering firms were investing boldly in the new technology with little experience to guide them, in high hopes that their entrepreneurial risk taking would pay off.

State five was not reached until knowledge of crystal yields and of manufacturing process costs was sufficient to make reasonable predictions of the ultimate technology and its profitability. But, by then, the leaders were entrenched and those who originally held back had to pay a high cost of entry into the industry.

We should note in passing that the information *in each state* of ignorance may be certain, uncertain, or risky in the sense of definitions commonly used in statistical decision theory. The table shows only the variability of *content,* not the *state of uncertainty.* The dimension of uncertainty can be easily added orthogonally to the table, thus creating a cube of possible states of information. In this cube, the states of information treated in statistical decision theory would be included in slice number five.

As indicated by the growing number of YESs in figure 3–4, ignorance is reduced and information is enriched as a threat/opportunity evolves from State one to State five. In the history of a given threat/opportunity, this evolution takes place over time. The speed of the evolution limits the time available to the firm for mounting a response. A useful measure is the time remaining before the impact of the discontinuity on the firm passes a critical profit benchmark. For a threat this is the level of loss at which the survival of the firm is threatened; for an opportunity this is the point beyond which it is too late: the cost of climbing on the bandwagon can no longer be recovered through profits.

Two hypothetical threat histories are illustrated in figure 3–5. Threat No. 1 appears to develop favorably for the firm. State five information, adequate for strategic planning, becomes available at T_1 in advance of the unacceptable threat level, allowing time for planning and response. Threat No. 2, on the other hand, is a potential source of surprise. It arises late, leaving little time before crisis; the crisis level is reached at State S_1, before the information is concrete enough for strategic planning.

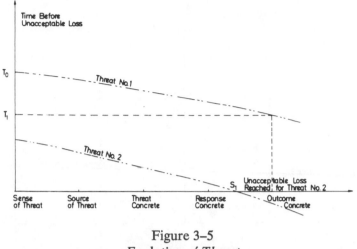

Figure 3-5
Evolution of Threat

It is clear that Threat No. 2 is a troublemaker; the quality of Threat No. 1 is less clear. The answer depends on whether the time T_1 is adequate to prepare a strategic plan and to execute it in a timely manner. This, in turn, depends on how well the firm uses the period since the sense of threat was felt, T_0 before the critical point. Beyond this point content of threat and response are well understood. But information will continue to get better, thanks to progressive reduction of uncertainty. A firm which requires State five information before it responds will at best monitor the evolution of the threat. A firm prepared to respond to partial information can use the period T_0-T_1 to enhance the responsiveness of the firm in a way so that the residual time T_1 *becomes adequate!* It is to this possibility that we now turn.

ALTERNATIVE RESPONSE STRATEGIES

Just as we have expanded the states of information to include poorer knowledge, we need to enlarge the repertoire of responses to permit weaker responses. Such a repertoire is shown in figure 3-6, where management options are subdivided into two groups: (1) responses that change the firm's relationship with the *environment* and (2) responses which change the *internal dynamics and structure* of the firm. For each group there are three categories of response strategies:

(i)   those that enhance the firm's awareness of its outer and inner worlds;

(ii)   those that increase the firm's flexibility for response to vague threat/opportunities; and

(iii) those that pinpoint the threat and respond directly to it.

Thus the entries in the table provide a total of six response strategies.

RESPONSE STRATEGIES / DOMAIN OF RESPONSE	DIRECT RESPONSE	FLEXIBILITY	AWARENESS
RELATIONSHIP TO ENVIRONMENT	EXTERNAL ACTION (STRATEGIC PLANNING AND IMPLEMENTATION)	EXTERNAL FLEXIBILITY	ENVIRONMENTAL AWARENESS
INTERNAL CONFIGURATION	INTERNAL READINESS (CONTINGENCY PLANNING)	INTERNAL FLEXIBILITY	SELF- AWARENESS

Figure 3–6
Alternative Response Strategies

The *External Action* strategy, as its name implies, mounts a direct counteraction against identified threats or opportunities. It proceeds through selection of the attack strategy, translation into plans and programs, and implementation of the latter. The end result is a threat averted, or an opportunity captured, an enhanced potential for future profits. Preparation for direct action is the object of strategic planning. The range of specific actions available under the direct action strategy can be divided into two groups: (i) aggressive actions, which treat the discontinuity as an opportunity, and (ii) defensive actions, which regard it as a threat. Some of the specific action alternatives are shown in the upper part of figure 3–7.

The lower part of figure 3–7 shows measures available in the *internal readiness* strategy, which match the skills, the structure, and the resources of the firm to the demands of specific threat/opportunities. The result of internal readiness is a state of preparedness for external action. In strategic planning internal readiness is commonly referred to as "strategy implementation" signifying that preparedness must await selection of the course of action that it will support. In Chandler's words "structure follows strategy." Thus, the prescribed sequence is: Strategic planning → internal readiness → action.

For triggering off this sequence, it is essential that the strategic informa-

EXTERNAL ACTION
- Optimize Timing of Response
- Seize Opportunity — Enter New Product Market
- Convert a Threat to Opportunity
- Change Competitive Strategy

DIRECT RESPONSE
- Share Risks with other Firms
- Secure Supply of Scarce Resource
- Diversify Threatened Resource Technology
- Reduce Commitment to Threatened Area
- Divest from a Threatened Product Market

INTERNAL READINESS
- Preplan
- Adapt Structure and Systems
- Acquire Technology
- Preposition Resources
- Acquire Skills
- Build Facilities
- Develop New Products Services
- Develop Operational Capability

Figure 3–7

Measures for Direct Response Strategy

tion be in the highly developed State five on our ignorance scale (figure 3–4). But many of the measures can be successfully carried out in State three, as soon as the shape of the impending threat/opportunity becomes concrete and before State five is reached. Thus, it is possible to accelerate response by reversing the sequence to: internal preparedness → strategic planning → action.

The earliest possible response to an opportunity/threat is offered by the pair of *awareness strategies,* shown at the right hand of figure 3–6 and elaborated into action alternatives in figures 3–8 and 3–9. In most firms a degree of environmental awareness is provided through economic fore-casting, sales forecasting, and analysis of competitive behavior. All of these are essentially extrapolative, based on a smooth extension of the past into the future. To broaden the awareness to include discontinuities, the firm can add special types of environmental analysis shown in figure 3–8. An examination of these shows that most of them do not require informa-tion about specific threats and opportunities. Knowledge at ignorance level one, a *sense of threat,* is adequate. State one is also adequate for many of the self-awareness measures.

The *flexibility strategy* shown in the middle column of figure 3–6 and elaborated in figures 3–10 and 3–11 differs from the direct action strate-gies in the fact that its end product is an enhanced *potential* for the firm's future, rather than tangible changes in profits and in growth.

The *external flexibility* sub-strategy concerns itself with positioning the firm in the environment in a way which satisfies two criteria: (i) satis-factory expected *average* potential for profitability over the long term,

ENVIRONMENTAL
- EXTRAPOLATIVE ECONOMIC FORECASTING
- SALES ANALYSIS
- SALES FORECASTING
- MONITORING of ENVIRONMENT
- STRUCTURAL, TECHNO, ECONO, SOCIO FORECASTS
- MODELLING of ENVIRONMENT
- THREATS and OPPORTUNITIES ANALYSIS

Figure 3–8
Alternatives for Awareness Strategy (1)

SELFAWARENESS
- PERFORMANCE DIAGNOSIS (DuPont Ratio Analysis)
- VALUE ANALYSIS
- CRITICAL RESOURCE AUDITS
- CAPACITY AUDITS
- STRENGTHS – WEAKNESSES ANALYSIS
- CAPABILITY PROFILES
- FINANCIAL MODELLING
- STRATEGIC MODELLING

Figure 3–9
Alternatives for Awareness Strategy (2)

(ii) adequate diversification of the firm's position to assure coping with *deviations* from the expected average: capture of attractive major opportunities and minimization of catastrophic reversals.

Formulation of the external flexibility strategy (commonly known as "position strategy") and of the external action strategy ("development planning") are both a part of the strategic planning process. In most instances of strategic planning it is usually assumed that the same level five information input is needed for both planning activities. But an examination of the measures in figure 3–10 shows that a flexibility strategy can be substantially planned *and implemented* if the state of ignorance is no better than level two, long before threats become concrete.

Unlike external flexibility, internal flexibility received relatively little attention from strategic planners. But recent history shows it to be a crucial ingredient in strategic preparedness. In the area of managerial flexibility the preparation of managers along the lines described in figure 3–11 is now recognized as essential and vital if the firm is to anticipate and deal with the growing turbulence of the environment. Without it, efforts to introduce strategic planning typically encounter strong "resistance to planning."

In the past *logistic flexibility* (lower part of figure 3–11) has received

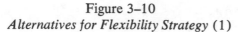

Figure 3–10
Alternatives for Flexibility Strategy (1)

Figure 3–11
Alternatives for Flexibility Strategy (2)

even less attention than managerial flexibility. A major reason is the fact that the concept of flexibility runs contrary to the fundamental organizational design principle of the Industrial Age, which holds that maximum profitability is to be gained through the maximum possible specialization of logistic activities. This calls for special facilities, specialized machinery, largest possible capacity, maximum capital-labor substitution, and longest possible production runs. In a world of strategic surprises the principle of maximum specialization has already been repeatedly compromised, when expensive capacities have been made prematurely obsolete by unexpected technological changes, or when the length of production runs has been cut short by shrinking product life-cycles. Thus, it is safe to predict that, in the coming years, logistic flexibility will be used increasingly as a measure of strategic preparedness. We note that, as with external flexibility, the mere knowledge of the source(s) of threat/opportunities is sufficient to start a rigorous program of logistic preparedness.

FEASIBLE RESPONSE STRATEGIES

The preceding discussion shows that much can be done to prepare the firm for strategic discontinuities if the firm is ready to respond to weak signals. But it also shows that the range of feasible responses is limited by the state of ignorance. Figure 3–12 summarizes the relationship between states of ignorance and feasible responses. As already discussed, environmental awareness requires only a conviction that the potential threat(s) is serious enough to warrant an early presentation. An examination of the options of figure 3–8 would show that not all response actions are imme-

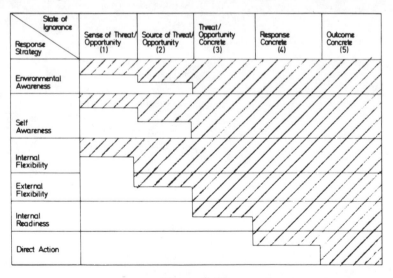

Figure 3–12
Feasible Ranges of Response Strategies

diately feasible. But such activities as monitoring of the environment, structural forecasting, and analyses of critical capacities and resources can be instituted right away. Others can be added as the environmental information matures.

Reference to figure 3–11 shows that in the internal flexibility strategy virtually all of managerial preparedness as well as a significant number of logistic measures can also be launched under sense of threat conditions. External flexibility work can be started as soon as the sources of threat are identifiable.

For direct response strategy, it is necessary to have a good idea of the threats which one is proposing to attack. But even here, a sufficiently clear idea of the origin and shape of threat is sufficient to launch a substantial percentage of internal readiness measures: acquisition of necessary technological, production, and marketing skills, new product development, development of sources of supply.

Even direct external action need not, and *in practice frequently does not,* await information which makes possible reliable cash and profit flow calculations. For example, adventurous firms will typically launch their entry into a new industry at stage 4, before the technology, the market, and the competition are well enough defined to permit such calculations. Other more conservative firms will prefer to wait on the sidelines until the "ball game" is better defined.

Figure 3–12 is a *response feasibility table:* given knowledge of the state of ignorance, the table yields the currently feasible range of strategies. But the ability to use these strategies depends also on the dynamics of the situation: the time left before the threat becomes overwhelming as compared to the time needed by the firm to respond.

DYNAMICS OF RESPONSE

Each of the six response strategies makes a complementary contribution to the firm's ability to handle strategic discontinuities. But the sequence in which they are used will vary from firm to firm. As mentioned in the preceding section, conventional strategic planning suggests a sequence in which measures for flexibility and awareness are derived from the analysis of direct response. Figure 3–12 suggests that a reverse procedure enables the firm to start the response much earlier.

One such reverse sequence is shown on the horizontal axis in figure 3–13. The vertical axis measures the time needed by the firm to complete a response to an opportunity/threat. The two solid curves show that the less prepared the firm is at the time it responds, the more time it will need to complete the response.

The upper curve shows the times for a normal response, in which existing processes, structure, systems, and procedures are used to handle the threat/opportunity. The lower solid curve, the "ad hoc crash response," shows the time savings that can be effected if "all the stops are pulled out," when everything that is possible is done to speed up the response: normal rules and procedures are disregarded, other priorities are pushed into the background, organizational lines are crossed, activities are duplicated, overtime is incurred.

The mere "pulling out of the stops" in a crash response when a crisis looms is not the only procedure open to the firm. If, in spite of best efforts to anticipate the threat/opportunity, the firm still expects to be confronted occasionally with very fast-developing threats, a program of training in *crisis management* can lower the ad hoc crash response line to the dotted line level labelled "organized crisis response," thus increasing the capability for handling fast-developing discontinuities.

The envelope of response times defined by the three curves will of course differ from firm to firm and from one discontinuity to another. Size, complexity, rigidity of structure will lengthen the response times. The nature of the threat/opportunity will be equally influential. Important factors will be size of the discontinuity as well as the "degree of unfamiliarity" of the threat/opportunity, both of which determine the magnitude of the response effort.

In an earlier section, we have shown that each threat will develop over time, leaving less and less time before the critical moment, but yielding increasing information about the threat/opportunity. As the information gets better, figure 3–12 can be used to determine the newly feasible state of preparedness; and figure 3–13 will provide the time needed to complete the response starting from that state. This relatively simple procedure can combine the history of threats and history of responses in the manner shown in figure 3–14. The vertical scale measures, using the same units of time, first, the response time needed, as shown by the response curves, and second, the time available, as shown by the threat curves. Two matched horizontal scales are given. The lower one shows the state of ignorance at the various stages of the threat. On the upper scale are the states of preparedness feasible in the respective states of threat.

Thus when Threat No. 1 reaches State one, the firm does not have enough time for a normal response. An urgent response is needed in its early stages. But at point A on figure 3–14, response finally catches up with the threat. Management can "take a breath" and treat the remainder of the response through normal business procedures. On the other hand, Threat No. 2, as anticipated earlier, turns out to be "bad news." It arises, like a low-flying attack airplane, too near the target, and moving too fast to be intercepted. Inevitably, it will lead to higher losses than the firm considers acceptable.

Figure 3–14 illustrates the superiority of the gradual preparedness approach over conventional strategic planning in handling a fast-developing T/O. The former can handle Threat No. 1 with time to spare. But in con-

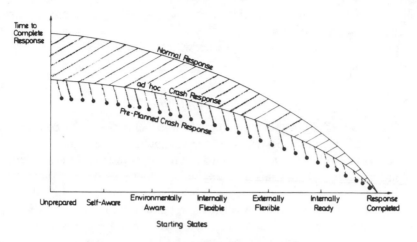

Figure 3–13
Internal Dynamics of Response

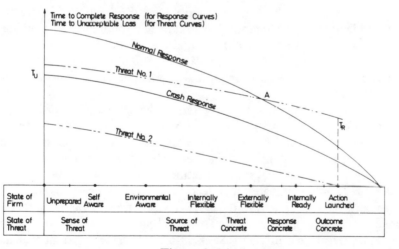

Figure 3–14
Dynamics of Response vs Availability of Information

ventional strategic planning the firm has remained unprepared (requiring T_U time to respond) until the threat is fully developed, leaving only T_R, which is less than T_U, for reaction! To put this differently, the stringent information requirements of strategic planning limit the useable forecasting horizon and make the firm lose the benefits of early warnings about the T/O. On the other hand, gradual preparedness expands the useable forecasting horizon and permits response to start early. One necessary consequence of this expansion is to broaden the firm's attention to the weak signals and trends in the environment. By responding to these the firm prepares itself to live in a climate of uncertainty and turbulence and thus respond early to threats/opportunities which arise suddenly and develop very rapidly.

Practical Application

Discussion of figure 3–14 completes the development of a conceptual framework which matches weak responses against weak signals. Clearly, the curves sketched in the preceding figures are illustrative. Most actual situations will lack the information needed for constructing them. We need, therefore, to reduce concepts to practice, to construct a step-by-step approach which will enable the firm to respond to weak signals. A necessary basis for such an approach is environment surveillance systems which can prepare and interpret vague trends and threats. We next turn to a brief discussion of such a system.

OPPORTUNITY-VULNERABILITY ANALYSIS

No matter how high the state of ignorance, three types of information can be identified in each impending strategic discontinuity: (1) timing of its probable occurrence; (2) the magnitude of the positive or negative impact on the firm; and (3) information about its specific characteristics: where it will occur, what changes it will introduce in products, in technology, in marketing, etc.

A reference to figure 3–4 shows that in the earlier states of ignorance the third type of information is scarce, while estimates of timing and impact based more on judgment than analysis are imprecise and span a broad range of possibilities. Nevertheless, even such estimates can provide a basis for substantial strategic action.

To obtain such estimates, it is necessary to make a systematic analysis of the firm's environment. In the early days of strategic planning this was done by examining the strategic future of each self-contained organizational unit, usually a division. After a time it became apparent that unit-by-unit analysis gives a confusing picture of the future, particularly when a division has a number of product lines and operates in many markets.

Recently, an alternative approach has emerged which subdivides the firm's environment into relatively independent *strategic business areas,* (SBAS), each of which is a segment of the firm's environment with distinctive trends, threats and opportunities. Current strategic changes in the availability of key resources, as well as increasing strategic interaction between the firm and society, focus attention on *strategic resource areas* and *strategic influence areas.* Thus, a complete analysis of strategic vulnerability would include these two in addition to strategic business areas. However, we can illustrate the method of analysis by confining our atten-

tion to the latter. Such a breakdown in strategic business areas is illustrated in figure 3–15, in which a firm has identified four SBAs and their
respective contributions to the firm's profit. In actual analysis, both present profit contributions and their trends would be analyzed. Again, to
keep the argument simple, we shall use only current profits.

		STATE OF IGNORANCE				
STRATEGIC BUSINESS AREAS	PROFIT CONTRIBUT.	SENSE OF T/O	SOURCE OF T/O	T/O CONCRETE	RESPONSE CONCRETE	OUTCOME CONCRETE
SBA₁	50 %			T 3–5 yrs 0,2–0,5		
SBA₂	30 %	T–O 10–15 yrs 0,0–2,0				
SBA₃	15 %					OF 1–2 yrs 2,5–3,0
SBA₄	5 %		O 4–8 yrs 2,0–5,0			
STATUS: ENVIRON-MENTAL AWARENESS		VERY POOR	POOR	EXCELLENT		ADEQU

Figure 3–15
Opportunity-Vulnerability Analysis

The entries in the table of figure 3–15 identify the impending strategic
discontinuities along four dimensions. The first is the state of ignorance
within the firm. This is indicated by the choice of an appropriate column
for each SBA. Next, each entry is identified as a potential threat or an opportunity, or both. This is entered into the appropriate columns, together
with the ranges of the possible impacts on the profit of the firm. This is
shown as a range of variation in the SBA's contribution to profit (0.2–
0.5 for SBA₁). (A number of techniques are available for estimating profit
impact of strategic discontinuity. The best known among them is *impact
analysis*.)

As illustrated, the variability of the respective estimates becomes higher
as ignorance increases. Thus for SBA₂ it is not even clear whether it is a
threat or an opportunity, but it is clear that the impact is likely to be very
serious. Clearly this discontinuity needs close watching. On the other

hand, the profit estimates for the opportunity in SBA₃ can be estimated within a narrow range of both occurrence and impact. Thus the various entries in the table will be the result of different computational approaches. In the higher states of ignorance techniques based on expert judgment, such as Delphi, must be used. For the lower states of ignorance it is possible to introduce quantitative modelling and cash stream projections.

PREPAREDNESS DIAGNOSIS

The next step is to assess the firm's readiness to respond. This can be accomplished through a *preparedness diagnosis,* which is illustrated for SBA₁ on figure 3–16.

SBA *1	FEASIB.	STATUS	RELAT. IMP.	CRASH TIME	CRASH COST	NORMAL TIME	NORMAL COST
SELF AWARENESS		0% ●———— 100%	VH	3		6	
ENVIRONMENTAL AWARENESS		————————●	H	1		2	
INTERNAL FLEXIBILITY		——●————	M	2		4	
EXTERNAL FLEXIBILITY		——●————	L	4		8	
ACTION READINESS		————●———	M	2		4	
ACTION		————————	VH	2		4	
COMPLETED RESPONSE		0% ———●—— 100%		4 YRS	4,0	8 YRS	1,0

Figure 3–16
Preparedness Diagnosis

First, feasible response strategies are identified by using the state of ignorance information for each SBA from figure 3–15 in conjunction with figure 3–12. As shown in figure 3–15, SBA₁ is an advanced state of information. Therefore all strategies short of direct action are feasible.

Next, using figures 3–7 through 3–11 as check-off lists, the current state of readiness (as well as of ongoing readiness-enhancing projects) is examined to determine the adequacy of the respective readiness states. The results are indicated as fat dots on figure 3–16, on a scale from 0 percent to 100 percent.

The "relative importance" in the following column assesses the importance of the respective sub-strategies to the ultimate success of the firm's response. Thus, in the illustration, external flexibility does not appear to be a problem, and internal readiness is medium important. This might signify that much of the firm's current capability appears applicable to the discontinuity.

The last four columns estimate the times and costs for normal and crash responses, respectively. A useful measure is the estimated cost of the total response program (shown in the last line of the table) as a fraction of the percentage of current profits contributed by the SBA. For example, if a crash program will cost 4.0, as indicated in figure 3–16, and if the response will prevent a loss of 0.2 to 0.5 of this profit, the "investment" will amortize itself in 8 to 20 years. This suggests that the threat will be "written-off" and allowed to run its course to avoid "sending good money after the bad." On the other hand, the normal response (if it will be timely enough), costing 1.0, will be worth the effort, because the amortization period will be only two to five years.

Preparedness diagnosis needs to be repeated for each discontinuity identified in figure 3–15, because the characteristic of the discontinuity will differ, and because the firm's capabilities will be better suited to some discontinuities than to others. Therefore, a serious effort to assess the firm's preparedness would involve two steps. The first would be a general *capability profile*[4] analysis which determines the firm's capabilities and capacities. In the second step the general profiles would be compared to specific discontinuities to determine the respective compatibilities, or synergies.

VULNERABILITY PROFILE

The results of discontinuity and of preparedness analyses are next combined in a summary *vulnerability profile* to produce a bird's-eye view of the firm's future prospects. This is shown in figure 3–17.

The respective rectangles enclose the "regions of probable impact" on the respective SBAs. Rectangles below the horizontal axis spell potential losses in profitability, those above indicate gains. The height of the rectangle spans the probable range of loss/gain, the base spans the probable times when the discontinuity will impact on the firm.

The horizontal dotted lines span the times of probable completion of successful response. Thus, the normal response for SBA₃ would be late, but the firm can assure itself of capturing the opportunity through a crash program. SBA₂ is "safe," normal response will capture it, provided the firm "moves right along." SBA₁ is in trouble because even a crash response may be late; it looks like a "surprise" in the making.

On a first examination, the overall picture for the firm is not bad. It has a very promising, near-term prospect in SBA₄. SBA₁ and SBA₃ may balance out. The potential problem is in SBA₂ which, because of the current state of ignorance may turn out either way. SBA₂ certainly should be carefully

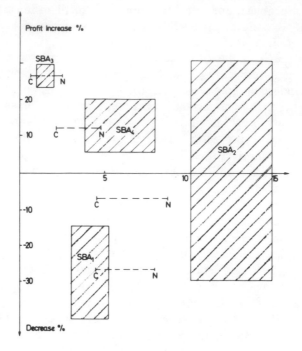

Figure 3–17
Vulnerability Profile

monitored, but a more vigorous response program can be delayed at least a year.

A closer look at the firm's position may suggest that the four SBAs of the firm, with their respective vulnerabilities, do not provide the firm enough long-term security, because so much rides on the future of SBA₂. If this conclusion is reached, an increase in external flexibility through diversification will be indicated. But this indication is one of several suggested by the vulnerability profile. Each of the SBAs requires attention and each competes with others for management attention and for resources. Therefore, we need a systematic procedure by which the alternatives can be compared and the resources allocated.

STRATEGIC ISSUE ANALYSIS

For this purpose, we shall use an extended version of *Strategic Issue Analysis* (SIA), a decision technique already in use. This technique emerged within the last few years as a means for overcoming a number of shortcomings that were found in applications of strategic planning. One shortcoming was the inability of strategic planning systems to respond to significant discontinuities that occurred outside the planning cycle. Another was a typical long planning delay of six to nine months between initiation and completion of planning, which made the response too slow for fast-moving threats. A third shortcoming was an organizational inflexibility of strategic planning: when an issue fails to fit neatly into one of the planning units, it tends to fall "between two stools." The fourth, and perhaps most important, shortcoming is a typical difficulty of converting plans into action.

Somewhat different varieties of Strategic Issue Analysis (SIA) have been used, sometimes as an addition, and sometimes as a replacement for annual organization-wide strategic planning. The technique has been applied both to business firms and to complex governmental organizations. When the various positive aspects are synthesized, four major features emerge:

(1) SIA embraces all potential discontinuities no matter what their source: markets of the firm, changes in characteristics of demand, changes in technology, in availability of resources, changes in political constraints, in conditions of work. For example, today the following would be scanned as potential *strategic issues:* "limits of growth," petroleum politics, environmental pollution, industrial democracy, thermonuclear fusion, technology of nonpetroleum power generation, scarcity of strategic resources, etc. Thus SIA broadens the much narrower preoccupation with products-markets-technology found in typical strategic planning systems.

(2) SIA assigns responsibility for response, not according to the firm's organizational jurisdiction, but according to the logic of the issue. If resolution of an issue cuts across organizational lines, a special task force is set to handle it.

(3) SIA, unlike most other management systems, does not operate on a fixed calendar basis. Rather, a perpetual list of strategic issues is continually modified and updated and temporary task forces are organized and launched whenever urgency and priority dictate.

(4) Finally, SIA is treated not as a planning but as a *result-oriented* activity. The charge to the task force is not limited to planning studies. Instead, the charge is to produce a change in the strategic posture of the firm.

In figure 3–18, we present the decision flow in an SIA system which is specifically oriented towards "amplification of weak signals." As shown in figure 3–18, SIA is a "real time" system triggered by two inputs: (1) a continual surveillance of the environment for "upstream" information of discontinuities; and (2) a continual appraisal and reappraisal of the changing capacities and capabilities of the firm.

The external surveillance activity yields a continually updated list of

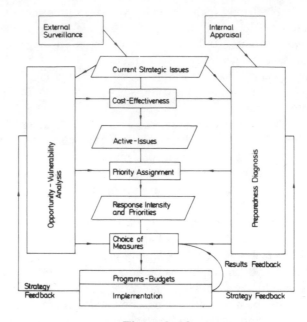

Figure 3–18
Dynamic Response to Strategic Discontinuities

current strategic issues which have important relevance to the firm. The central stem of figure 3–18 shows how this list is translated into ultimate strategic action. The issues are subjected to three successive stages of analysis. First, cost-effectiveness comparison, in the manner discussed in conjunction with figure 3–17, is used to eliminate from the current list those issues whose cost would not be justified, either by the amount of potential losses saved, or the profit opportunity foregone.

The vulnerability profile (figure 3–17) shows that what matters is neither the timing of the threat, taken by itself, nor the timing of the response, but the combination of the two. An imminent near-term threat may present no problems if the firm is able to respond to it quickly. On the other hand, a long-term threat may result in a strategic crisis, if the changes needed in the firm are major and time-consuming.

This interaction between timing of threat and timing of response can be combined into a single concept of *urgency,* which is measured by the overlap of the two time periods. Thus, if we use C and N (see figure 3–17) to denote the respective times required for normal and crash responses, and E and L for the earliest and latest times of probable impact of discontinuity, a scale urgency can be defined as follows (see figure 3–17 for examples) :

1. Low urgency if $N < E$
2. Moderate if $E < N < L$, and increasing as N approaches L
3. High urgency if $N > L$ but $C < E$
4. Very high urgency if $E < C < L$
5. Crisis urgency if $L < C$.

But urgency alone would not by itself determine the priority of an issue. Equally important will be the *cost-effectiveness* measured by the difference between the impact and the cost of response. Relative cost-effectiveness will differ from firm to firm, depending on the number of strategic issues and on the total budget available. A working table, shown in figure 3–19, can be used for assigning the relative priorities among the active strategic issues, as well as for selecting the appropriate speed of response.

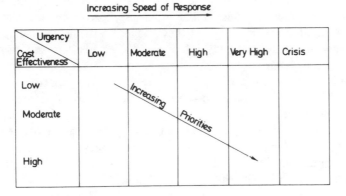

Figure 3–19
Determining Priorities for Active Strategic Issues

With priorities established, the next step is to select the specific measures to be implemented. The *vulnerability-opportunity analysis* shown on the left-hand side of figure 3–18 will provide one input to this decision. The key instrument is the feasibility table of figure 3–12 (which would be supplemented by Strategic Resource and Societal Influence Areas), used to find the feasible strategies. These in turn are translated into feasible measures with the aid of figures 3–7 through 3–11.

The second input comes from *preparedness diagnosis* shown on the right of figure 3–18. The current state of readiness for dealing with each of the active issues, as well as the status of the current projects to enhance readiness, can be determined using, again, figures 3–7 through 3–11, this time as diagnostic checklists.

DYNAMICS OF STRATEGIC ISSUE ANALYSIS

A two-dimensional graph, such as figure 3–18, cannot properly reflect the dynamic properties of the process it represents. In the case of SIA, dynamics are very important because they distinguish SIA from the much more static strategic planning process.

The latter is typically periodic, conducted according to a set calendar. Since strategic planning embraces the totality of the firm's future and since it is typically a decentralized process, it is time-consuming and usually cumbersome. The complexities of the systems, of interlocking relationships, and of decision responsibilities focus attention on the dynamics of the planning system. As a result, preoccupation with system dynamics leads to a neglect of the threat dynamics.

Strategic Issue Analysis is a complement to strategic planning designed to remedy this deficiency. It might be called a "real-time" component of the total system. The external surveillance and internal surveillance activities are conducted continuously, providing new signals and issues for management as soon as they surface on the horizon. The current list is continuously updated and projects are activated and terminated throughout the year.

The dynamic nature of such a process, involving early response to vague, imperfectly understood discontinuities, naturally creates the possibility of overresponsiveness, of the firm's going off "half-cocked" at the slightest provocation. An examination of the process described in the preceding pages shows that, while valid and necessary, this concern is anticipated in the nature of SIA. In the first place, there is a built-in protection against overreaction in the fact that limited information permits only limited measures. Secondarily, the strategies and measures are designed for *graduated response* which increases the firm's commitment in step with developing information. Nevertheless, maximum possible protection against overreaction must be built in. This can be helped by proper use of feedback. Two types of feedback are shown at the bottom of figure 3–18: *performance feedback* and *strategic feedback*. The former informs management about progress in implementing selected measures. The latter provides information on whether the strategy pursued and the measures selected are the proper ones.

When a threat is in the higher states of ignorance, the knowledge of whether one is on the right track is more important than results. But as time passes, the firm progressively has to commit itself to a specific approach, even at the risk of error. Thus another necessary dynamic feature of SIA, not immediately evident from figure 3–18, is to select measures which give the type of feedback desired. Through the life of the threat, in the manner illustrated in figure 3–20, the emphasis shifts from measures

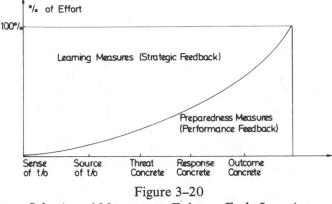

Figure 3–20
Selection of Measures to Enhance Early Learning

which produce strategic feedback to measures which yield preparedness results.

SIA AND STRATEGIC PLANNING

As already discussed, strategic issue analysis is not a replacement but a complement to strategic planning. Strategic planning deals with the totality of the firm's future, but it lacks responsiveness to weak strategic signals. While SIA provides the latter, it is essentially an *opportunistic* approach, seeking to protect and prepare the firm for singular events. A comparison of the salient features of the two approaches is given in figure 3–21.

The choice of the appropriate technique is almost obvious from the preceding.

(1) A firm which confronts a strategically unsatisfactory future, or a firm which seeks to make a discontinuous improvement on the past, but which finds itself in a relatively surprise-free environment, would choose strategic planning.

(2) A firm whose overall strategic trends appear satisfactory, but whose environment is highly turbulent, can limit itself to SIA.

(3) A firm with both problems would be wise to use both.

The existence of SIA alongside strategic planning will not only provide insurance against surprises, but also, when properly used, speed up the strategic planning process. This is illustrated in figure 3–22.

Shown above the horizontal time axis is the typical sequence of events involving strategic planning. Annual environmental surveillance identifies major trends, as well as threats and opportunities. These would be based on strong signals; weak signals would be filtered out. This informa-

Strategic Planning	Strategic Issue Analysis
• Deals with firms' total strategic future.	• Deals with probable discontinuities
• Focussed on Products-Markets-Technology	• Embraces discontinuities from all sources
• Applicable when major Strategic reorientation is desired	• Applicable when insurance against surprises is desired
• Responds to strong signals	• Responds to weak signals
• Strategic information needs derived from decision	• Feasible decisions determined by available information
• Prepared periodically	• A continuous process
• Organization-focussed	• Problem-focussed

Figure 3–21

Comparison of Strategic Planning and Strategic Analysis

tion is translated into strategy which serves as a basis for plans and programs. The first step in implementation is to develop new product/markets, the second is to develop the needed capability, and the third is to launch the new product/markets. The strategic action sequence is completed when the new product attains a profitable position at point A.

As shown in the lower part of figure 3–22, outputs of SIA can be fed to respective steps in strategic planning, thus expediting the entire chain of events and advancing the profitable position from time A to time B.

APPLICATION TO PRACTICE

In the preceding pages we have travelled a long road, first developing a conceptual framework and, then a practical procedure by which a firm in a turbulent environment can cope with "weak signals" and minimize the chances of surprise.

The result is a new planning approach that, to become effective, must be accepted and used by practicing managers. However persuasive and logical the approach, neither its acceptance nor its use can be taken for granted. To do so would be to disregard the numerous instances during the past twenty years, when similarly logical approaches encountered "resistance to planning," and were either rejected or emasculated by the using organizations.

To gain acceptance for this particular approach, it is necessary to as-

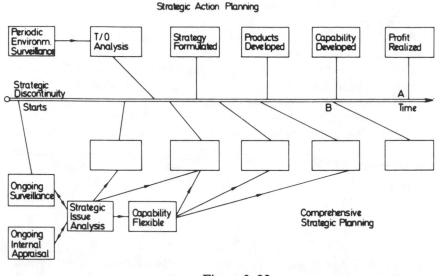

Figure 3–22
Time Compression through Strategic Preparedness

sure within the firm a climate of openness to strategic risk and preparedness to face unfamiliar and threatening prospects. This problem of creating
a climate of strategic decisiveness is at least equally as complex and as important as the one we have just treated. Therefore, we have explored
decisiveness in the companion paper cited in note 1.

In that paper we argue that in the absence of strategic decisiveness, we
would find little acceptance of Strategic Issue Analysis. However, diagnosis of strategic decisiveness is not easy. Firms who lack it do not necessarily appear sleepy, environmentally inactive. Many of them will be
quite active, but deeper analysis would show that their environmental en-
gagement is *competitive* and not *strategic,* confined to dealing with familiar
fluctuations in the environment[5] and unaccustomed to discontinuities.
Such firms will be active in marketing, new product development, long-
range forecasting, even long-range planning. But all these activities will
cling to a historical perception of the environment and its extrapolations.
As one researcher put it, such firms use environmental information to
confirm their prior models of reality, and not to change and enlarge their
understanding. A vivid example of such behavior is furnished by the
U.S. automotive industry which, during the past fifteen years, has persisted
in clinging, in spite of a flood of contrary data, to the belief that its customer is still in love with the luxurious "gas-guzzling monster."

Therefore, in a large percentage of cases, an effort to introduce strategic preparedness based on weak signals is likely either to encounter resistance, or to be rejected altogether, unless strategic decisiveness is substantially enhanced.

But this does not mean that preparedness analysis must be delayed until after the influential managers change their perceptions. The two processes can proceed in parallel, interacting and reinforcing each other. Thus, for example, enhancement of managerial flexibility will at the same time contribute to enhanced decisiveness (see figure 3–11).

What is needed, therefore, is a two-way feedback organizational change process in which both the *willingness to act* and the *ability to act* are developed in a coordinated and mutually supportive manner. The technology for designing such change processes now exists and has been tested in practice,[6] and has been described in the literature.

NOTES AND REFERENCES

1. Ansoff, H. Igor; Eppink, J.; and Gomer, H. "Management of Surprise and Discontinuities: Increasing Managerial Responsiveness," *EIASM Working Paper No. 75–29*, Brussels, 1975.
2. I owe this happy phrase to W. W. Bryant, Manager of TEO Central, in the Philips Company.
3. My thanks to Mr. Leslie Smith, Chairman of the BOC Limited, London.
4. Ansoff, H. Igor. *Corporate Strategy*. New York: McGraw-Hill, 1965.
5. Ansoff, H. Igor; Hayes, R. L.; and Declerck, R. "From Strategic Planning to Strategic Management." In *From Strategic Planning to Strategic Management*. New York: John Wiley, 1976.
6. Davous, Pierre and Deas, J. "Design of a Consulting Intervention for Strategic Management." In *From Strategic Planning to Strategic Management*. New York: John Wiley, 1976.

4

Product Portfolio Strategy, Market Structure, and Performance

WILLIAM E. COX, JR.

During the past decade there have been countless studies seeking to relate some or all of the elements of strategy, structure, and performance of large diversified corporations. Many of these studies have been conducted by economists specializing in industrial organization. They have developed an approach to the economic analysis of markets known as markct structure analysis. The essence of this approach is summarized in the scp paradigm: "the *structure* of a market is assumed to determine the *conduct* of the participants in the market, and the conduct, in turn, to determine the economic result that flows from the market, i.e. the market's *performance*." (Vernon 1972, p.7.)

The scp paradigm, which is drawn from the microeconomic theory of markets, has proved difficult to test empirically; the absence of relevant information on conduct has led most analysts to seek relationships between market structure and performance. Yet there is general disappointment and pessimism among industrial organization economists regarding the existing and prospective findings about the structure-performance relationship. Vernon (1972, p.117) concluded that the "overall state-of-the-art in market structure analysis is unimpressive." After reviewing the literature on structure-performance relationships, Marion and Handy (1973, p.43) stated: "Empirical results do not present a clear, consistent picture of the determinants of market performance. This inconsistency can be interpreted in different ways, depending largely on the biases and beliefs of the interpreter." Stern (1970, p.19) presented a very pessimistic outlook for market structure analysis in his review of the approach:

The problems of obtaining objective measurements of the elements of market structure are legion and should not be understated. In fact, some of the problems are so critical that there is real doubt as to whether any theory grounded on these elements can ever be verified.

The disappointment and pessimism reflected in the preceding quotations has resulted in a call for a return to the "industry study," an approach that had been eased aside in favor of SCP paradigm analyses and cross-sectional interindustry regression models. Vernon (1972), Shubik (1970), and Weiss (1971) have all concluded that it is time to turn to detailed *intra*-industry models, while continuing to employ quantitative methods for analysis, in contrast to the descriptive industry studies of the 1930–1960 period.

Grether, in a comprehensive review of the industrial organization field, suggested that the critical question about market structure analysis is not that of methodology but one of relevance:

The most important issue for the field of industrial organization is how to bring the large diversified corporation within the framework of analysis. The crux of the matter is whether the market structure framework can be employed at all; in other words, is it relevant? If such large organizations are free of the market, as some allege, it would seem futile to try to analyze their behavior and performance results in a market structure framework. The focus of research then should be on internal organizations, policies and strategies and their performance results. Orientation should then be from performance results back into internal organization and decision making. But if there is a significant amount of market determinism and constraint, even if only for a period of time under given structural characteristics, it would seem reasonable to use the market structure framework of analysis. (Grether 1970, p.35.)

A series of studies have appeared recently that seek to explain the behavior and performance of large diversified corporations without recourse to market structure analysis. Based on the premise that "structure follows strategy" (Chandler 1966), these studies of large manufacturing enterprises in a number of countries indicate that a prevailing strategy of product diversification was accompanied by the adoption of decentralized, divisionalized organization structures, and by relatively high levels of profitability (Rumelt 1974; Channon 1973). These studies provide valuable insights into the relationships between corporate strategy, organization structure, and economic performance of large firms. There will continue to be industrial organization studies conducted without regard to market influences, but as Grether, Vernon, and others have noted, new approaches to market structure analysis are needed. This paper presents one such approach, based on the SCP paradigm.

Market Structure

Studies of market structure have tended to focus on three primary areas of investigation: (1) the distribution of firm sizes within an industry; (2) concentration measures, usually based on the share of output or capital held by the 4th, 8th and 20th largest firms in the industry; and (3) the variation in market shares over time among leading firms in an industry. Each of the three areas has generated a sizable literature, particularly the latter two. A recently completed study by Cooke and Cox (1975) reviews the literature associated with the first area and finds that there is a demonstrated and specific relationship between firm size, as measured by market share percentage for specified time periods, and the firm's market share rank in an industry in which all important firms (those with significant market shares) are identified. More specifically, it was found that the market share distributions of the important firms in ten industries may be described by a semi-logarithmic function:

$$\log s_j = k_0 - k_1 j \tag{1.1}$$
$$c = \text{antilog } k_1 \tag{1.2}$$

where:

s_j = the market share of the jth firm in a market
j = the market share rank of the firms in a market
k_0, k_1 = regression coefficients
c = the proportionality constant, a parameter of the semi-logarithmic function

The nature of this semi-logarithmic relationship is such that each market share (s_j) is some constant percentage (c) of the next higher market share position (s_{j-1}) in the market:

$$s_j = c \, s_{j-1} \tag{1.3}$$

The parameter c, the proportionality constant, is the transformed slope of a semi-logarithmic function, and describes the structural relationship of the market shares held by firms within an industry.

Additional equations useful for calculating market share values and proportionality constants are:

$$s_n = c \, s_{n-1} \tag{1.4}$$
$$s_i = (1 + c + c^2 + \ldots + c^{n-1})^{-1} \tag{1.5}$$

where:

s_n = market share of the firm with the lowest important market share, i.e., the last important firm in the market. In this study of ten industries, $s_n > 0.1\%$.

The choice of the semi-logarithmic function instead of the Pareto, log-normal (Gibrat's Law), Yule, or other similar distributions is shown by Cooke and Cox (1975) to be based on the properties of the parameter c. There is very little difference between the alternative functions in terms of their goodness of fit to empirical distributions of firm size. Thus, the relative ease of computing the parameter c and its usefulness in measuring a variety of structural relationships lead to the selection of the semi-logarithmic function as the preferred measure for market structure analysis.

The Cooke and Cox study (1975) fitted equation (1.1) to data for the ten industries in table 4–1 and calculated the c values from equation (1.2). The coefficient of multiple determination, r^2, which is a measure of the least squares fit of the semi-logarithmic function to the actual data, was 0.936 or greater for seven of the ten industries (air transport, beer, cereals, diesel engines, gasoline, steel, and sulphur). In the other three industries (automobiles, cigarettes, and trucks), the values of r^2 ranged from a low of 0.868 to a high of 0.914.

Table 4–1

The Distribution of Market Shares

Industry	c	Number of Important Firms
Automobiles	.420	4
Sulphur	.539	6
Diesel engines	.566	6
Cereals	.599	7
Cigarettes	.735	6[a]
Air transport	.785	11
Steel	.812	16
Trucks	.850	6[a]
Beer	.893	25
Gasoline	.898	40

[a]Exceptions to the direct relationship between the value of c and the number of important firms in an industry.

Source: Ernest F. Cooke, *Market Share Measures of Rivalry.* Unpublished Ph.D. dissertation, Case Western Reserve University, 1974.

Table 4-1 also presents the number of important firms in each of the ten industries studied. It is apparent that there is a direct relationship between the value of c and the number of important firms in eight of the ten industries. The only exceptions to the direct relationship are the cigarette industry, in which the c value suggests that the rivalry approximates that of eight important firms rather than six; and the truck industry, in which the *c* value indicates a degree of rivalry that approximates that of twenty important firms rather than six. Cooke (1974, chapter 6) has shown that these two industries have displayed the greatest amount of competitive instability and rivalry among the ten industries during the periods studied, resulting therefore in higher *c* values than would be expected on the basis of the number of important firms in the two industries.

Based on the observed relationship between the value of *c* and the number of important firms in an industry, we may estimate an "equilibrium" value or range of values for *c,* as indicated by the number of important firms in an industry. "Equilibrium" values of *c* are normative positions based on empirical regularities, which may be used to calculate an "equilibrium" distribution of market shares toward which the industry may be expected to move.[1]

The "equilibrium" distribution of market shares for the breakfast cereals industry, assuming that it continues to be composed of seven important producers (six firms plus an "all other" firm), is shown in table 4–2, together with the actual market share distribution for the industry for the 1954–64 period, and the 1969–74 period. There is virtual correspondence between the actual "equilibrium" market share distributions for the breakfast cereal industry during the 1954–64 period and a very close correspondence during the 1969–74 period. This is the result of the high stability in both market share rank and values for individual firms within the periods. Between the periods, however, there were significant

Table 4–2
"Equilibrium" and Actual Market Share Distributions in the Breakfast Cereal Industry, 1954–1964 and 1969–1974

Firm Rank	"Equilibrium" Distribution[a] ($c = 0.596$)	1954–64 Average Actual Distribution[b] ($c = 0.599$)	1969–74 Average Actual Distribution[c] ($c = 0.604$)
S_1 — First	41.0%	40.8%	40.3%
S_2 — Second	24.5	24.4	24.3
S_3 — Third	14.6	14.6	14.7
S_4 — Fourth	8.7	8.8	8.9
S_5 — Fifth	5.2	5.2	5.4
S_6 — Sixth	3.1	3.1	3.3
S_7 — Seventh (all others)	1.8	1.9	2.0

Sources: [a]Calculated from equations (1.1–1.5) of this chapter.
[b]Based on data in Markham and Slater (1966).
[c]Based on data from three sources: *Advertising Age,* March 24, 1975, p. 52, *Barron's,* October 2, 1972, p.14; *Barron's,* July 26, 1971, p.18.

shifts in both market share rank and values for individual firms. General Foods, the second-ranked firm from 1954 to 1963, lost its position to General Mills in 1964 and trailed General Mills by five to six share points during most of the 1969–74 period. Nabisco, the fourth-ranked firm during the 1954–64 period, lost its position to Quaker Oats between the periods and continued to lose ground to Quaker from 1969 to 1974. Quaker more than doubled its market share between the two periods, while Ralston lost the gains made in the latter part of the earlier period. The return to an "equilibrium" distribution in the years 1969–74 after competitive turmoil from 1964 to 1969 provides additional support for the concept of an "equilibrium" distribution of market shares, based on the empirical regularities in this case.

There are close similarities between c and the Herfindahl index of concentration as measures of market structure and competition. (Vernon 1972, pp.43–44.) Both measures are useful and relatively easy to calculate, but the c value appears to have broader application. It is capable of generating an "equilibrium" distribution of market shares and measuring the relative stability of market shares in an industry, besides serving as a measure of concentration.[2] Accordingly, the distribution of market shares in an industry, described by a semi-logarithmic function and c, the transformed slope of the function, will be used as the measure of market structure in the paradigm.

Conduct

The element of conduct has been consistently ignored in statistical studies of market structure (Vernon 1972, p.39), primarily for the reasons noted by Bain (1968, p.329):

> Actual   patterns of market conduct cannot be fully enough measured to permit us to establish empirically a meaningful association either between market conduct and performance, or between structure and market conduct. It thus becomes expedient to test directly for net associations of market structure to market performance, leaving the detailed character of the implied linkage of conduct substantially unascertained.

However, as noted previously, the numerous attempts to relate market structure to market performance have been basically unsuccessful. Thus Vernon (1972, p.39) has concluded that "future research in classification and measurement of conduct appears to be warranted."

Bain (1968, p.9) has defined conduct as the "patterns of behavior which enterprises follow in adapting or adjusting to the markets in which they sell (or buy)." This broad definition thus focuses on the marketing strategy of firms in the largest sense, including product, price, promotion, and place policies. Among the various marketing strategies that might be selected, advertising has been perhaps the most widely studied. There are at least three reasons for the frequent choice of advertising expenditures as a measure of conduct:

1. Advertising expenditures are used as a proxy variable to measure the extent of product differentiation within an industry. Since product differentiation occupies a central role in modern economic theory, its measurement is deemed relevant and useful by economists. The following relationships are generally postulated: high advertising expenditures in an industry → high product differentiation → high barriers to entry → high concentration → high profitability → low performance or rivalry.[3] For a comprehensive review of studies on these relationships, see Vernon (1972, chapter 4).

2. Advertising is an important element in the marketing strategy of many consumer goods industries that are important, highly visible participants in American economic life.

3. Advertising expenditure data are readily available for all industries from government sources, while comparable data on other elements of marketing strategy are not available.

Although dozens of studies have used advertising expenditures as a measure of conduct, there is little agreement among analysts on its value. Vernon (1972, chapter 4) and Bass (1974 and chapter 8 of this volume) have offered persuasive evidence to show why this is so. There does seem to be general agreement that other measures of conduct should be investigated. Accordingly, a conceptual and methodological approach to marketing strategy, product portfolio strategy, is examined next as a measure of conduct.

The Boston Consulting Group (BCG), a management consulting firm, introduced the concept of product portfolio strategy, based on their development of "experience curve" analysis. Experience curve analysis, derived from the similar learning curve phenomenon, suggests that the total unit costs (in constant dollars) for a product or service will tend to decline by a consistent percentage (20–30 percent) with each doubling of accumulated output. Thus the competitor with the largest accumulated output will tend to have the largest market share, the lowest unit costs, and the highest profits (Cox 1975, p.466). The relationship between market share and profitability has been independently verified in the PIMS (Profit Impact of Market Strategies) study and illustrated in figure 4–1. (See also chapter 5 of this volume.) Dominant market share tends to be associated with very high profitability, with firms that hold market shares over 36 percent having an average profit return on investment of 30.2 percent. One basic focus of product portfolio strategy is thus on the strategic im-

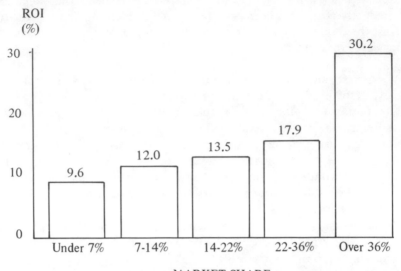

SOURCE: Sidney Schoeffler, Robert D. Buzzell and Donald F. Heany, "Impact of Strategic Planning on Profit Performance," *Harvard Business Review* (March-April 1974), p. 141.

Figure 4–1
Relationship of Market Share Level to Profitability

portance and value of obtaining and maintaining a dominant market share position in the firm's chosen markets.

A second focus of product portfolio strategy is the rate of growth in the firm's markets. Experience curve analysis shows that accumulated experience is doubled rapidly in high-growth markets. Unit costs should therefore decline substantially for all competitors, and even more substantially for those firms that are rapidly increasing their market share. Accordingly, a relatively high investment in improving or maintaining market share in high-growth markets is indicated on the basis of potential cost reductions and consequent relative profitability.

Product portfolio strategy is therefore based on two measures, market share and market growth rate. These measures may be related by the use of a growth/share matrix, shown in figure 4–2, in which each measure is categorized on a high/low basis. In figure 4–2, the categorization is based on (1) 36 percent and over market share levels, and (2) 10 percent and over market growth rates. The four categories thus created are:
1. Stars—high growth, high share
2. Problem Children—high growth, low share

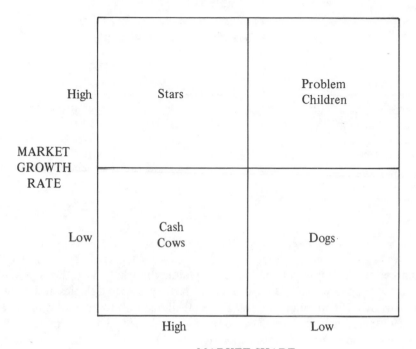

MARKET SHARE

Figure 4–2
Growth/Share Matrix: Product Portfolio Strategy

3. Cash Cows—low growth, high share
4. Dogs—low growth, low share

Each category of the growth/share matrix has an associated set of marketing strategies that are appropriate for the businesses and products within the category. (Cox 1975, p.469; Day 1975, pp.14–18.) In order to illustrate the application of product portfolio strategy, the breakfast cereals industry was selected from the ten industries listed in table 4–1. Table 4–3 shows the market share distribution for the ready-to-eat (RTE) breakfast cereal industry in 1974 and indicates that the Kellogg Company held a dominant market share of the industry with a 41.0 percent market share. The market growth rate (in constant dollars) from 1970 to 1974 was approximately 8 percent annually.

Figure 4–3 shows the growth/share matrix for the Kellogg Company. Its dominant market share coupled with a market growth rate of less than 10 percent make RTE cereals a Cash Cow for Kellogg. Accordingly, its

Table 4–3

Market Shares of Producers in the Ready-to-Eat
(RTE) *Cereal Industry, 1974*

Producers	Market Shares (based on dollar sales)
Kellogg	41.0%
General Mills	21.0
General Foods	16.6
Quaker Oats	10.7
Nabisco	4.3
Ralston Purina	2.9
All other producers	3.5
Total	100.0%

Source: Advertising Age, March 24, 1975, p.52.

marketing strategy has focused on maintaining market share through advertising and new product introductions. Kellogg's Rice Crispies and Corn Flakes held the number two and three positions in the RTE cereal market in 1974 with market shares (based on dollar sales) of 6.1 percent and 5.8 percent, respectively. (*Advertising Age,* 1975b, p.149.) A primary effort in new product introduction was centered in 1974 on a continuing national rollout of its Country Morning brand in the rapidly-growing "natural" cereal segment of the total RTE market.

With a variety of new products other than cereals competing for breakfast food expenditures, Kellogg's entry in the toaster pastries market, Kellogg's Pop-Tarts, held a dominant 55 percent share of the fast-growing market, placing the product in the Star category in the growth/share matrix. Again, the basic marketing strategy was to maintain share through advertising support ($1 million in 1974 against estimated sales of $47 million, for an advertising to sales ratio of 2.1 percent). (*Advertising Age,* 1975b, p.149.) Kellogg was also positioned in the high-growth frozen breakfast products market, with its Eggo brand holding 30 percent of the market, thereby creating a Problem Child in the growth/share matrix. Marketing strategy was directed toward increasing market share through modest advertising support ($600,000 on a sales volume of $18 million) and new product introductions.

While the Kellogg Company has achieved market dominance in the RTE cereal market by concentrating its resources and attention on that market (approximately 80 percent of its worldwide sales are in RTE cereals), each of its five major U.S. competitors is much more diversified in products and markets. Ralston Purina Company, with total sales over $3 billion in 1974, obtained only 1 percent of its total in the U.S. RTE cereal market;

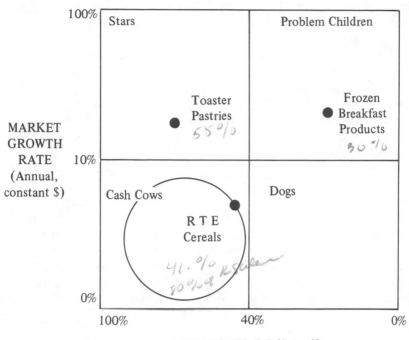

A third factor of importance in product portfolio strategy, market size, may be shown in the Growth/Share Matrix as a circle, with the size of the circle proportional to relative market size.

SOURCE: *Advertising Age* (August 18, 1975), pp. 149-50.

Figure 4–3
Growth/Share Matrix: Kellogg Company

Nabisco, Inc., 5 percent; General Foods Corporation, 8 percent; Quaker Oats Company, 11 percent; General Mills, Inc., 12 percent; while the Kellogg Company received 53 percent of its total sales in the U.S. RTE cereal market.[4] In addition, each of the five major U.S. competitors of the Kellogg Company have achieved positions of market dominance in other markets. Ralston Purina dominates the fast-growing dry pet foods market; Nabisco dominates the cracker (Ritz brand), dog snack food (Milk Bone), tonic (Geritol), and sedative (Sominex) markets; General Foods dominates the coffee, instant breakfast drink (Tang), powdered soft drink (Kool-Aid), and semi-moist dog food markets; Quaker Oats dominates the hot cereal market; and General Mills dominates the family flour (Gold Medal) and casserole products (Betty Crocker) markets. In their quest for market dominance and high-growth markets, the six primary competitors in the RTE cereal market have tended to converge repeatedly in the same markets, with the pet foods markets as perhaps the best example.

General Foods, with 16.6 percent of the RTE cereal market and no dominant brands in any major segment of the market, has a balanced product portfolio as shown in the growth/share matrix in figure 4–4. Its low share of the RTE market (third among the six major producers) and the low (8 percent) market growth rate place its RTE business in the Dog category of the growth/share matrix. Examination of marketing strategy suggests that General Foods has engaged in an aggresive advertising effort to position its long-time Grape Nuts brand as an entry in the rapidly growing "natural" cereal segment of the market. Selected other brands have also received relatively high advertising support, despite the traditional admonitions regarding the futility of aggressively supporting the Dogs in a product portfolio. Actually, General Foods appears to be giving heavy advertising support to brands that are being repositioned in relatively high-growth segments of the RTE cereal market. The "natural" cereal segment, a case in point, is actually in the Problem Child category in the growth/share matrix, and an aggressive advertising effort by General Foods to increase its market share is a logical marketing strategy in this situation.

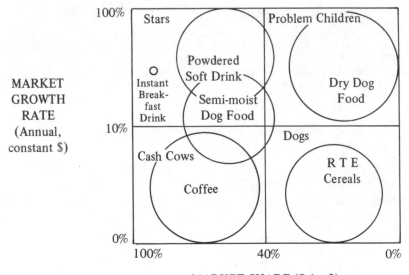

SOURCE: *Advertising Age* (August 18, 1975), pp. 133-34.

Figure 4–4
Growth/Share Matrix: General Foods Corporation

Coffee is the most important product to General Foods; it dominates each segment of the market: ground (Maxwell House and Yuban), instant soluble (Maxwell House, Yuban, Maxim), and decaffeinated (Sanka and Brim), with an aggregate market share over 40 percent. This dominant share and the relatively low market growth rate combine to place coffee in the Cash Cow category of the growth/share matrix. Marketing strategy has emphasized maintenance of market share through advertising and periodic new product introductions.

There are several Star businesses in the General Foods growth/share matrix: instant breakfast drink (Tang), powdered soft drink (Kool-Aid), and semi-moist dog food, with each market enjoying a growth rate in excess of 10 percent annually. Tang was the most heavily advertised General Foods product in 1974, and held more than 80 percent of its market. Kool-Aid has had to meet new competition from Borden's Wyler's brand, but continues to hold its number one position in the overall market. General Foods has four entries in the very fast-growing semi-moist dog food market (Gaines-burgers, Top Choice, Gaines Variety, and Prime) that collectively hold more than half of the market. Marketing strategy for the Stars in the portfolio is clearly that of heavy advertising support to maintain the dominant market share positions that have been achieved.

The dry dog food market creates a Problem Child for General Foods. It has two entries in this large, fast-growing market (Gravy Train and Gaines Meal) that have a combined market share of less than 15 percent, while the combined share of the Ralston Purina brands exceeds 60 percent. Marketing strategy appears to be directed primarily towards maintenance of market share through a modest level of advertising effort, limited product improvements, and new product introduction.

Additional insight into the marketing strategy and conduct of the major producers of RTE cereals may be gained through the application of the "Fundamental Theorem of Market Share Determination" (Kotler 1971, p.92): the market shares of various competitors will be proportional to their shares of total marketing effort, which may be expressed symbolically as:

$$s_i = m_i = A_i/A$$

where:

s_i = firm i's market share
m_i = firm i's share of total market effort
A_i = firm i's advertising effort in dollars
A = total industry advertising effort in dollars

Table 4–4 shows the market and advertising shares for the six major competitors in the RTE cereal industry. Although the "Fundamental Theorem" is generally supported, there are several obvious departures from proportionality between market share and advertising share in the cases of the Kellogg Company and General Foods.

Table 4–4

Adjusted Market Shares and Advertising Effort Shares in the
RTE Cereal Industry, 1974

Firm	Adjusted Market Share[a]	Advertising Effort Share[b]
Kellogg	42.5%	36.2%
General Mills	21.8	22.8
General Foods	17.2	21.7
Quaker Oats	11.1	12.4
Nabisco	4.4	2.9
Ralston Purina	3.0	4.0
Total	100.0%	100.0%

[a]Adjusted market shares are based on the six major firms listed and do not include the other firms in the industry.

[b]Advertising effort share figures are based on advertising expenditures for the six major firms in measured media: newspapers, magazines, spot TV, network TV, spot radio, network radio, outdoor.

Sources: Market share data from *Advertising Age,* March 24, 1975, p.52; advertising share data calculated from information in *Advertising Age,* August 18, 1975, p.133.

Kellogg's Rice Krispies held a 6.1 percent market share and an advertising share of 5.2 percent; Kellogg's Corn Flakes had a 5.8 percent market share and a 3.0 percent advertising share. Both brands are longtime, well-established products, and it is apparent that Kellogg was providing less than proportional advertising support to its major brands and most of the remaining brands in its product line. Only the Country Morning "natural" cereal brand received disproportionately high advertising support in 1974, with an advertising share of 3.8 percent and a market share of less than 2.0 percent.

General Foods, in contrast to Kellogg, followed a 1974 marketing strategy of providing greater than proportional advertising support to its RTE cereal line. Much of the relatively heavy advertising support was placed with the two leading brands: Grape Nuts, with an advertising share of 7.4 percent, accounted for an estimated 2.5 percent market share, while General Foods' leading brand, Raisin Bran, had an advertising share of 5.9 percent against a market share of about 3.4 percent. Both brands have received disproportionately high advertising support as a result of General Foods' attempt to position these well-established products in the "natural" segment of the RTE market that has shown such rapid growth in the past few years.

Marketing strategy and conduct in the RTE cereal industry is therefore focused on the use of advertising effort to establish and maintain target market share positions. There is an approximate proportionality between market share and advertising share, with most departures from proportionality due to the use of relatively heavy advertising support to establish new products or reposition old products in new, higher-growth market segments. Use of the product portfolio strategy concept and the "Fundamental Theorem of Market Share Determination" helps to direct attention to a series of key measurable variables: market share, market growth rate, market size, and marketing effort (advertising) share. Analysis of these variables within the conceptual frameworks suggested here provides a basis for evaluating conduct (marketing strategy) as an element in the SCP paradigm.

Conduct may be related to market structure by examining two sets of complex relationships:

1. the relationship between the actual and the "equilibrium" distribution of market shares within an industry; and

2. the relationship between the direction and the magnitude of the variance in the market share distributions and marketing strategies in an industry, as indicated by the four measures of structure and conduct (market share, market growth rate, market size, and marketing effort share), using the conceptual framework of product portfolio strategy and the theorem of market share determination.

Such inquiry, conducted on an "industry study" basis with the use of appropriate statistical methodology, should provide a significant advance in market structure analysis.

Performance

Market performance, the third and final element in the SCP paradigm, deals with the economic results of structure and conduct. Many dimensions of performance have been advanced in the literature, but the rate of profit is the measure most often used in empirical studies. The rate of profit, as the most available indicator of the relationship between price and average costs in a firm and its industry, has been used to determine allocative efficiency. The classic school of economic theory suggests that firms and industries with relatively high rates of profit indicate inefficient market performance; if resources were efficiently allocated under conditions of perfect competition, the returns on capital would tend to be equal for all firms and industries. Inequality in returns on capital is therefore considered to be indicative of market power, tendencies toward monopoly, and poor performance. This position predicates perfect competition as the standard for judging market performance; the position adopted in this paper is that the characteristics and assumptions of perfect competition (product homogeneity, many buyers and sellers, freedom of entry, perfect information, profit maximization) constitute an ideal that has little relevance in modern society as a basis for judging market performance. There are other theories regarding high profits: (1) profits are rewards for bearing risks, and (2) profits are rewards for successful innovation. (Dean 1951, chapter 1.) Both of these profit theories suggest that inequality in returns on capital is both normal and desirable in the American economy. As Dean has noted, "profits are the acid test of the individual firm's performance," and profit rates are therefore an appropriate and useful measure of market performance (Dean 1951, p.3.).

Profit rate has been calculated in a variety of ways in previous studies, with two measures predominating: (1) rate of return on equity, and (2) rate of return on total assets. There is controversy regarding the merits of either measure (Vernon 1972, pp.51–53) and some authors have elected to use both (Vernon and Nourse, 1972). However, problems even more important than the choice of measure have been ignored in virtually all of the statistical studies on the relationship between market structure and performance in multiple product, multiple industry, multinational firms. Each of the six major firms in the RTE cereal industry falls into such a category, and data on their profits in the U.S. market are not available. Since RTE cereal sales are less than 15 percent of total U.S. sales for five of the six firms (only Kellogg derives more than half its U.S. sales from RTE cereals), it is meaningless to use total domestic profits as a measure of the firm's performance in the RTE cereal market.

It is disappointing to conclude that profit rates do provide an appropriate and useful measure of market performance and then find that the required profit data are not available publicly. The Federal Trade Commission has sought for the past three years to require firms to provide data on profits by products and lines of business through its Line of Business Reporting Program. Hearings have been held periodically during this time with considerable debate over the feasibility of establishing standards for the allocation of joint costs in the firm. Although Line of Business reports are now required as a result of recent legislation, the diversity of current managerial accounting practices makes it unlikely that reliable public data on profits by products and lines of business will be available in the near future. The only feasible approach would therefore seem to be cooperative efforts such as the PIMS project, in which firms would attempt to provide data that could be used for approximate comparisons.

Alternative measures of performance do not appear very promising at this time. Bain (1968) suggested five dimensions for measuring performance; his work has served as the starting point for many studies of each dimension. Profit rates have been widely used as the primary measure of the first dimension, allocative efficiency. The second dimension, technical efficiency, also depends on cost data that are not available. Selling cost level relative to production cost level was suggested as the third dimension. Not only does it require cost data that are unavailable, but it also involves arbitrary distinctions with respect to the purposes for which the costs are incurred. Product characteristics, including design, quality, and variety, were offered as a fourth dimension and have proved very difficult to measure. The fifth dimension referred to the rate of progressiveness in product and process development as measured by research and development expenditures, innovation rate, and diffusion rate. Of the five dimensions, the last two are perhaps the most promising. Development of these measures will be difficult, however, for they should be based primarily on buyer behavior, rather than seller behavior. Studies of buyer behavior have advanced significantly during the past decade and it is now technically possible to develop the measures, but to do so will require specially designed and conducted studies.

Summary

After two decades of research based on market structure analysis, there is general agreement on the need for new approaches. This paper emphasizes the relationship between market structure and conduct, in contrast to the prevailing practice of seeking relationships between market structure and performance. A measure of the distribution of firm sizes within an industry developed by Cooke (1974) is employed as a measure of market structure, providing an opportunity to determine the variance between the actual and "equilibrium" market share distribution within an industry.

Conduct, the element usually ignored in most statistical studies of the structure-conduct-performance (SCP) paradigm, is examined within the context of the ready-to-eat breakfast cereal industry, one of the ten industries analyzed in the market structure section of this paper. The analysis of conduct is facilitated primarily through the application of the product portfolio strategy concept, and secondarily through the use of the "Fundamental Theorem of Market Share Determination." The relationship between market structure and conduct within the cereal industry is examined and suggestions are offered for further study.

Serious methodological difficulties are identified in the performance element of the SCP paradigm, especially when profitability is used as a measure of performance, as is the prevailing practice in market structure analysis. Suggestions for further research in the measurement of performance are offered, but the unavailability of relevant data precluded the analysis of performance in the cereal industry.

Emphasis in recent years on the structure-performance relationship has created an impasse in market structure analysis. The most promising way out lies in taking new approaches to the study of the structure-conduct relationship; at the same time we must try to improve the measurement of performance so that in future studies it may be related to structure and conduct more meaningfully.

NOTES

1. In the discussion of the present paper at the conference it was suggested by Frank Bass that the number of important firms in an industry may also be used to approximate the market share percentage of the leading firm in the industry:

$S_1 = 1/\sqrt{n}$, where n is the number of important firms.

Application of this formula to the ten industries studied indicates that it does provide a fairly close estimate of the actual share held by the leading firm in most of the ten industries.

2. The concentration ratio, the most commonly used measure of concentration in market structure studies, fails to indicate the relative distribution of firm sizes in an industry and is thereby severely limited in its usefulness as a measure of market structure. To illustrate, assume two industries have the following distributions of firm sizes, measured in terms of market share percentages:

$$One = 20\%, 20\%, 20\%, 20\%, 20\% \text{ (all others)}$$
$$Two = 60\%, 10\%, 5\%, 5\%, 20\% \text{ (all others)}$$

The four-firm concentration ratio for both industries is 80%, but no one would claim that the market structure of the two industries is similar. In spite of these limitations, the easy availability of concentration ratio data from government sources results in their widespread use.

3. Although the present paper treats advertising expenditures as a measure of conduct, it should be noted that economists have considered them measures of market structure. This position may be traced to Bain (1968), who postulated that among the key dimensions of market structure were (1) the degree of product differentiation and (2) the conditions of market entry (barriers to entry); the relationships of these to advertising expenditures have been treated as market structure measures. It is argued here that advertising expenditures are more properly classified as a measure of market conduct, in that they constitute a form of "adaptive behavior" on the part of firms responding to market demand. Other forms of such behavior include pricing, sales promotion, and product strategies of firms, which are interrelated with advertising, and as previously noted, are appropriately classified as measures of conduct by Bain.

4. These and other 1974 data for the RTE cereal industry are from *Advertising Age*, August 18, 1975, pp.133–72. Market size and share estimates are

developed by John C. Maxwell, Jr., of Wheat First Securities. Advertising expenditures are estimated by *Advertising Age*.

REFERENCES

1. *Advertising Age*, March 24, 1975 (a), p.52.
2. *Advertising Age*, August 18, 1975 (b), pp.133–72.
3. Bain, Joe S. *Industrial Organization*. 2d ed. New York: John Wiley and Sons, 1968.
4. Bass, Frank M. "Profit and the A/S Ratio," *Journal of Advertising Research*, Vol. 14, No. 6, December 1974, pp.9–19.
5. Buzzell, Robert D.; Gale, Bradley T.; and Sultan, Ralph G. M. "Market Share—A Key to Profitability," *Harvard Business Review*, Vol. 53, No. 1, January–February 1975, pp.97–106.
6. Chandler, Alfred D., Jr. *Strategy and Structure*. New York: Anchor Books, 1966.
7. Channon, Derek F. *The Strategy and Structure of British Enterprise*. Boston: Graduate School of Business Administration, Harvard University, 1973.
8. Cooke, Ernest F. *Market Share Measures of Rivalry*. Unpublished Ph.D. dissertation, Case Western Reserve University, 1974.
9. Cooke, Ernest F., and Cox, William E., Jr. *The Relationship Between Market Shares and Rank as a Measure of Market Structure*. Unpublished working paper, 1975.
10. Cox, William E., Jr. "Product Portfolio Strategy: A Review of the Boston Consulting Group Approach to Marketing Strategy." In Curhan, R. (ed.). *Marketing's Contribution to the Firm and to Society*. Chicago: American Marketing Association, 1975, pp.465–70.
11. Day, George S. "A Strategic Perspective on Product Planning," *Journal of Contemporary Business*, Spring 1975, pp.1–34.
12. Dean, Joel. *Managerial Economics*. Englewood Cliffs, N.J.: Prentice-Hall, Inc., 1951.
13. Grether, E. T. "Industrial Organization: Retrospect and Prospect," *American Economic Review*, Volume 60, No. 2, May 1970, pp.83–89.
14. Kotler, Philip. *Marketing Decision Making*. New York: Holt, Rinehart and Winston, 1971.
15. Marham, Jesse W., and Slater, Charles C. "Standards of Competition and the Food Industries." In Wright, J. S., and Goldstucker, J. L. (eds.). *New Ideas for Successful Marketing*. Chicago: American Marketing Association, 1966, pp.19–45.
16. Marion, Bruce W., and Handy, Charles R. *Market Performance: Concepts and Measures*. Agricultural Economic Report No. 244. Washington: Economic Research Service, U.S. Department of Agriculture, 1973.
17. Rumelt, Richard P. *Strategy, Structure, and Economic Performance*. Boston: Graduate School of Business Administration, Harvard University, 1974.

18. Schoeffler, Sidney; Buzzell, Robert D.; and Heany, Donald F. "Impact of Strategic Planning on Profit Performance," *Harvard Business Review*, Vol. 52, No. 2, March–April 1974, pp.137–45.

19. Shubik, Martin. "A Curmudgeon's Guide to Microeconomics," *Journal of Economic Literature*, Vol. 8, No. 2, June 1970, pp.405–34.

20. Stern, Louis W. *Market Structure as a Measure of Market Performance*. Cambridge, Mass.: Marketing Science Institute, 1970.

21. Vernon, John M. *Market Structure and Industrial Performance: A Review of Statistical Findings*. Boston: Allyn and Bacon, Inc., 1972.

22. Vernon, John M., and Nourse, Robert E. M. *Profitability and Market Structure*. Cambridge, Mass.: Marketing Science Institute, 1972.

23. Weiss, Leonard W. "Quantitative Studies of Industrial Organization." In Intriligator, M. D. (ed.). *Frontiers in Quantitative Economics*. Amsterdam: North-Holland Publishing Co., 1971.

COMMENTS ON THE ESSAY
BY WILLIAM E. COX, JR.

Joseph C. Miller

In one trained in industrial organization economics, the paper by William E. Cox, Jr., evokes feelings of both admiration and concern. The economist must admire the imaginative (and objective) application of the ssp paradigm to important problems at the firm level. In their search for answers to pressing social problems, many economists have neglected to follow Cox's good example of examining the effects especially of strategy in the large corporation and in oligopolistic industries. Cox follows in the grand tradition of Preston, Thorelli, Moyer, Buzzell, and Schoeffler in creatively extending the paradigm to important problems of marketing.

At several points, however, the Cox paper raises concern about the interpretation of concepts. Although industrial organization economists should not feel possessive about the strategy-structure-performance framework, it is true that the lion's share of research has been done by them. They have learned through experience to beware of several pitfalls in the application of ssp concepts. Cox correctly emphasizes the benefits of ssp relationships, but he has not fully recognized the costs of applying them. The comments that follow point to specific questions of methods or conceptualization raised by Cox.

Structure

The first question that should be raised about any proposed new structural variable is whether it will better explain conduct or performance. Cox's market share proportionality variable (c) is presented as a market concentration variable similar to the Herfindahl index, and said to be superior to the simple concentration ratio. However, there is no demonstration of any relationship between the structural variable and the strategy or performance variables later discussed. The studies referred to (e.g., Cox 1975; and Schoeffler, Buzzell, and Heany 1974) do examine structure-performance relationships, but the structural variables in these studies are one-firm or multi-firm market concentration ratios. If market share proportionality is similar to the Herfindahl index of concentration, it probably will not explain very much more of the variations in conduct or performance than either the Herfindahl index or the concentration ratio has, since the correlation between the latter two measures has been consistently found to be very high (e.g., 0.94, by Nelson 1963).

The formulation of the c parameter by Cox also raises some questions. As the semi-logarithmic function of the slope of a linear equation relating the firm's market share with its share rank in the industry, the proportionality parameter c appears to be directly correlated with the number of important firms (n) in the ten industries examined and inversely related to the four-firm (or eight-firm) concentration ratio in each industry.[1] In two of the ten industries the coefficient of multiple determination was less than 0.9, and Cox describes these two industries (cigarettes and trucks) as 'exceptions to the direct relationship between c and n.' Clearly, many more than ten industries will need to be tested before generalizing further about the properties of the c parameter. Market shares are relatively stable over time, but shifts will change the proportionality "constant" in a given industry. As a general matter, it seems unwise to speak of any measure of concentration as being a constant, because of the well-known sensitivities of such measures to the product- and geographic-market specifications on which they are based.

Cox acknowledges the major shifts in market shares and share rankings that occurred in the breakfast cereal industry between 1964 and 1969, but he argues that stability during the 1954–64 and 1969–74 periods gives the c values for those periods "equilibrium" significance. The close correspondence between actual and c-computed market shares (table 4–2) cannot be denied, but the term *equilibrium,* like *constant,* should be used advisedly and with more substantiation. One line of research, suggested by the work of Gort (1963) and Schneider (1966), is to test the effect of various marketing strategies on the stability of market shares. A second area of related research looks at the stochastic growth processes of business firms' market shares (e.g., Simon and Bonini 1958).

Strategy

The past decade has seen significant growth in research on firms' conduct.[2] Among a large and diverse range of studies, a great deal of work has focused on pricing, product innovation, and advertising. Cox is concerned primarily with advertising, although he argues that other promotion variables and measures of physical distribution should be investigated as well. The particular strategy variable on which Cox relies exclusively in his analysis of the breakfast cereal industry is a ratio of each firm's annual advertising expenditures to the total industry advertising expenditures. Testing Kotler's (1971) hypothesis that this ratio is proportional to the firm's market share, Cox observes that the proportionality is only approximate with exceptions occurring when new brands are introduced or old brands are repositioned.

As Cox himself implies, his analysis of the structure-strategy relationship should examine other strategy variables and set them against the *c* index of industry structure. Within a given industry such as RTE cereals, promotional expenditures may be broken down into amounts spent on different media, direct mail and premium advertising, and in-store advertising. Another strategy variable in the cereal industry might well be the number of brands of each firm, as an indicator of shelf-space coverage, and the rate of new brand introductions. Interindustry research provides a further basis for comparison of these promotional and product variables, and may also permit the analysis of other strategy variables. For example, Michael E. Porter (1974) investigated the effects of convenience and non-convenience marketing outlets in his interindustry research on consumer goods manufacturers and retailers.

Performance

Cox refers briefly to the structure-performance relationship, which has been a focus of attention in the research literature longer than the other two relationships,[3] and mentions rate of return on assets as related to sales growth in the section on conduct. However, the unavailability of product-line data prevents his applying these concepts to the RTE cereal industry. Alternative measures of performance are discussed, including economies of scale, product quality, and technological innovativeness, but other data deficiencies are obstacles to their application.

Cox concludes that the PIMS approach to obtaining performance data seems the most promising, and, until companies agree to the FTC request for linc-of-business reporting, he may be correct. However, much work can be done in the meantime. Interindustry studies of price-cost margins, such as that by Collins and Preston (1968), arc promising, and Cox refers to the need for further research on the demand side of changes in product quality and innovations. In all research of this kind, as in work on the structure-strategy relationships, there is always room for fresh ideas and concepts, especially at the micro-level.

NOTES

1. Frank Bass and F. M. Scherer suggest that nearly the same result can be obtained without the regression computations by estimating the market share of the largest firm (s_1) as being equal to one divided by the square root of n, where n is the number of firms in the industry. The following table com-

pares s_1 values estimated by the Cox formula (equation [1.5, $s_1 = [1 + c + c^2 + \ldots + c^{n-1}]^{-1}$), the Bass/Scherer suggestion, and actual (1974) one-firm concentration ratios:

	Cox	$1/\sqrt{n}$	Actual (1974)
Automobiles	59.9%	50.0%	49.6%
Sulphur	54.8	40.8	
Diesel engines	44.9	40.8	
RTE cereals	40.8	37.8	41.0
Cigarettes	31.5	40.8	
Air transport	23.1	30.2	
Steel	19.5	25.0	
Trucks	22.1	40.8	36.1
Beer	11.4	20.0	
Gasoline	10.3	15.8	

2. F. M. Scherer's excellent text (1971), with its unprecedented emphasis on conduct, has contributed in no small measure to this growth. See also the survey article by Weiss (1971), especially pp.379–97, for a critical discussion of the research.

3. See Weiss (1971), pp.363–75.

REFERENCES

1. Collins, Norman R., and Preston, Lee E. *Concentration and Price-Cost Margins in Manufacturing.* Berkeley: University of California Press, 1968.
2. Cox, William E., Jr. "Product-Portfolio Strategy: A Review of the Boston Consulting Group's Approach to Marketing Strategy." In Curhan, R. (ed.). *Marketing's Contribution to the Firm and to Society.* Chicago: American Marketing Association, 1975, pp.465–70.
3. Gort, Michael. "Analysis of Stability and Change in Market Shares," *Journal of Political Economy*, February 1963, pp.58–69.
4. Kotler, Philip. *Marketing Management: Analysis, Planning, and Control.* 3d Edition. Englewood Cliffs, N.J.: Prentice-Hall, 1976.
5. Nelson, Ralph L. *Concentration in the Manufacturing Industries of the United States.* New Haven: Yale University Press, 1963.
6. Porter, Michael. *Retailer Power, Manufacturer Strategy, and Performance in Consumer Goods Industries.* Ph.D. dissertation, Harvard University, 1973.
7. Scherer, F. M. *Industrial Market Structure and Economic Performance.* Chicago: Rand McNally, 1970.
8. Schneider, Norman. "Product Differentiation, Oligopoly, and the Stability of Market Shares," *Western Economic Journal*, December 1966, pp.58–63.

9. Schoeffler, Sidney; Buzzell, Robert D.; and Heany, Donald F. "Impact of Strategic Planning on Profit Performance," *Harvard Business Review,* March–April 1974, pp.137–45.

10. Simon, Herbert A., and Bonini, C. P. "The Size Distribution of Business Firms," *American Economic Review,* September 1958, pp.607–17.

11. Weiss, Leonard W. "Econometric Research in Industrial Organizations." In Intriligator, M. (ed.). *Frontiers of Quantitative Economics.* Amsterdam: North-Holland, 1970.

5

Cross-Sectional Study of Strategy, Structure, and Performance: Aspects of the PIMS Program

SIDNEY SCHOEFFLER

The PIMS (Profit Impact of Market Strategies) program of the Strategic Planning Institute is a large-scale, continuing empirical inquiry into the interrelationships among a group of factors representing the strategy, the competitive position, the business environment, and the operating results of businesses producing manufactured products or services. The program is organized around a data base reflecting the business-strategic experiences of about 600 individual businesses operated by 50-plus major corporations.

This paper discusses some of the methodological issues that need to be confronted in this kind of empirical approach to microeconomic phenomena, and presents some of the conclusions.

The PIMS program is a *cross-sectional* study of business-strategic *experience*. It attempts to explain the experienced differences in operating results across the 600-plus businesses on the basis of differences in the strategic moves being made and differences in the competitive setting in which they were made. The statistical approaches employed are those appropriate to cross-sectional analyses.

History and Organization

The program originated as an internal planning study in the General

Electric Company about 15 years ago. The GE study interpreted the experience of that company, in a considerable variety of product and service businesses, as if that company were a large business-strategy testing laboratory. Each of the various operating divisions was visualized as conducting a series of "experiments" designed to find out the consequences of business strategy in its particular market setting. The overall study interpreted these experiments with a view to detecting the underlying regularities—the "laws of nature" that operate in the marketplace—that govern which business action, in which business environment, produces what consequences.

In early 1972 the study was organized on a multicompany basis, under the umbrella of the Harvard Business School, and located initially in the Marketing Science Institute. The first two directors of research were Ralph G. M. Sultan and Robert D. Buzzell of Harvard Business School. The research team was drawn largely from General Electric, Harvard Business School, and the University of Massachusetts.

Effective as of the beginning of 1975, the program was organized as the Strategic Planning Institute (SPI), an independent nonprofit body, dedicated to empirical cross-sectional investigations in the microeconomic area. The executive secretary of the SPI is Sidney Schoeffler and the director of research is Bradley T. Gale of the University of Massachusetts.

The Institute is governed by its member companies as to priorities, finances, and policy. The small central staff is augmented by university researchers at several leading schools of business as well as by staff members of participating companies. Each participating company contributes data on several of its business experiences (under confidential conditions) plus a pro-rata share of the cost of the program. It receives, in return, reports on the general findings of the research program, plus a series of diagnostic analyses, in the light of these findings, on each business it has contributed to the data base.

Data Coverage

At present, the data base includes 600-plus "businesses" for the five-year period from 1970 through 1974. The unit of observation, here called a "business," is a specific product line (or service line) that is reasonably homogeneous in terms of market served and technology employed.

Each "business" is documented by about 100 data items, supplied in standardized format by the company operating that business. The data items describe the *market* served by the business (in terms of growth, stability, etc.), the *competitive environment* (number and size of competitors, number and size of customers, etc.), and the *position* of the business (market share, comparative product quality, comparative price, etc.). These data about market structure are supplemented by critical characteristics of the *strategy* of the business (changes in position, discretionary budget allocations, product quality, etc.), and finally, with information concerning the *operating results* obtained (profit, cash flow, and so on).

The businesses, at present, are mainly North American; only about 10 percent of them are located in Europe and South America. A major effort is currently under way to strengthen the non-North American portion of the data base.

Operating Principles

The program operates as a *continuing* activity, with an annual update of data, an annual recalibration of the research findings, and an annual analysis (in the light of the research findings available to date) of the individual businesses in the data base.

The focus of attention is on *observables,* i.e., observable actions under observable environmental characteristics producing observable results. This excludes consideration of intentions and purposes. We concentrate, in other words, on what people *do,* not on *why* they do it, and observe the consequences.

The research emphasizes *robust* relationships, those that stand up under a variety of ways of measuring the phenomena and of structuring the analysis. These robust patterns are so powerful and diverse, and we are currently so far from exhausting them, that it would be a misallocation of scarce resources to devote much time to the subtle or weak relationships among the variables. Hence, the exploration of subtle patterns has been deferred to a later time.

We are taking a very *conservative* approach vis-à-vis *data errors* and *outliers.* That is, we go out of our way to minimize the risk of having the analysis contaminated by large data errors or dominated by real but extreme individual cases. The research objective is to identify robust patterns that hold true for, say, 95 percent to 98 percent of the observed cases. The vehicle for implementing this conservatism is a limitation on the range of permissible values for the key variables. Each variable is confined to a range of approximately 2.75 standard deviations around its mean. When a business falls outside of these limits for *many* variables, it is *deleted* from the analysis; if for only a *few* variables, it is allowed to remain in the data base, but the extreme values are compressed upward or downward to the limit. This maneuver removes both the large data errors (small errors, not being very damaging, do not require equally heroic preventive actions) and the extreme values. Since there is no convincing way of differentiating between the two, it is especially important to neutralize both.

Tests of Validity

We "believe" a particular observed pattern if it meets at least three tests:

1. It is *statistically significant,* at the 95 percent level or better.
2. It conforms to the best available *theory* of the case (which occasionally is constructed after the empirical observation).
3. It *makes sense* to knowledgeable businessmen, who have direct experience with the phenomenon concerned.

The tests of statistical significance operate at both the micro-level (i.e., individual variables) and the macro-level (i.e., functions as a whole), with the latter being the more useful of the two. Since the key variables employed (to explain, say, ROI) are highly multicollinear, one should not attach much importance to individual coefficients of individual variables, and hence also not to the significance tests on such coefficients. The more useful test, though far more difficult to construct, is at the level of the function as a whole. The critical test is: Does the "black box," taken as a whole, behave in the same way the "reality" does, as visible in the data base? Specifically, does the black box generate closely the same kinds of graphs and cross-tables, for example, as can be constructed from the original data? The key questions is: How close is close?

Basic Findings

Taking our cross-sectional ROI-explaining equation as an example, we have so far identified 37 variables (each of them significant in the micro sense at the 95 percent level or better, and theoretically sensible) that jointly explain about 80 percent of the variance of ROI. Several of these variables are identified later in this paper. These 37 variables operate in a highly interactive way, being compounded into 58 separate cross-products or other combined terms. With over 500 degrees of freedom, plus good computer programs, even such a frighteningly complex equation becomes quite manageable. One of the main advantages of large-scale, cross-sectional analysis is that it allows the delineation of very complex patterns. (In the more customary longitudinal analysis, equations with more than five variables quickly become rather difficult to handle.)

Part of the 80 percent explanation of variance is definitional, rather than empirical. This comes about because some of the profit-explaining variables, such as Investment Intensity, contain elements that are also present in the construction of the dependent variable. We have made an effort to remove such redundancy from the analysis, but may not have fully succeeded. Fortunately, this problem does very little damage to a robust analysis.

One of the more interesting findings to date is that the 80 percent level of explanation appears to be a kind of *upper limit* for explaining ROI (or other measure of operating performance) with strategy/structure/environment kind of data. Including the previous study in General Electric, so far there have been six separate attempts to estimate a cross-sectional ROI-explaining equation with that kind of data, covering the time period from the middle 1950s to the early 1970s, and also covering several different groups of businesses. In each case, the R^2 could be pushed to about 80 percent, but not beyond.

Equally interesting is that the *same key explanatory variables* (see the appendix) appeared each time as being powerful and significant. There *is* some turnover in the relatively *minor* variables as we move from time period to time period, and from sample to sample, and also some change in the precise values of the coefficients, but no major alterations in the patterns.

Some Research Issues

1. MULTICOLLINEARITY

The ROI-explaining variables are highly multicollinear. This is a problem that must be managed rather than removed, because the cure is far worse than the disease. A multiple-factor analysis disclosed that the 37 major variables collapse into 17 orthogonal principal components; but these principal components were not very easy to understand. It seemed better to stay with 37 comprehensible factors.

The problem turned out to be not much of a problem at all. If there are multicollinear terms in a regression equation, one cannot put any interpretation on the individual coefficients of individual terms. But there is no particular need to do so.

One can get a rather good reading on the impact of changes in the regression terms by making sure that multicollinear clusters of variables *are moved together,* in a pattern consistent with their historical covariation. Our tool for accomplishing that was a set of "consistency equations," estimated on the basis of the past three years, that were used to constrain the behavior of multicollinear clusters. A set of eight such equations seemed to do the job.

Each consistency equation links a strategy-descriptive variable, such as "change of market share," with the variables representing the moves empirically associated with it, such as price changes, marketing expenditures, inventory levels, new-product introductions, etc. The equation plays the role of prohibiting inconsistent assumptions about the strategy-descriptive variables and the detailed action variables.

2. SINGLE UNIVERSE VS MULTIPLE UNIVERSES

The 600-plus businesses in the PIMS data base are very *diverse*. They include industrial products and consumer products, goods and services, domestic businesses and foreign businesses, growing markets and maturing markets, and many other dimensions of difference.

When one examines the impact of the various explanatory variables on ROI, it quickly becomes apparent that the impact differs from group to group. For example, while Market Share always has a favorable impact on ROI, this impact is far stronger for industrial products than it is for consumer products. We found it productive to proceed in a two-step fashion: First, to *identify* such differences, and then to *explain* them. The first step is important because it raises interesting questions; the second step is important because it yields important insights. For example, the differences in the Market Share coefficient between industrial and consumer products appear due in large measure to differences in the number of customers served.

It is interesting to note that when one identifies several universes of cases, and then explains the differences and builds these explanations into the model, one arrives at a single universe represented by a single model. To continue the above example another step, if we find that, for *consumer* products,

$$\text{ROI} = a + b \text{ (Market Share)}$$

and, for *industrial* products,

$$\text{ROI} = c + d \text{ (Market Share)},$$

then, if we estimate the coefficients of

$$\text{ROI} = e + f \text{ (Market Share)} + g \text{ (Number of Customers)} + h \text{ (Market Share)} \cdot \text{ (Number of Customers)}$$

using the *entire* data base, consumer plus industrial products, we capture both the information contained in the original two models plus an insight into the reason for the difference.

Thus we have deemed it expedient in the PIMS Program to adopt a "single universe resolution," i.e., a methodological resolution to push the explanation of profitability to the point where a single model covers all cases. We have not yet succeeded to the degree we would like; but we have made considerable progress. That is why our model is so highly interactive and complex. True, this complexity presents some problems, particularly in testing validity and in explaining to users what is going on; but the benefits seem to outweigh the costs considerably.

3. THEORY VS DATA

Conventional research wisdom decrees that hypotheses and models be specified first, and confronted with data second. While this approach has, of course, sound methodological justification, it does, however, deprive us of a very productive source of ideas. It is sometimes very useful to "rummage" through the data to see what is going on, especially when looking at phenomena that have not been extensively studied yet.

We have found it helpful to *combine* the theory-first and the observed-patterns-first approaches into a kind of cyclical thinking process that moves back and forth from one to the other, i.e., an inductive-deductive approach. I would estimate that about 70 percent of our current model derives from the theory-first approach, and about 30 percent from the observed-patterns-first approach.

4. MEASURED VARIABLES VS JUDGMENTS

Most businesses measure many strategically unimportant variables very well (e.g., petty cash) and many strategically very important variables not at all (e.g., product quality). Hence, in trying to get at the important phenomena, we must learn to make do with rough estimates. Our approach has been

—to try very hard to give our members clear descriptions of the *concept* (for example, "product quality" is something seen by the *customer,* covers both the article sold and the associated service package, and can take on only three values: clearly superior to competitors, clearly inferior to competitors, and not clearly different);

—to try to give no incentive to knowingly supply wrong information;

—to ask *many simple* questions rather than a few *complex* questions, and then to check for internal consistency in the answers;

—to make maximal use of *redundancy* within the group of questions; and, finally,

—to delete from the sample those few businesses that exhibit patterns wildly at variance with the greater part of the data base.

5. COMPLEX VS SIMPLE MODELS

It was Mencken, I believe, who remarked that for every complicated problem there is a clear, simple answer, which is wrong. A similar principle may apply to models of complicated realities. This is not to say, of course, that a particular model is "right" just because it is complex. Moreover, simplicity has great aesthetic appeal. But, since the main advantage of a large, cross-sectional data base is that it permits us to sort out the individual separate impacts of many factors operating on a dependent variable, it seemed unwise in PIMS to pay a very high price for simplicity.

Accordingly, we have not hesitated to complicate our models wherever that bought a significant gain in statistical fit (say another percentage point or two in R^2) plus a more appealing functional form (a variable that "should" interact with another in fact interacting with it). The presence of multicollinearity among the explanatory variables did limit this ability somewhat, but, as noted above, not very seriously. However, to satisfy inveterate simplicity-lovers among our group of users, and also to facilitate applications in special areas, we have developed, and are using alongside our full-scale models, a "limited-information model." This focuses on the 13 most powerful impacts on profitability and keeps the interaction terms simple and relatively few. We recommend to our members that they use this model whenever information is indeed very limited (as, for example, in the typical acquisition study) or where easy explainability of research findings is especially important.

Some Specific Results

Our operating rules specify that the major models may not be published, but must remain proprietary to the companies whose experiences are included in the data base. But *some* of the findings can be presented here.

All data presented here are *three-year* averages covering the period 1970–72. This period includes one poor year, one middling year, and one good year, and thus comes close to reflecting trend-line results. The number of cases is about 550 in each exhibit, so that the bar charts include about 110 cases per bar, and the cross-tables include about 30 to 80 cases in each box. We define ROI here as *pre-tax, operating* ROI at the *business* level, exclusive of financial charges, with investment measured at *book* value. (The effects of inflation, depreciation, and financial charges are controlled in the model, but not reflected in the exhibits here. In every case, however, the pattern remains essentially the same after adjustment.) In each exhibit, a difference of three points of ROI is significant at the 95 percent level or higher. Cash flow is defined as cash generated by after-tax earnings and depreciation minus cash absorbed by increases in gross investment.

(a) *Market Share* has a strong positive impact on ROI. See figure 5–1. Market Share is shown in the form of Relative Market Share, which is the market share of the business divided by the combined market shares of its three largest competitors. (So, if a particular business has an absolute market share of 20 percent, and its three largest competitors have a combined 40 percent, its relative share is 20 percent/40 percent, or 50 percent.)

Market share is measured here in relation to the *served market* of the

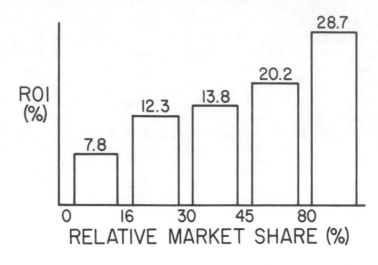

Figure 5-1

business. Of the total potential market the *served market* is that segment within which the business is in fact competing, i.e., it has a product offering suitable for that segment and focuses its marketing effort on that segment. Some of the reasons for the favorable impact on ROI are given in a recent article by Buzzell, Gale, and Sultan.[1]

As a side point, while *having* strong market share is profitable, *getting* strong market share costs money; it entails reductions in ROI and negative cash flows. So, there is a positive relationship between market share and ROI, but a negative relationship between the rate of change of market share and ROI. The specific price paid (in the form of transitionally reduced ROI) per point of market share gained is a function of several characteristics of the business environment in which the move is attempted. For example, the price per point gained is less in a fast-growth market than in a slow-growth market.

(b) *Market Share* interacts with the *R & D* level of the business. (See figure 5-2. Numbers in blocks are percentages of ROI.) Weak businesses are hurt by operating at high R & D levels, while strong businesses benefit from high R & D levels. The major apparent reason for this pattern is that it requires market clout to make an R & D program profitable. In the absence of market clout, as measured here by relative market share, the stronger competitors of the business usually succeed in "taking the play away" by coming out with a quick imitation of any new developments that may be produced by R & D, or by making offsetting pricing or marketing moves. Another probable reason lies in the area of economies of scale in R & D.

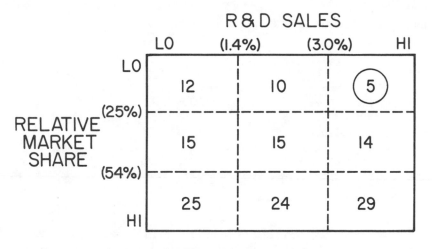

Figure 5-2

(c) *Product Quality* has a favorable impact on ROI. See figure 5–3. Quality is measured here as the percent of sales volume originating in products judged by the market to be *superior* to those of the competition *minus* the percent of sales coming from products judged to be *inferior*. To be more accurate, it is the management's judgment of the market's judgment, subject to an audit of internal consistency.

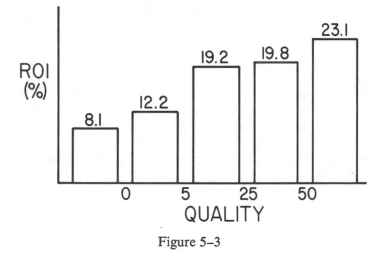

Figure 5-3

(d) The *Investment Intensity* of the business has a sharply *negative* effect on ROI. Investment intensity is here defined as the *total investment* in the business (working capital plus fixed capital at book value, including both that investment financed by equity and that financed by long-term debt) per dollar of *value added* by the businesses (sales minus purchased materials, with above-average profit removed from sales).

INVESTMENT/ VALUE ADDED	ROI	ROS*
Below 70%	20%	8%
70%–90%	14%	8%
95%–120%	10%	6%
120%–160%	2%	2%
Over 160%	−1%	0%

*ROS (Return on Sales) is measured by operating earnings (net of a capital charge of 10% pre-tax) per dollar of sales.

There are at least two reasons for this pattern. First, it is a matter of arithmetic. When a business becomes more mechanized, or automated, or otherwise investment-intensive, it puts a large number of dollars into the denominator of the ROI ratio, thus depressing the value of the ratio. But this is far from the whole story, as the ROS pattern suggests. High investment-intensity affects the character of competition; the various competing firms anxiously try to keep their expensive plants fully loaded. This anxiety, often desperation, can turn competition into a volume-grubbing contest, replete with price wars and very costly marketing campaigns. The net effect (when we average good years with bad) is very damaging to all the businesses concerned, and may well be a major contributor to currently expected capital shortage in the economy.

(e) When we interact *Investment Intensity* with *Relative Market Share*, the impact on cash flow becomes even clearer. See figure 5–4. Here we are measuring cash flow *before* any financial changes; and even then highly investment-intensive businesses with a low relative market share are below the level of self-sustainability.

(f) *Fixed Capital Intensity* interacts with the *Industry Concentration Ratio* and ROI in a major way. See figure 5–5. We are measuring fixed capital intensity by the ratio of plant and equipment (at first cost, undepreciated) to sales volume. Industry concentration is the joint share of the four largest sellers. Fixed-capital-intensive businesses in *unconcentrated* markets are very unprofitable, as the lower left corner of the table shows. (Government efforts to deconcentrate the market in fixed-capital-intensive industries are unwise; such action tends to deprive those industries of the ability to sustain their growth. Their own cash flow would be clearly inadequate, while their poor profitability would preclude access to the capital markets.)

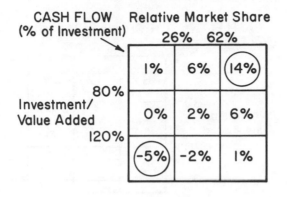

Figure 5–4

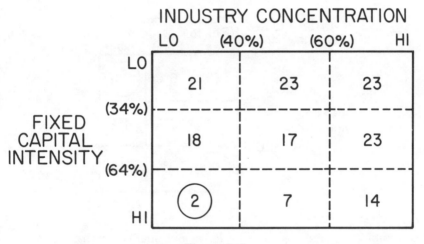

Figure 5–5

(g) Focusing specifically on cash flow again, we see in figure 5–6 that *Investment Intensity* and *Industry Long Range Growth Rate* interact in a rather damaging way. The lower right corner is a disaster area from the cash flow standpoint, and clearly requires particular attention from corporate planners and public-policy makers. Growth normally "eats" cash, because of the increased investments required to stay with a growing market. However, noncapital-intensive businesses usually can generate the required cash internally. Capital-intensive businesses, for the reasons previously discussed, cannot.

(h) *Investment Intensity* also interacts with the *Breadth of the Product Line*. See figure 5–7. It is very dangerous to manufacture a narrow product line in an investment-intensive way, probably because such businesses

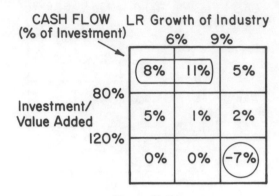

Figure 5–6

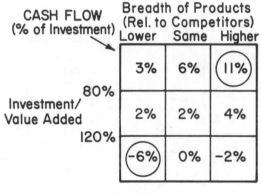

Figure 5–7

lack flexibility in adapting to quantitative and qualitative changes in the market.

Concluding Observations

The PIMS Program is uncovering a large number of impacts on profit and cash flow of the kind shown here. In the aggregate, these impacts account for about 80 percent of the cross-sectional variance in ROI (or in other profit measures) across the whole data base, excepting only a small number (about 5 percent) of extreme outliers.

It seems safe to conclude that microeconomic processes are indeed phenomena that obey "laws of nature." These can be discovered in the way usual in many empirical sciences, and also applied in the usual way.

The laws operating in the marketplace are not simple, or at least not yet. We can *simulate* simplicity by *fragmenting* the universe, particularly if we use simplicity of the resulting descriptive equation as the criterion for choosing a particular fragmentation scheme. But this approach loses many important insights, and is therefore not good despite its many obvious operational advantages. Elegant simplicity will have to be won the hard way, by the formulation of new theory.

APPENDIX

Some Key Variables Explaining ROI

1. *Attractiveness of Business Environment*
   Market Growth, Long-Term
   Market Growth, Short-Term
   Percent Industry Exports
   Industry Concentration Ratio
   Customer Concentration Ratio
2. *Strength of Competitive Position*
   Market Share
   Relative Market Share (relative to three largest competitors)
   Relative Pay Scale (level of compensation relative to competition)
   Relative Product Quality
3. *Effectiveness of Use of Investment*
   Investment Intensity
   Value Added/Sales
   Sales/Employee
   Percent Capacity Utilized
4. *Discretionary Cost Allocations*
   Marketing Expenses/Sales
   R & D Costs/Sales
   Rate of New Product Introductions
5. *Characteristics of the Owning Corporation*
   Company Size
   Company Diversity
6. *Current Changes in Position Variables*
   Change in Market Share
   Change in Vertical Integration
   Change in Relative Price
   Change in Product Quality
   Change in Capacity

REFERENCE

1. Buzzell, Robert D.; Gale, B. T.; and Sultan, R. G. M. "Market Share—A Key to Profitability," *Harvard Business Review*, January–February 1975, pp.97–106.

6

Marketing Costs in Consumer Goods Industries

ROBERT D. BUZZELL AND PAUL W. FARRIS

The magnitude of marketing costs, in specific industries and in the economy as a whole, has long been a source of concern both to business executives and to those involved in formulating and administering public policy regarding competition. Managers responsible for establishing marketing plans and budgets are very often uncertain about how much to spend, or how to modify their spending in response to changes in market conditions (McNiven, 1969). Economists and legislators, for their part, have frequently criticized particular industries—or the marketing system itself—on the grounds that expenditures are "excessive" and that they tend to deter entry and reduce competition (Comanor and Wilson, 1974, especially chapter 4).

Some critics regard any marketing costs, beyond perhaps some bare minimum, as undesirable from a social viewpoint. Others, adopting a more pragmatic approach, are more concerned with those industries or markets in which marketing expenditures are relatively "high." But what standard should be used to judge whether a given level of spending is "high"? The usual approach has been to compare an industry or product category with one or more other industries or product categories; those that are above average are, by definition, "high." It is obvious that there are serious drawbacks in this kind of interindustry comparison. There is no reason to believe, for example, that marketing costs for ready-to-eat cereals *should* be equal to those incurred by fruit and vegetable canners, even though both produce food products. Differences in customer buying patterns, in market structure, in competition, and in companies' strategies—all can be expected to influence the amounts spent by particular firms or groups of firms in any given period of time. Marketing executives are well aware of differences in the characteristics of products and markets, and some attention has been given to such differences in published studies.[1] But there has been very little systematic research on marketing costs, considering the importance of the subject. The principal reason for this is, of course, the lack of adequate data on marketing expenditures.

This paper is a partial progress report on a study aimed at improving our understanding of marketing costs. Specifically, the work summarized here is an analysis of *variations* in marketing expenditure levels among a sample of more than 100 consumer-product manufacturing "businesses." The purpose of the analysis was to "explain" variations in the ratios of marketing cost (and specific components of total marketing cost) to sales by relating these variations to differences in the characteristics of the businesses themselves, in the characteristics of their markets and customers, and in their competitive positions.

The PIMS *Data Base*

The data used in this study were drawn from the PIMS (Profit Impact of Market Strategy) project. The PIMS project is a large-scale statistical study of the market and competitive characteristics, strategies, and financial performance of individual "business" units operated by a group of corporations participating in the project. Each business is a distinct product-market unit that can be distinguished from other components of its parent corporation by any or all of the following: production technology, customers served, strategy employed, and financial results. Data for Phase III of the PIMS project, on which this paper is based, cover the 4-year period 1970–73.[2]

Overall, the PIMS–Phase III data base includes information for 547 businesses. The analysis reported here, however, is based on only the *consumer-products manufacturing* businesses in the data base, of which there were 103.[3] Further research, currently in progress, will extend the analysis of marketing costs to the businesses primarily engaged in manufacturing products for industrial, commercial, professional, and institutional markets.

The PIMS data differ from the *industry* level data typically used in industrial organiation studies in that they pertain to more narrowly defined product markets. The company personnel who assembled the data for each business unit were requested to define the size of its "market," the identity and relative size of competitors, etc., in such a way as to limit the market to that which a given business actually serves. Markets thus defined are typically much narrower than 4-digit or even 5-digit SIC industry classifications. The scope of a "market," as generally conceived in the

PIMS project, is much closer to that of a "product category" as the term is commonly used in market research studies. For example, "dentifrices" or "color television sets" might constitute markets as defined here. In some cases, markets were restricted to geographic *regions,* either because a business restricted its activities to one region or because differences in competition, etc., made it necessary to separate a national market into two or more dissimilar components.

The distinctive aspect of the PIMS data is that they combine, in a single source:

1. Information about the *market* served by a business, including its growth rate, the number of customers in it, and their buying patterns;
2. Information about the competitive structure of the market, i.e., the number and relative size of competitors;
3. Information about the *competitive behavior* of sellers in the market, in terms of relative prices, relative product quality, and (to a limited degree) relative breadth of product line and market segments served; and
4. *Financial data,* including annual balance sheets and profit-and-loss statements.

All of this information has been assembled for the primary purpose of explaining differences in profitability among businesses.[4] As a byproduct of this primary research goal, the data base permits analysis of marketing costs in relation to all of the factors listed.

METHOD OF ANALYSIS

The principal method employed in the analysis was linear multiple regression. Numerous cross-tabulations were also done in an effort to identify curvilinear relationships and interactions in the effects of independent variables. The regression models were estimated using the time-shared AQD (Analysis of Quantitative Data) program collection designed by Robert Schlaifer.

The results summarized in this paper are for linear regression models in which three different measures of marketing costs are used as *dependent* variables:

Sales Force Expenditures as a Percentage of Sales (SF/S): This includes all costs incurred by a business for compensation (salary, commissions, bonuses, etc.) and fringe benefits of field sales personnel, sales supervisors, home office and district office sales managers; travel and other expenses of sales personnel; and sales force administrative costs such as sales office occupancy, secretarial personnel, communications, and so on.

Advertising & Sales Promotion as a Percentage of Sales (A&P/S): Included here are all costs of advertising media; salaries, fees, and other expenses of company employees and outside contractors involved in planning and preparation of media advertising, displays, catalogs, brochures, etc.; and costs of promotional materials or programs such as contests, premiums, and the like. Strictly temporary price reductions, e.g., trade and consumer deals, are also treated as promotional expenses, *except* in cases where price "dealing" is a regular, continuing form of competition; then it is treated as a reduction in realized prices.

Total Marketing Expense, as a Percentage of Sales (MKTG/S) : Total marketing includes, in addition to sales force and advertising and sales promotion, marketing administration, product and customer service expense, marketing research costs, and miscellaneous expenses related to marketing. It does *not* include physical distribution costs.

These dependent variables were defined as percentages of net sales primarily because past research on marketing costs has concentrated on cost/sales ratios. We did, however, also experiment with other forms of the dependent variables, including ratios of each expense category to value added and to gross margin. These alternate versions of the dependent variables did not, however, produce results significantly different from those obtained using the percentage-of-sales versions.

All three dependent variables, as well as all of the continuous independent variables in the models, are *4-year averages* (combined dollar amounts) for the period 1970–1973.

Empirical Results

In the interests of conserving space and simplifying the presentation, the format of this article diverges somewhat from that usual in similar work with far fewer independent variables. Essential results of the regressions are first presented, along with brief definitions of the independent variables. Subsequently, these independent variables, their definitions, and the implications of the regression results are discussed in more detail.

Table 6–1 lists the dependent and independent variables, their means, and where applicable, their standard deviations within the sample. Table 6–2 shows regressions performed on each of the three dependent measures —MKTG/S, SF/S, and A&P/S. Simple correlations of independent and dependent variables are given in table 6–3.

The regression equations explain an unexpectedly high proportion of the variation in marketing cost/sales ratios—75 percent for total marketing cost, 57 percent for sales force, and 77 percent for advertising and promotion. High R^2s are not, however, the only criterion by which this work should be evaluated. Prediction of the marketing costs required for dif-

Table 6–1

Means and Standard Deviations of Variables
in Marketing Cost Regressions

Variable	Mean	S.D.
Marketing/Sales	17.57	10.66
Sales Force/Sales	5.95	3.67
Advertising & Promotion/Sales	8.53	8.01
Percent Household Consumer Sales	90.87	13.82
Low Importance to User Dummy	.53	—
High Purchase Frequency Dummy	.21	—
Low Purchase Amount Dummy	.39	—
Consumer Durable Dummy	.33	—
Percent Sales to Wholesalers	43.97	36.63
Percent New Products	16.16	24.24
Mature Stage Dummy	.75	—
Decline Stage Dummy	.14	—
Market Share	23.61	16.59
Pioneer Dummy	.66	—
Late Entrant Dummy	.10	—
Regional Marketer Dummy	.15	—
Combined Share, largest three competitors	45.84	15.87
Combined Share^2	2,853	1,575
Sum of Absolute Market Share Changes	15.32	10.39
Trading Margin	32.85	13.80
Relative Price	−1.58	4.31
Capacity Utilization	78.57	15.32

ferent businesses is more useful if the model aids our understanding of "why" these variations occur. We can accept the model only if we are confident that the regression coefficients do indeed represent real relationships, that they are not mere statistical artifacts. This confidence, in turn, depends on the statistical procedures used and the degree to which the indicated relationships make sense, both theoretically and intuitively.

The regression models in table 6–2 were developed by means of a procedure somewhat analogous to stepwise regression. Other independent variables were tested in various versions of these "best" regressions. The decision to retain a particular independent variable in the model was made primarily, but not exclusively, on the basis of the incremental *increase* in the standard deviation of residuals if that variable were removed. Not all independent variables contribute significantly to R^2 for all three dependent measures of marketing cost ratios, but each contributes significantly to explaining the variance of at least one of the three dependent measures. Besides this, it was considered desirable to maintain identical models for each dependent measure so that differences in coefficients would not be functions of differing degrees of collinearity among the independent variables in each model.

Perhaps the most interesting aspect of table 6–2 is that many of the independent variables either have different signs in the SF/S and A&P/S regressions, or exhibit marked changes in size and/or significance of their coefficients. These variables include Percent Household Consumer Sales, Percent Sales to Wholesalers, Regional Marketer Dummy, Pioneer Dummy, Relative Price, Percent New Products, Low Purchase Amount Dummy, Trading Margin, and High Purchase Frequency Dummy. Variables associated with the most variation in A&P/S are, however, also dominant in the regression of MKTG/S. This is not surprising, since advertising and promotion make up the bulk of marketing costs for the consumer-goods manufacturers in our sample.

MULTICOLLINEARITY

There is a high degree of multicollinearity among the independent variables used in each of the three regression models. Indeed, when the PIMS data forms were originally designed, closely related measures were deliberately included in order to determine which of them would be most useful in explaining differences in profitability, marketing costs, and other dependent variables.

For example, we have included measures of both *purchase frequency* and *average purchase amount*. Obviously, frequency and amount are related: high unit-value products, such as automobiles and major appliances, are not purchased frequently. (On the other hand, some low-value products, such as shoe polish, are not bought very often, either.)

In some instances, either of two highly related variables gave about the same result when included in a model, but coefficient estimates were distorted when both variables were included. In these cases, we discarded one of the variables, retaining the one for which the statistical significance of the coefficient was highest. Even after several independent variables were eliminated in this way, the "best" models, as shown in table 6–2, still contained several variables that are correlated with one another (table 6–3 is a correlation matrix). We have allowed significantly correlated independent variables to remain only when a priori expectations suggested that *both* variables ought to be related to marketing costs. For example, businesses with large market shares tend to have lower marketing costs, as do businesses that were pioneers in a particular market, the latter having the advantages of obtaining distribution, establishing consumer awareness, and getting trial before the entry of others. The regression models include both market share and a dummy variable for "pioneer."

Table 6–2

Regression Equations Explaining Marketing Cost Ratios
(Natural Coefficients — "*t*" Ratios in Parentheses)

Independent Variables	Dependent Variables					
	MKTG/s		SF/s		A&P/s	
Intercept	5.338	(−.713)	11.200	(3.305)	−8.641	(1.620)
Percent Household Consumer Sales	−.017	(−.290)	−.039	(−1.515)	.060	(1.470)
Low Importance to User Dummy	6.168	(4.156)	2.178	(3.250)	2.450	(2.337)
High Purchase Frequency Dummy	−2.841	(−1.170)	−.068	(−.068)	−2.664	(−1.560)
Low Purchase Amount Dummy	5.750	(3.230)	−.501	(−.624)	5.318	(4.220)
Consumer Durable Dummy	−2.502	(−1.406)	−.732	(−.917)	−2.510	(−2.010)
Percent Sales to Wholesalers	−.048	(−2.090)	−.036	(−3.460)	.010	(.604)
Percent New Products	.067	(2.250)	−.009	(−.676)	.054	(2.575)
Mature Stage Dummy	−2.682	(−1.355)	−.635	(−.714)	−1.120	(.801)
Decline Stage Dummy	−6.949	(−2.879)	−2.260	(−2.080)	−4.638	(−2.720)
Market Share	−.066	(−1.357)	−.005	(−.203)	−.041	(−1.175)
Pioneer Dummy	−.364	(−.241)	−.044	(−.064)	−1.450	(−1.357)
Late Entrant Dummy	3.017	(1.260)	.797	(.745)	2.120	(1.260)
Regional Marketer Dummy	11.160	(3.341)	5.310	(3.560)	−2.296	(−.979)
Combined Share, largest three competitors	.298	(1.630)	.116	(1.410)	.051	(.395)
Combined Share^2	−.003	(1.670)	−.002	(1.612)	−.001	(−.257)

Sum of Absolute Market Share						
Changes	.184	(2.360)	.028	(.796)	.185	(3.363)
Trading Margin	.389	(6.960)	.036	(1.428)	.295	(7.480)
Relative Price	.319	(2.210)	−.047	(.723)	.268	(2.630)
Capacity Utilization	−.107	(−2.260)	−.056	(−2.630)	−.031	(−.940)
Sample R^2	.788		.641		.812	
Adjusted R^2	.745		.568		.774	
Est. Residual S.D.	5.460		2.450		3.860	
(adjusted for degrees of freedom)						
Correlation of Absolute Value of						
Residuals with Regression Estimate	.093		.064		.125	

Table 6–3

Correlations of Independent and Dependent Variables

	MKTG/S	SF/S	A&P/S	% Household Sales	Low Importance	High Frequency	Low Amount	Consumer Durable	% to Wholesalers
MKTG/S	1.00								
SF/S	.62	1.00							
A&P/S	.76	.08	1.00						
% Household Sales	.42	.19	.40	1.00					
Low Importance	.09	−.11	.37	.25	1.00				
High Frequency	.25	.49	−.19	.29	−.42	1.00			
Low Amount	.47	.34	.26	.53	−.15	.45	1.00		
Consumer Durable	−.46	−.36	−.35	−.48	−.01	−.32	−.57	1.00	
% to Wholesalers	−.22	−.48	.16	−.26	.26	−.44	−.42	.46	1.00
% New Products	−.01	−.18	.07	−.12	−.01	−.29	−.28	.29	.01
Mature Stage	−.04	.17	−.16	−.04	−.18	.25	.06	−.07	−.12
Decline Stage	−.01	−.18	.12	.25	.31	−.14	.02	−.10	.09
Market Share	.30	.25	.19	.31	.05	.20	.34	−.28	−.09
Pioneer	.05	.15	−.17	.09	−.18	.27	.21	−.15	−.10
Late Entrant	.07	−.04	.16	.02	.04	−.17	.00	−.09	−.13
Regional	.43	.66	−.13	.27	−.44	.79	.51	−.29	−.50
Big 3 M.S.	.01	−.06	.09	−.12	.00	.00	−.06	−.13	.04
Big 3 M.S.²	−.04	−.12	.07	−.11	.00	−.01	−.07	−.13	.01
Sum M.S. Changes	.47	.18	.51	.25	.22	.05	.00	−.16	.18
Margin	.56	.05	.72	.21	.19	−.13	.13	−.18	.34
Relative Price	.12	.00	.08	.04	−.19	.19	−.09	−.06	−.16
Capacity Utilization	−.28	−.42	.04	−.12	.31	−.48	−.16	.22	.15

Most businesses with large market shares were pioneers, and vice versa, as table 6–3 shows. What this means, of course, is that the coefficients of these two variables cannot be treated as separate, distinct factors influencing marketing costs. Since many of the independent variables in our models are correlated, the relationship of each to marketing costs must be interpreted in the context of the model as a whole.

INDEPENDENT VARIABLES

This section briefly reviews the rationale for selecting the independent variables included in the regressions on marketing cost ratios.[5] These factors fall into seven general categories: Customer Characteristics, Purchase Patterns, Distribution Channels, Product Life Cycle, Competitive Position, Competitive Environment, and Price/Cost Structure.

% New Products	Mature Stage	Decline Stage	Market Share	Pioneer	Late Entrant	Regional	Big 3 M.S.	Big 3 M.S.²	Sum M.S. Changes	Margin	Relative Price	Capacity Utilization
1.00												
−.29	1.00											
.12	−.68	1.00										
−.30	.00	.05	1.00									
−.19	−.09	.05	.41	1.00								
.32	−.11	.06	−.31	−.46	1.00							
−.22	.24	−.16	.29	.30	−.13	1.00						
−.26	.09	−.01	−.26	−.09	.11	−.11	1.00					
−.22	.06	.02	−.29	−.10	.16	−.15	.98	1.00				
−.08	−.27	.31	.37	.00	−.11	.10	.09	.03	1.00			
−.08	−.06	.06	.40	.06	−.13	−.06	.02	−.03	.49	1.00		
.08	−.07	.00	−.15	−.06	.03	.10	.17	.21	.09	−.08	1.00	
.06	.06	−.09	.00	−.18	.06	−.50	−.05	−.06	−.15	.04	−.13	1.00

Customer Characteristics

Percent Household Consumer Sales: This variable represents the percent of business sales used by household and individual consumers. Although all businesses in the sample identified themselves as "consumer-products" manufacturers, some market a significant amount of total sales to other businesses or institutions (up to 49 percent of total sales). Examples might include soap companies that sell to industrial as well as wholesale and retail customers.

This variable, not surprisingly, exhibits a positive relationship with A&P/S and the reverse pattern for SF/S. These two effects appear to cancel each other, however, and the net association with MKTG/S is negligible.

In considering the true impact of this variable, it is important to remember that the minimum value is 50 percent (mean = 91 percent). Much of this variable's impact can therefore be described as bringing the "true" intercept of the equations closer to zero: Percent Household Consumer Sales has a positive coefficient for A&P/S (negative intercept) and negative coefficients for SF/S and MKTG/S (positive intercepts).

Purchase Patterns

Low Importance to User Dummy ($= 1$ if the product typically accounts for less than .25 percent of end user's total annual purchases).

High Purchase Frequency Dummy ($= 1$ if a typical consumer buys the product weekly or even more often).

Low Purchase Amount Dummy ($= 1$ if the typical purchase amount is less than $1.00).

Consumer Durable Dummy ($= 1$ if the product is durable).

The effects of different combinations of purchase amount, purchase frequency, and product durability are shown in table 6–4.

Table 6–4

Purchase Patterns and A&P/S Ratio

Purchase Amount	Purchase Frequency	
	High	Low
	Average Ratio of A&P/S	
Low	5.85	15.17
	($n = 18$)	($n = 23$)
High:	4.30	10.23
Nondurable	($n = 3$)	($n = 25$)
		4.53
Durable	—	($n = 34$)

For infrequently purchased nondurables A&P/S tends to be higher than for those bought once a week or more often. But, although durable goods are purchased infrequently, average A&P/S is *lower* for these products. Within the nondurables category, average A&P/S is significantly lower for products generally bought in amounts of more than $1.00 than for those with smaller average transactions. All of these effects are reflected in the coefficients of the three dummy variables in the regression equations shown in table 6–2.

An additional dummy variable, Low Importance to User, is included to represent its significant effect on the other three variables. Our interpretation of the relationships between marketing costs and purchase importance, amount, frequency, and product durability is as follows:

Products that are of little importance to the consumer and/or are of low unit value are those for which the consumer is not likely to engage in extensive information search activity, since the perceived risk of such purchases is relatively small.[6] Since the "cost" of obtaining information from advertising is very low, advertising and promotion may be expected to be important for such products. Cox, for instance, cites evidence that reliance on marketer communications is highest when the perceived risk of the purchase is low (Cox, 1967). Even though the purchase decision itself may be of little consequence to the consumer, if advertising is the main source of "information," it may play an influential role in the outcome of the purchase decision. In a similar vein, Krugman has argued that TV advertising may be most effective for "low involvement products" (Krugman, 1965). In addition, the concept of a minimum "transaction cost" may be important in increasing marketing cost ratios. Given the self-service nature of many outlets, a minimum amount of advertising may be required to make consumers aware of the product's existence. This may well result in higher marketing cost ratios when unit value is low and/or product purchases constitute a small proportion of annual expenditures. As shown in table 6–2, both Low Importance to User and Low Purchase Amount dummy variables are positively and strongly related to A&P/S and MKTG/S. Regressions on marketing cost ratios done by the Conference Board resulted in a *positive* coefficient for the dummy variable "major purchase for most consumers," in contrast to these results (Bailey, 1975).

Only the Low Importance Dummy appears significant in the SF/S model, however. This may suggest that products "unimportant" to users are also relatively unimportant to distributors, and hence require more sales-force efforts to maintain distribution.

Frequency of purchase is often mentioned in the marketing and economic literature as a potential determinant of marketing cost levels. It has been suggested that more frequently purchased items offer the marketer more opportunity to influence the consumer's purchase decision (Buzzell, 1972). On the other hand, Comanor and Wilson suggest that product use experience for frequently purchased items should reduce the consumer's need for advertising (Comanor and Wilson, 1974). While both views have merit, studies done on an earlier version of the PIMS data base suggest that the relationship may be more complex. When Durable Good is used as a surrogate for low frequency of purchase and compared with the High Purchase Frequency Dummy, it can be seen that *both* have negative coefficients in the A&P/S model. This suggests that those products bought less frequently than weekly but more often than durable goods are advertised and promoted more intensively. The Conference Board study of marketing costs indicated *higher* total marketing costs for products "generally purchased more often than yearly" than for less frequently purchased goods (Bailey, 1975). This is probably due to the implied durable/ nondurable split that is treated separately here.

For advertising to generate sales, there must be a sufficient number of consumers "in the market" for the product within a reasonable time period after ad exposure. Also, consumers must be willing to re-evaluate their purchase decision for the product being advertised (or need reinforcement to remain loyal). Thus, the products that employ the most advertising and promotion are those that are purchased frequently enough so that a substantial proportion of the advertising audience is "in the market" at any particular time, but not so frequently that the decision to buy is habitual or that the consumer relies entirely on product use experience.

The manufacturers of durable goods, perhaps because their products are usually big-ticket items and purchased very infrequently, appear to spend proportionately less on all forms of marketing costs. Previous empirical work by Comanor and Wilson (1974) supports a negative relation between durables and the A/S ratio. The negative coefficient for SF/S is somewhat surprising, but may reflect higher dealer-purchase amounts and/or lower sales-call frequency. The system of franchising dealers for durable goods may also play an important role in the underlying reasons for the negative coefficient, i.e., fewer dealers to service, and a more stable manufacturer-dealer relationship.

In summary, frequency and amount of purchase, durables versus nondurables, and importance to the consumer are so intertwined that they must be considered together. They provide a significant degree of explanatory power in the regressions on marketing cost levels. (It should also be noted that they are intrinsic to a particular product-market; thus, despite their considerable impact on the required level of marketing costs, little or nothing can be done by management to moderate their effects.)

Distribution Channels

Percent Sales to Wholesalers: The percentage of total sales made to wholesalers.

The reasons for including this variable are quite straightforward. Generally speaking, the more sales made at wholesale level, the more consumer "pull" a manufacturer should have to generate, i.e., there would be little or no "push" for product (unless, of course, missionary salesmen are employed). Sales-force efforts, however, should be reduced because fewer salesmen are required to service wholesalers than are needed for retail channels or direct sales. Regression coefficients for this variable strongly support a negative relationship with SF/S, but are only slightly positive for A&P/S. The net impact on MKTG/S is negative. There is, however, a high degree of collinearity between this variable and several others (see table 6–3). Only certain kinds of products lend themselves to a distribution strategy that employs wholesalers. For these products wholesale outlets do not require the higher sales-force expenditures necessary for those sold through retailers or direct to end users.

Product Life Cycle

Percent New Products: The percentage of total sales resulting from sales of products introduced during the three preceding years.

Mature Stage Dummy (= 1 if the product class is judged to be in the mature stage of its life cycle).

Decline Stage Dummy (= 1 if the product class is judged to be in the decline stage of its life cycle).

Much has been written that suggests that promotional activity is highest in the earlier stages of the life cycle of the product. The two dummy variables in this category represent different stages in the product life cycle, while Percent New Products is a continuous variable measuring that proportion of the total business in the introductory or growth stage of either the brand or product life cycle. It is interesting to note that the correlation of Percent New Products with the "mature" stage is negative, while with the "decline" stage it is actually positive (.12). This may indicate attempts to launch new products in order to extend the life cycle (Levitt, 1965). The coefficients of these variables in regressions on A&P/S and MKTG/S lend support to the contention that the intensity of marketing expenditures tends to decline over the product and brand life cycles. Percent New Products has a positive coefficient in equations predicting A&P/S and MKTG/S, while Mature has a negative coefficient, and Decline is even more strongly negative. In equations predicting SF/S, however, only Decline Stage Dummy is associated with a significant coefficient. The coefficient is negative, indicating lower sales-force efforts at the end of the life cycle.

Competitive Position

Market Share: The business's share of the total served market (dollar value).

Pioneer Dummy (= 1 if the business was one of the first entrants into the served market).

Late Entrant Dummy (= 1 if business entered market after several competitors were well established).

Regional Marketer Dummy (= 1 if business serves only a particular geographic region within the national market).

Market share's relationship to the intensity of marketing costs, particularly advertising, has received much attention from marketers and economists. It is possible to formulate different hypotheses about the association of market share and marketing costs, some of which may be a function of differing views of the marketing cost/sales response function. An "S" curve would suggest that over a certain range larger market shares might be associated with smaller marketing cost ratios, while response functions that suggest only decreasing marginal returns to marketing expenditures would imply rising cost ratios.

However, two other factors seem to support the idea that marketing costs decline with market share, whatever the nature of the sales response function. First, businesses with large market shares are more likely to pursue a strategy of maintaining or "milking" the business; further growth is probably not as viable a strategy when share is already quite large. Secondly, because of the cumulative effects of advertising, total sales for a business with a large share of market are apt to depend less on marketing efforts in the current period. While marketing expenditures may have been instrumental in building a large market share, it is not obvious that a large marketing cost/sales ratio must be continued once that share is obtained.

This view of market share's association with marketing cost ratios is not, however, strongly supported by the regression coefficients. The coefficients are negative but not highly significant, and there is evidence of collinearity that might bias the coefficients in this direction.

Closely related to the market share variable is the type of entry into the market. Although Pioneer and Late Entrant dummy variables are correlated with market share (.41 and −.30 respectively), these variables also reflect other dimensions of a business's competitive position. In general, firms that enter the market later must promote more heavily to gain position. This argument is like that used for the cumulative effects of advertising on market share. Both variables have regression coefficients consistent with this reasoning in each of the three equations. Although the coefficients are not highly significant, the combination of early entry and high market share almost certainly leads to lower marketing costs. By the same token, late entry and a low market share cause marketing costs to rise.

Regional Marketer Dummy provides yet another measure of the nature of a business's competitive position. For consumer businesses, it seems likely that regional marketers will tend to spend less for advertising and promotion. This pattern should be expected because of the relative inefficiency of utilizing local media as compared to national media. Regional Marketers in our sample also tend to supply products that are purchased very frequently (correlation of Regional Marketer and High Purchase Frequency Dummy = .79). Again, although the sign of the coefficient indicates lower advertising and promotion expenditures, it is not obvious whether these lower ratios are attributable to frequency of purchase, lower effectiveness of local media, or some other factor.

The correlation with frequency purchased products presents a problem in the interpretation of the coefficient for SF/S as well. Frequently purchased products may well be "sold" and delivered by the same person. Are higher sales-force expenditures due to call frequency, typical low amount of purchase, or the shifting of more marketing expenditure into sales-force efforts?

The coefficient for Regional Marketer Dummy is relatively weak in regressions on A&P/S, but increases markedly in significance in the SF/S equation; this supports the hypothesis that regional marketers, other things being equal, tend to spend more for sales force and less for advertising and promotion efforts. Their total marketing expenditures tend to be higher in relation to sales than those of national marketers.

Competitive Environment

The regression models include two variables that reflect the competitive environment in which a business operates:

Big 3 Market Share: The sum of the market shares of the three largest competitors.

Competitive Turmoil: The sum of the *absolute values* of year-to-year changes in market shares, over the period 1970–73, for the business and its three largest competitors.

The Big 3 Market Share is a measure of the strength of competition faced by a business. Not surprisingly, this variable is positively associated with all three measures of marketing cost intensity. The stronger the competition, the more a business must spend. In addition, the combined share of the largest competitors is related to the more familiar measures of market concentration. Firms competing with a few powerful rivals are more likely to base their strategies on nonprice elements, since price changes are relatively easy to detect and imitate in such markets.

The positive association between Big 3 Market Share and marketing costs appears to diminish after a certain point. To reflect this, we have included the *square* of Big 3 Share in the models and, as expected, its sign is negative. The coefficient of (Big 3 Share)^2 is not significant, however, in the regression equation for advertising and promotion expenditures.

The Competitive Turmoil variable reflects the total amount of *change* that has occurred in the market positions of leading competitors over the 4-year period covered by the PIMS data. This variable is strongly and positively related to both MKTG/S and A&P/S, but its coefficient is not significant in the regression for SF/S.

Markets with a high level of turmoil may be those in which important changes have occurred in consumer buying patterns, distribution channels, or other aspects of market structure. Under these conditions, there is greater opportunity to gain sales via market efforts—and, perhaps, greater need to spend for defensive purposes. We had expected that the turmoil measure would correlate positively with the extent of new product activity in a market, but this was not the case ($r = -.085$).

Price/Cost Structure

Trading Margin: Percent of total sales revenues that contribute to covering depreciation, nonmanufacturing expenses, and profits.

Relative Price: Percentage by which a business's selling price differs from that of leading competitors ($+$ or $-$).

Capacity Utilization: Percent of total manufacturing capacity utilized, on average.

Trading Margin is the most significant of all the independent variables shown in table 6–2 for explaining variations in marketing cost intensity. Assuming that this measure is a good approximation of a business's marginal contribution from incremental sales volume (this assumes approximately constant marginal cost over some wide range of output) and that marketing expenditures are decreasingly marginally effective in generating sales, businesses with large trading margins should be willing to spend more on marketing efforts. In other words, the more a sale is "worth" in terms of contribution to overhead, the more a business can profitably spend to obtain that sale. If returns from promotional efforts are diminishing, it follows that marketing cost/sales ratios should be positively related to Trading Margin. Trading Margin may vary for a number of reasons. Increased vertical integration, more efficient production methods, a higher proportion of fixed costs (i.e., more capital intensity) are all, other things being equal, likely to increase the value of this variable. Some of these factors, together with the possibility of scale economies in purchasing and distribution, may explain the positive association of Trading Margin with Market Share (see Buzzell, 1975).

In addition to the cost and volume factors, market and business price elasticities of demand will also exercise an influence on the price charged and thus the resulting Trading Margin. Relative Price is not strongly correlated with Trading Margin ($-.08$), however, and this suggests that, at least for our sample, Trading Margin is not a surrogate for high relative price. High price strategies may be associated with costs that negate the influence of this variable on Trading Margin. Relative Price *within* a market says little, however, about the overall market price elasticity of demand, which we assume is related to the level of Trading Margin a particular business earns on sales.

Coefficients for Trading Margin in the three marketing cost regressions confirm the expected positive relationship, but are weaker for SF/S than A&P/S and MKTG/S. The weaker influence on sales force might be interpreted as stemming from the high fixed-cost component of sales-force expenditures.

An appropriate question at this point is whether Trading Margin is a legitimate independent variable for regressions on marketing cost ratios. The answer is twofold. First, Trading Margin may vary for reasons that have little to do with market response to advertising—such as those associated with different fixed/variable cost relationships. Second, it makes sense in our opinion to differentiate between those variables that impact on marketing costs through their association with higher trading margins and those that appear to influence levels of marketing costs in other ways. Relative Price, for instance, may impact on marketing costs regardless of its relationship with Trading Margin. To the extent that higher relative prices are justified to the consumer by higher quality, then that superiority must be communicated to the consumer. When such higher quality is not apparent from inspection (for example, Borden's "hidden values," Borden, 1942), then this is likely to result in higher advertising and certain forms of sales promotion. The regression coefficients for Relative Price confirm this relationship to A&P/S and MKTG/S, but indicate little association with SF/S.

The last variable in this category, Capacity Utilization, is included because of the likelihood that businesses operating at or near manufacturing capacity will tend to promote their products less intensively. There is no gain from stimulating demand that cannot be met. Although the signs in all regressions are negative, as expected, the impact appears to be larger for SF/S. This is perhaps because sales-force expenses are generally more fixed than advertising and promotion, and thus less subject to short-term modifications. The more liquid advertising budget can be easily adjusted by management if the objective is to maintain a constant A/S ratio or to generate short-term profit.

MARKETING COSTS AND PROFIT RATES

There has been considerable debate among industrial economists regarding the relationship, if any, between marketing expenditures and profitability. Published studies of the subject have concentrated on *advertising costs* because, as noted earlier, data are generally not available for other components of total marketing expense.[7] Moreover, previous studies have dealt with the relationship between advertising intensity (usually measured in terms of the ratio of media advertising costs to sales) and profitability at the *industry* level. Thus, a typical approach has been to explain variations in return on stockholders' equity (or on total assets) among SIC 3-digit "industries" by relating them to variations in the A/S ratio, usually in conjunction with other variables such as capital requirements, rate of demand growth, and the level of industry concentration.

The theoretical arguments for expecting a *positive* association between advertising intensity and profitability are generally stated as follows:

1. High levels of advertising expenditure, in and of themselves, constitute a barrier to entry that (possibly in conjunction with other barriers) enables established firms to enjoy above-normal rates of profit; and/or

2. A high A/S ratio is a symptom of a high degree of "product differentiation," and advertising, in turn, may help to *create* consumer perceptions of differentiation. Either way, the differentiation acts as a barrier to new entry and permits high profit rates; and/or

3. Firms that earn high profits, for whatever reason, are more likely to spend on advertising. Conversely, if profits are low, advertising budgets are often reduced because it is a discretionary type of outlay (see especially Comanor and Wilson).

Although this study was not designed specifically as a test of the hypothesized positive association between advertising intensity and profitability, our data do permit us to examine the relationship, and also to ascertain how profit rates are related to other, broader measures of marketing expenses.

Table 6–5 shows simple correlations between two measures of profit rates (Net Profit as a Percent of Sales and Net Profit as a Percent of Investment) and ratios of marketing expense to sales (MKTG/S, SF/S, A&P/S, and media Advertising/Sales). The profit measures are defined at the individual *business* level before income taxes and interest charges; "investment" is likewise measured at the business level and is equal to total assets *minus* current liabilities.

Correlations are also shown between each of the two profit measures and the *residuals* from the three regression equations described in table 6–2. Our rationale for relating the residuals to profit rates was that if marketing expenditures, or a specific component such as A&P/S, were utilized by firms as a barrier to entry, then variations in the residuals—after "accounting for differences in market and customer characteristics via the regressions"—might be expected to be even more closely related to profits than the marketing cost ratios themselves.

As shown in table 6–5, correlations between each of the profit measures and MKTG/S, SF/S, and A&P/S are zero or *negative*. Only ADV/S (media

Table 6-5

Simple Correlations of Profit Measures with Marketing Cost Ratios
and with Residuals from Marketing Cost Regressions

	MKTG/s	SF/s	A&P/s	ADV/s	MKTG/s Residual	SF/s Residual	A&P/s Residual	NP/s	NP/ Investment
MKTG/s	1.00								
SF/s	.62	1.00							
A&P/s	.76	.08	1.00						
ADV/s	.58	−.02	.85	1.00					
MKTG/s Residual	.46	.30	.32		1.00				
SF/s Residual	.23	.60	.03		.51	1.00			
A&P/s Residual	.34	.04	.43		.74	.07	1.00		
Net Profit/s	−.23	−.27	−.05	.03	−.28	−.12	−.23	1.00	
Net Profit/Investment	−.20	−.31	.00	.16	−.24	−.28	−.21	.85	1.00
Trading Margin	.56	.05	.72	.72	.00	.00	.00	.48	.43

advertising expense only) exhibits any positive correlation, and the correlations are slight. Moreover, *all* of the correlations between the profit measures and the residuals from the marketing cost regressions are negative.

These results lend no support to the theoretical arguments in favor of a positive association between marketing cost ratios and profitability. If anything, the data indicate negative relationships between most of the cost measures and profit rates. Such a negative relationship might exist because (1) high levels of marketing expense reflect intense competitive rivalries in which profits are dissipated; and/or (2) businesses with high ratios of marketing/sales tend to be those that are engaged in bulding market share (see Buzzell, 1975).

How can the results in table 6–5 be reconciled with previous studies showing positive relationships between average industry profits and A/S ratios? A plausible explanation is that both A/S and the two profit measures are strongly related to *trading margin*. Businesses with high trading margins tend to have higher net profits, too; and, for reasons outlined previously, their optimal rates of marketing cost tend to be higher. To the extent that high trading margins reflect successful "product differentiation," the results in table 6–5 are not necessarily inconsistent with earlier findings. However, to the extent that larger trading margins indicate greater manufacturing efficiency and/or a greater degree of vertical integration, the explanation for the A/S-profit relationship is quite different from that usually advanced.

The issue of the relationship between profits and advertising, or marketing more broadly defined, is too complex to be resolved in this paper. Our results do, however, suggest the need for a reappraisal of the conventional wisdom on the subject. We hope to be able to explore the topic further in future analyses of the PIMS data base.

Summary and Conclusions

The regression models reported here account for very high proportions of the variance in marketing cost ratios among consumer-goods businesses. The value of the analysis is enhanced by the use of independent variables that are more generalizable than business or industry-specific factors. Of course, regressions can never prove causality, only association. This means that the relationships between some of the independent and dependent variables are subject to "chicken or egg" arguments. Among the variables for which causality may possibly operate in both directions are Trading Margin, measures of industry concentration, Market Share, and Relative Price. Others, however, such as Frequency of Purchase, Amount of Purchase, Importance of Purchase, and Percent New Products, are not likely to be *results* of marketing cost ratios themselves; for these variables, the direction of causality seems clear.

Many of the variables related to marketing cost ratios are *not* controllable by management. There is little a manager can do to change these factors, and he must accept them as inherent in the type of business he operates. Because these factors appear to exercise a considerable influence on marketing cost ratios, the degree of latitude about marketing expenditure decisions within a particular business may be narrower than is often presumed by market researchers and economists.

The regression estimates of marketing cost ratios offer management some insight into these constraints. The coefficients should *not* be interpreted as tools for fine-tuning a promotional budget, but the information in these regressions may be of value to managers of new businesses where experience in judging budget levels is scant. They may also help managers to plan for anticipated changes in product, market, customer, and strategy factors—for example, changes in the product life cycle or shifts in consumer purchasing behavior.

Public policy makers and economists may also find the work useful because of the reported relationships between marketing cost ratios and the "uncontrollable" factors that characterize businesses. Our analysis indicates that differences in marketing costs between companies and industries can, to a large extent, be explained by differences in the characteristics of customers and markets. To the extent that this is true, the fact that a given industry's marketing costs are higher than those of another industry does *not* necessarily indicate an "abnormal" or economically unjustifiable pattern of competition.

More generally, this work can be viewed as accounting for differences in the amount managers have *decided* to spend for marketing. The nature of many of the independent variables suggests that much of this variation is due to differences in the market response to promotion of different consumer goods. This, in turn, suggests that descriptive studies of this nature may provide researchers with some interactive variables they need to start measuring the *differences* in the effectiveness of advertising and sales-force expenditures for various businesses. We have too long asked the simplistic question, "Is advertising effective?" Such a question cannot be answered meaningfully in absolute terms. On the other hand, the mass of research done to measure the response of sales to marketing effort, for *one* particular brand in *one* particular situation, contributes little to our general theories of marketing. Instead, we should begin to explore those characteristics of a business that determine the extent to which advertising, sales promotion, and/or sales-force efforts are useful in generating sales.

This chapter constitutes a status report on the research directed at finding general patterns of spending among consumer businesses. Other work, currently in progress, will extend the analysis to industrial businesses and also examine advertising's effect on business performance.

NOTES

1. For example, several studies have shown that advertising expenditures, as a percentage of sales, tend to decline as a product category passes through succeeding stages of the Product Life Cycle (Buzzell, 1966).

2. This was one of the phases of the PIMS project carried out at the Marketing Science Institute during the years 1972–74. Since early 1975, further PIMS research has been done under the auspices of the Strategic Planning Institute (Cambridge, Mass.), an organization established for this specific purpose.

3. Consumer-products manufacturers are defined, for purposes of this analysis, as those who (1) designated themselves as being engaged in the manufacture of durable or nondurable consumer goods and (2) reported that at least 50 percent of their sales were to individuals or households. The data submitted to the PIMS project did *not* include identification of the specific products manufactured by each business or, in some cases, even a SIC industry classification.

4. Published reports of the profitability analysis include work by Schoeffler, Buzzell, and Heany (1974); and Buzzell, Gale, and Sultan (1975).

5. A more extensive discussion of the theoretical rationale for each independent variable will be given a forthcoming doctoral thesis by Farris.

6. Psychological importance is, of course, not captured by either the amount of purchase or portion of total annual expenditures variables. While their importance is acknowledged, few surrogates for such concepts were available, and these failed to explain a sufficient amount of total variance to warrant inclusion in the final models.

7. One of the most extensive studies of advertising and profits, which also contains a bibliography of previous work, is summarized in Comanor and Wilson (1974).

REFERENCES

1. Bailey, Earl L. *Marketing Cost Ratios of U.S. Manufacturers.* New York: The Conference Board, 1975.
2. Borden, Neil. *The Economic Effects of Advertising.* Chicago: Richard D. Irwin, 1944.
3. Buzzell, Robert D. "Competitive Behavior and Product Life Cycles," in Wright, J. S. and Goldstucker, J. L. (eds.), *New Ideas for Successful Marketing.* Chicago: American Marketing Association, 1966, pp.46–68.
4. Buzzell, R. D.; Gale, Bradley T.; and Sultan, Ralph G. M. "Market Share —A Key to Profitability," *Harvard Business Review*, January–February 1975, pp.97–106.

5. Buzzell, R. D.; Nourse, R. E. M.; Matthews, J. B.; and Levitt, T. *Marketing: A Contemporary Analysis*, 2nd ed. New York: McGraw-Hill, 1972, chapter 20.
6. Comanor, William S., and Wilson, Thomas A. *Advertising and Market Power*. Cambridge: Harvard University Press, 1974.
7. Cox, Donald F. "Risk Taking and Information Handling in Consumer Behavior," in Cox, Donald F. (ed.), *Risk Taking and Information Handling in Consumer Behavior*. Boston: Division of Research, Graduate School of Business Administration, Harvard University, 1967, pp.604–40.
8. Krugman, Herbert. "The Impact of Television Advertising: Learning Without Involvement," *Public Opinion Quarterly*, Vol. 39, No. 3, Fall 1965, pp.349–56.
9. Levitt, Theodore. "Exploit the Product Life Cycle," *Harvard Business Review*, November–December 1965, pp.81–94.
10. McNiven, Malcolm A. (ed.). *How Much to Spend for Advertising*. New York: Association of National Advertisers, 1969.
11. Schoeffler, Sidney; Buzzell, R. D.; and Heany, D. F. "Impact of Strategic Planning on Profit Performance," *Harvard Business Review*, March–April 1974, pp.137–45.

7

Reseller Strategies and the Financial Performance of the Firm

BERT C. McCAMMON, JR., AND ALBERT D. BATES

The structure of distribution in advanced economies is currently undergoing a series of changes that are as profound in their impact and as pervasive in their influence as those that occurred in manufacturing during the 19th century.

When money doesn't work, it doesn't count.

CNA Financial Corporation Advertisement

For too many companies, life consists of working very hard to make small differences in performance produce small differences in profitability. But, the really significant alterations in corporate fortunes depend on those relatively few and basic decisions that enable a company to fight corporate wars with its best weapons ... not those of its competitors ... and enable it to choose the time and place where competitive strength really counts.

BRUCE HENDERSON

Introduction

The 1970s have been a sobering experience for many retailing and wholesaling executives. After a decade of relatively rapid expansion, distribution companies were suddenly confronted by double-digit inflation, wage and price controls, product shortages, rising energy costs, record interest rates, and a major economic recession. Since retailers and wholesalers operate on relatively slender margins, the cumulative effects of these developments were much more severe in distribution than in manufacturing.

146

In addition to coping with a roller coaster economy, retailers and whole-salers were also confronted by rising competitive pressures. In the 1970s, conventional retailers were seriously threatened by furniture warehouse showrooms, home improvement centers, super drugstores, and other inno-vative forms of competition. Though less publicized, the turmoil in whole-saling was equally severe.

Given this background, it is not surprising to observe that many com-panies are in the process of reviewing their strategic posture in the market-place. During the first half of 1975, for example, Penney's, Federated, Oshawa, and Super Valu almost simultaneously announced that they were embarking on major long-run planning projects. Because of economic and market dislocations, strategic planning has emerged as a central corporate concern in the field of distribution.

The purpose of this paper is to explore the interrelationship between corporate strategy and financial performance. The findings of the paper are based on a careful analysis of all major publicly owned retailing and wholesaling corporations. Of the 391 companies analyzed, 269 are retail-ing concerns and the balance are wholesaling corporations.

The first section of the paper dramatizes the performance imperative in the field of distribution. Subsequent sections of the paper identify the mainstream strategies that have been most successful in retailing and wholesaling during the 1970–74 period.

The Performance Imperative

Analysts and executives agree that retailers and wholesalers are cur-rently confronted by a major performance imperative: Distribution com-panies must improve their profitability, liquidity, and growth potential ratios over forthcoming budget periods.

PROFITABILITY TRENDS

The strategic profit model is a useful frame of reference for understand-ing the profitability challenge in distribution. As shown in figure 7–1, the strategic profit model combines in a single profit-planning equation the principal elements of a company's operating statement and balance sheet. The model involves multiplying a company's profit margin by its rate of asset turnover and its leverage ratio to derive its rate of return on net worth.

The data in figure 7–1 show that retailers and wholesalers experienced a sharp decline in profitability between 1968 and 1974. Obviously, much of this decline can be attributed to the 1974–75 recession. It should be emphasized, however, that rates of return on net worth in the field of dis-tribution have declined steadily since the mid-1950s. Thus, recent devel-opments can be interpreted as a continuation of long-term trends.

Figure 7–1

Composite Strategic Profit Models for Retailing and Wholesaling Corporations,* 1968 and 1974

Retailing Corporations

	$\dfrac{\text{Net Profits (after taxes)}}{\text{Net Sales}}$	×	$\dfrac{\text{Net Sales}}{\text{Total Assets}}$	=	$\dfrac{\text{Net Profits (after taxes)}}{\text{Total Assets}}$	×	$\dfrac{\text{Total Assets}}{\text{Net Worth}}$	=	$\dfrac{\text{Net Profits (after taxes)}}{\text{Net Worth}}$
1968:	1.4%		2.6		3.8%		2.3		8.8%
1974:	1.0%		2.6		2.6%		2.7		7.0%

Wholesaling Corporations

	$\dfrac{\text{Net Profits (after taxes)}}{\text{Net Sales}}$	×	$\dfrac{\text{Net Sales}}{\text{Total Assets}}$	=	$\dfrac{\text{Net Profits (after taxes)}}{\text{Total Assets}}$	×	$\dfrac{\text{Total Assets}}{\text{Net Worth}}$	=	$\dfrac{\text{Net Profits (after taxes)}}{\text{Net Worth}}$
1968:	1.2%		2.9		3.6%		2.4		8.6%
1974:	1.1%		2.6		2.9%		2.6		7.5%

*The strategic profit model ratios may not multiply to the totals indicated because of rounding. Furthermore, the net profits to net sales ratios for 1974 have been recalculated to eliminate inventory profits and thereby minimize the effects of inflation.

Sources: Dun and Bradstreet, Inc., First National City Bank, Internal Revenue Service, and authors' calculations.

. As shown in figure 7–1, retailers and wholesalers are currently generating a composite rate of return on assets of less than 3.0 percent and a composite rate of return on net worth of less than 8.0 percent. By any criteria, these results are well below the levels of performance that will be required during the decade ahead.

Equally disquieting is the persistent increase in leverage ratios. As shown in figure 7–1, retailers and wholesalers are currently operating on leverage ratios of more than 2.5 times; this suggests, particularly in an era of capital shortages and high interest rates, that many firms have reached their effective borrowing capacity.

To place these trends in perspective, it is useful to examine the performance criteria currently being emphasized by profit planners. Executives and analysts agree that retailers and wholesalers should program their operations to achieve a rate of return on assets of *at least* 8.0 to 10.0 percent and a rate of return on net worth of *at least* 15.0 to 20.0 percent. Furthermore, they contend that leverage ratios in the field of distribution should be maintained in the 2.0 to 2.5 range. By these standards, it is apparent that most distribution companies are currently confronted by a major profitability challenge.

LIQUIDITY TRENDS

Retailers and wholesalers in recent years have also encountered liquidity problems, in part because of inflationary pressures and in part because of the collapse of capital markets. As indicated in table 7–1, distribution companies currently have a composite current ratio of less than 2.0 times. Their cash to current liabilities ratio is also relatively low, at least by historical standards.

More disquieting is the sharp decline in interest coverage ratios that has occurred since 1968. As shown in table 7–1, the composite interest coverage ratio for retailers fell from 4.7 times in 1968 to only 3.5 times in 1974. During the same period, the interest coverage ratio for wholesalers decreased from 4.9 to 3.7 times. Thus, at the present time, retailers are finding it more difficult to cover their interest payments than are wholesalers.

At the macro-level, it is difficult to determine how severe the "liquidity crisis" is. Liquidity requirements vary widely by line of trade and by season. In addition, many firms can "afford" to maintain low cash balances because of the predictability of their receipts and disbursements, or because they have a strong working relationship with commercial banks, merchandise suppliers, and other creditors.

Despite these and other qualifications, most analysts agree that liquidity ratios must be improved in the field of distribution. Certainly, there is agreement that interest coverage ratios have declined to a dangerously low level given the current and projected volatility of the economy.

Table 7–1

Composite Liquidity Ratios for Retailing and Wholesaling Corporations, 1968 and 1974

Liquidity Ratios	Retailing Corporations		Wholesaling Corporations	
	1968	1974	1968	1974
Current Assets to Current Liabilities (Times)	1.8	1.7	1.7	1.5
Cash[a] to Current Liabilities (Percent)	19.5	16.5	16.6	14.0
Net Profits (before interest and taxes) to Interest (Times)	4.7	3.5	4.9	3.7

[a]Includes marketable securities.

Sources: Federal Trade Commission, First National City Bank, Internal Revenue Service, and authors' calculations.

GROWTH POTENTIAL TRENDS

The ability of distribution companies to finance expansion is the final area of performance to be explored. Two growth potential ratios are particularly important in this regard. The first ratio, net profits (after dividends) to net worth, roughly measures the rate at which a firm can expand without a disproportionate increase in outside financing. The second ratio, net profits (before interest and taxes) to total assets, roughly measures a firm's ability to leverage its earnings through the use of borrowed funds.

As indicated previously, retailers and wholesalers are currently generating a rate of return on net worth of less than 8.0 percent. After dividend payments, however, this rate of return declines to less than 6.0 percent (see table 7–2). Obviously, this level of retained earnings can support only a modest rate of growth. Furthermore, the problem of internally financing expansion will become progressively severe as inflationary pressures persist.

To complicate matters further, retailers and wholesalers have also reached the limits of their borrowing capacity. As shown in table 7–2, distribution companies generate a rate of return on assets (before interest and taxes) that is well below their effective borrowing cost. Thus, for many firms earnings can no longer be leveraged through the use of borrowed funds.

MANAGEMENT IMPLICATIONS

The above analysis suggests that retailers and wholesalers are indeed confronted by a major performance imperative. During the next decade,

Table 7–2
Composite Growth Potential for Retailing and
Wholesaling Corporations, 1968 and 1974

	Retailing Corporations		Wholesaling Corporations	
Growth Potential Ratios	1968	1974	1968	1974
Net Profits (after dividends) to Net Worth	6.7%	5.6%	6.3%	5.7%
Net Profits (before interest and taxes) to Total Assets	8.2%	7.8%	7.9%	7.3%

Sources: Federal Trade Commission, First National City Bank, Internal Revenue Service, and authors' calculations.

distribution companies must improve both their rates of return on investment and their liquidity positions. Furthermore, these improvements must be engineered without a significant increase in leverage ratios.

In short, retailers and wholesalers must *simultaneously* program their operations to generate higher yields while maintaining a quality balance sheet. To an increasing extent, this combination of high-yield performance and conservative financing will be required to maintain continuous access to capital markets and to satisfy fully stakeholder expectations.

The Correlates of Profitability

Of the performance gaps identified above, the profitability challenge is the most severe. In particular, rates of return on assets must be improved. Preliminary analysis suggests that four factors are critically important in determining the rate of return on assets achieved by distribution companies.

SPACE PRODUCTIVITY

The effective use of space is a critical determinant of corporate profitability in numerous lines of trade. While important at all levels of distribution, space productivity is a particularly significant variable at the retail level. Table 7–3 (data were derived from extensive regression analyses) shows the importance of increasing sales per square foot in two lines of retail trade.

Supermarkets can significantly improve their rate of return on assets by increasing their sales per square foot, largely because supermarkets have a high level of fixed costs and, therefore, tend to be volume-sensitive operations. By comparison, furniture store profits are much less influenced by space productivity gains, in part because fixed costs are less significant in

Table 7–3

Space Productivity Requirements in Two Lines
of Retail Trade, 1974

| Line of Trade | Sales per Square Foot of Selling Area Required to Achieve the Following Rates of Return on Assets | | Percent Increase |
	5.0%	10.0%	
Supermarkets	$250	$325	30
Furniture stores	65	125	92

Source: Company annual reports and authors' calculations.

furniture retailing. In short, the relative importance of space productivity as a determinant of rate of return on assets varies widely by line of trade.

INVENTORY PRODUCTIVITY

Statistically, inventory productivity is a less important determinant of corporate profitability than is space productivity. The relationship between inventory productivity and rate of return on assets is still important, however, as table 7–4 suggests.

Table 7–4

Inventory Productivity Requirements in Two Lines
of Retail Trade, 1974

| Line of Trade | Sales to Inventory Ratios Required to Achieve the Following Rates of Return on Assets | | Percent Increase |
	5.0%	10.0%	
Drugstores	5.7	9.5	67
Variety stores	3.7	7.2	95

Source: Company annual reports and authors' calculations.

The data in table 7–4 show the importance of improving sales-to-stock ratios in the drug and variety store fields. Comparable increases in profitability can be achieved in other lines of retail trade through more aggressive inventory management programs. Furthermore, preliminary analysis suggests that improved inventory management has an even greater effect on profitability in wholesaling than in retailing.

SCALE OF OPERATIONS

Analysts have historically argued that economies of scale are required to achieve high levels of profitability in the field of distribution. On a preliminary basis, it appears that the size of individual firms does have an influence on profitability in some lines of trade.

In those lines of trade that are highly fragmented and in which the typical firm is relatively small, larger firms tend to generate higher levels of profitability than smaller ones. However, in those lines of trade in which most firms have crossed some minimal size threshold, the size of the firm plays little or no role in determining profitability. This appears to be true for both wholesalers and retailers.

MARKETING STRATEGIES

Space productivity, inventory productivity, and economies of scale—all are related to the daily operation of the firm and they can have significant effects on profitability. A much more important determinant of profitability, however, is the firm's strategic posture in the marketplace.

For virtually all the companies analyzed, the *critical* factor associated with high levels of performance, and certainly with exceptional levels of performance, is the firm's ability to establish a unique or differentiated position in the marketplace. This does not imply that a unique strategy is a guarantee of success or that the lack of a differentiated strategy is an absolute barrier to success. However, the authors' analysis of publicly held retailers and wholesalers indicates that most of the firms producing exceptional results follow well-defined and relatively innovative strategies. On the other hand, companies producing less attractive results are typically committed to more conventional approaches to the marketplace.

The balance of this paper examines the strategies that have been most successful in retailing and wholesaling during recent years. The high-performance companies used to document this analysis are profiled in the appendixes to this chapter.

Before examining the strategies used by these companies, it may be useful to describe their performance. As indicated in table 7–5, these "elite" firms achieved unusually high rates of growth between 1970 and 1974. Their sales increased at an annual rate of 21.3 percent a year, and their profits expanded even more rapidly. (The "elite" retailers increased their volume and profits even more rapidly than the wholesalers.)

The financial performance of these firms is even more compelling than their rates of growth. Table 7–6 shows that the "elite" companies in distribution are currently generating a median rate of return on assets of 10.1 percent and a median rate of return on net worth of 17.5 percent. Furthermore, they have achieved these results while maintaining a defensible

Table 7–5

Median Compound Annual Growth Rates for 42 Leading
Retailers and Wholesalers, 1970–71/1974–75

Type and Number of Companies	Compound Annual Growth Rates* (1970–71/1974–75)	
	Net Sales	Net Profits
Retailing Companies (19)	28.6%	31.6%
Wholesaling Companies (23)	18.9	27.8
All Companies (42)	21.3%	28.6%

*Adjusted for mergers and acquisitions.

Source: Company annual reports and authors' calculations.

liquidity position and a balanced capital structure. In short, the high performance of these companies underscores the importance of strategic planning in the field of distribution.

High Performance Strategies in Retailing

The history of retailing is the history of strategic innovation. In the early 1970s, retailers were continuously confronted by new and innovative forms of competition. Warehouse retailers, for example, emerged as an explosive competitive force; furniture warehouse showrooms, appliance and TV warehouse showrooms, and catalog showrooms expanded rapidly in most metropolitan markets. In addition, the most advanced form of warehouse retailing, the hypermarket, achieved a position of competitive saliency in Western Europe, and several units have recently been opened in North America. Thus, warehouse retailing has been a major source of competitive turbulence over the past five years.

As a group, however, warehouse retailers have yet to produce consistently attractive results. To phrase it charitably, their financial performance has been decidedly mixed. Thus, the warehouse retailing movement is ignored in this paper, even though both authors recognize its importance.

Also ignored are other strategic thrusts such as the fast-food service outlet in the restaurant field and the convenience food store in the grocery field. These latter developments are ignored because their impact has been for the most part confined to a single line of trade. In short, they are *specific* rather than *generic* strategies. In addition, the long-run potential of the convenience food store, given its low rate of return on assets and its high gross margin requirements, is yet to be demonstrated.

Our analysis concentrates on the *mainstream* strategies that have been

Table 7–6
*Median Financial Ratios for 42 Leading
Retailers and Wholesalers, 1974–75*

| | Type and Number of Companies | | |
| | Retailing Companies (19) | Wholesaling Companies (23) | All Companies (42) |
Financial Ratios			
Strategic Profit Model Ratios[a]			
Net Profits to Net Sales (Percent)	4.0	4.8	4.2
Net Sales to Total Assets (Times)	2.6	2.2	2.3
Net Profits to Total Assets (Percent)	10.0	10.2	10.1
Total Assets to Net Worth (Times)	1.7	1.8	1.8
Net Profits to Net Worth (Percent)	18.1	17.5	17.5
Liquidity Ratios			
Current Assets to Current Liabilities (Times)	2.4	2.3	2.4
Cash[b] to Current Liabilities (Percent)	40.4	7.5	21.6
Net Profits (before interest and taxes) to Interest (Times)	16.7	15.4	15.4
Growth Potential Ratios			
Net Profits (before interest and taxes) to Total Assets (Percent)	20.9	21.0	21.0
Net Profits (after dividends) to Net Worth (Percent)	15.4	14.8	15.2

[a]The strategic profit model ratios will not multiply to the totals indicated because the ratios are medians rather than weighted averages.
[b]Includes marketable securities.

Source: Company annual reports and authors' calculations.

most successful in retailing over the past five years. The taxonomy developed is neither exhaustive nor exclusive. It is, however, useful for understanding the importance of strategic planning in the field of retailing.

On the basis of line-of-trade and corporate data, it appears that seven mainstream strategies in retailing deserve particular emphasis. The strategies are discussed here; data on the firms using them are given in Appendixes A and B.

SUPERMARKET RETAILING

The supermarket concept, though originally developed in the food field, is not limited to the sale of food products. It involves the use of five key factors to improve productivity and reduce the cost of distribution. These factors are: (1) self-service and self-selection displays; (2) centralization of customer services, usually at the checkout counter; (3) large-scale, low-cost physical facilities; (4) a strong price emphasis; and (5) a broad assortment and wide variety of merchandise to facilitate multiple item purchases.

During recent years, an increasing number of retailers, in multiple lines of trade, have adopted the supermarket concept. In the process they have strengthened their market position and improved their financial results. The extension of the supermarket concept to other lines of trade is unquestionably a major competitive development. This strategy has been particularly successful in the drug, home improvement, sporting goods, and toy fields.

Long's, for example, pioneered the super drugstore movement in the early 1960s. Since that time, the company has consistently achieved outstanding results. Long's currently operates 82 super drugstores in California and contiguous states. A typical Long's outlet contains 26,000 square feet of selling space, generates annual sales of more than $4.5 million, and operates on a gross margin of 25 percent. Thus, Long's relies on an aggressive pricing policy and economies of scale to generate an adequate rate of return on investment.

Standard Brands is pursuing a similar strategy in the home improvement field. At the present time, the company operates 55 paint and home decorating supermarkets, each of which contains more than 11,000 square feet of space. Standard Brands obtains 41 percent of its volume from self-manufactured products; this partially accounts for the company's high profit margin.

Oshman's, a Houston-based firm, has pioneered the supermarket concept in the sporting goods field. The company currently operates 44 sporting goods supermarkets, which generate an annual volume of more than $1.0 million each. Thus, the Oshman units have a substantial scalar advantage over conventional sporting goods dealers.

As these examples suggest, supermarket operators project a strong price image, which appeals to a major segment of the market. Given the importance of this segment, the supermarket approach is likely to remain successful for some time to come.

STORE POSITIONING

As the consumer market becomes more fragmented, store positioning strategies become more important. A substantial number of retailers have already positioned (or are repositioning) themselves to capitalize on life style or demographic trends. Byerly's, Handy Andy, and Treasure Island, for example, have positioned themselves to appeal to the affluent grocery shopper. Crate and Barrel and Pottery Barn also concentrate on the affluent consumer, while Pier I focuses on the "under 35" market and Radio Shack on the electronics enthusiast. Positioning has emerged as a major strategic thrust. It can be particularly effective in the sale of "fashion" merchandise. In the apparel, home accessories, and home furnishings fields, for example, consumer preferences vary widely by social class and by life style. Thus there are numerous opportunities to focus on specific market segments.

Mervyn's and The Limited are retailers that have effectively positioned themselves in the apparel field. The Limited focuses on the 18 to 30-year-old "high fashion" shopper, while Mervyn's concentrates on the middle-income, middle-class, family market. Both companies have achieved enviable rates of growth, because they have developed a focused and competitively differentiated approach to the markets they serve.

In summary, store positioning offers numerous opportunities for creating a differential advantage. However, it is a difficult strategy to implement, because it requires a precise understanding of consumer buying behavior, as well as a sophisticated management team to capitalize on the opportunity.

NON-STORE RETAILING

Direct marketing is rapidly becoming a major force in the American economy. Established companies such as Sears and Ward's are continuing to expand their direct marketing programs. More important, however, is the entry of new and innovative firms, such as GRI, Mary Kay, and Unity Buying Service.

GRI sponsors the World of Beauty Club and other direct mail programs. Consumers belonging to the World of Beauty Club receive four to six cosmetics kits a year, each of which has a retail value of $15.00 or more. The membership price for these kits is approximately one-third the normal retail price. Thus, consumers can effect substantial savings by joining the World of Beauty Club. GRI has also developed direct marketing programs for flatware and vitamins. As a result, the company has emerged as a major competitor in the direct mail field.

Mary Kay has been equally successful in the cosmetics industry by using the party plan method of distribution. The company specializes in skin care products, which are marketed by 29,000 Sales Directors and Sales Consultants. As is the case with many direct marketing organizations, Mary Kay operates its own manufacturing facilities, thus increasing its profit margin.

Unity Buying Service is another high-performance company in the direct marketing field. The company sponsors the Unity Buying Club, which offers a wide variety of merchandise to consumers at "cost plus 8 percent." The Club's membership roll currently consists of 955,000 families. Furthermore, the membership renewal rate has increased steadily since the mid-1960s, which suggests that this program will continue to expand over the decade ahead.

Non-store retailing will become progressively more important in the 1970s as more and more consumers become disenchanted with the shopping process. In addition, of course, non-store retailing will continue to expand because of the innovative programs developed by GRI, Mary Kay, Unity Buying Service, and other leading firms.

EXPANSION INTO SECONDARY MARKETS

Retailers operating in secondary markets have consistently outperformed their metropolitan counterparts. Bi-Lo, Pamida, and Wal-Mart are companies that have achieved superior results by focusing on "fringe" markets. Bi-Lo operates discount supermarkets in small rural communities; Pamida locates its bantam discount stores in cities with populations of less than 10,000; and Wal-Mart operates discount department stores in county seat towns throughout the Southwest. By focusing on secondary markets, each of these organizations has been able to achieve a position of competitive dominance at a relatively low cost.

Obviously, secondary markets have several attractive characteristics, including a lower level of competition, a stable labor force, and a minimum number of zoning and environmental regulations. For these and other reasons, secondary market retailers are likely to outperform the "industry averages" over forthcoming budget periods.

MARKET INTENSIFICATION

Companies adopting a market intensification strategy pursue a programmed and disciplined approach to corporate expansion. They restrict their expansion efforts to a limited number of "core" markets rather than expanding erratically into geographically distant markets. Almost without exception, market concentration retailers have performed better than their "national" counterparts. Caldor, Lowe's, and Weis are among the leading proponents of the market concentration philosophy.

Caldor, a discount department store chain, operates a compact group of stores in the urban corridor between New York and Boston; Lowe's, a home improvement center chain, operates primarily in six southeastern states; and Weis, an extraordinarily well-managed food chain, operates in only three states. By concentrating their efforts on a limited number of markets, these and companies like them have been able to generate unusually attractive results.

Some very important advantages accrue to firms operating in a contained expansion mode. These include advertising economies arising from multiple outlets in a single market, maximum utilization of a small number of distribution centers, high levels of customer awareness, and easy access to top management to prevent or resolve operating problems at the store level.

In short, market intensification results in both strategic and operating advantages that can dramatically affect profitability. Consequently, it is a strategic approach that should be given more attention than it presently receives.

PRODUCT SPECIALIZATION

Analysts contend that "super" specialty stores could be the wave of the future. The explosive growth of Athlete's Foot, County Seat, The Gap, and Calculators, Inc. tends to confirm this hypothesis.

These and other specialty store operators have been conspicuously successful in rationalizing the distribution process. They have blended the advantages of product specialization with the economics of chain-store operation. As this trend develops, it will irretrievably alter the nature of competition in an increasing number of product categories.

Aaron Brothers, Child World, and Jerrico are among the leading proponents of the product specialization concept. Aaron Brothers specializes in artist's supplies, picture frames, and related lines of merchandise; Child World specializes in bicycles, toys, children's furniture, and leisure goods; and Jerrico is currently emphasizing its Long John Silver's Sea Food Shoppes. Each of these companies has achieved a distinctive niche in the marketplace by focusing on a limited number of product categories. Aaron Brothers and Child World achieve additional economies by operating on a supermarket basis.

RETAIL DIVERSIFICATION

The strategy of retail diversification produced mixed results between 1970 and 1974. Dayton Hudson, Supermarkets General, and Zale, for example, experienced operating difficulties as a result of their diversification programs. Other companies, however, coped successfully with the problems of managing multiple businesses. For these firms, diversification proved to be an effective growth vehicle. Currently, Edison Brothers and Melville Shoe are the most successful diversified retailers.

Edison Brothers operates 814 Edison Brothers shoe stores (under the Chandlers, Bakers, Leeds, Burts, The Wild Pair, and Joan Bari Boutiques names); 44 Handyman do-it-yourself hardware and building materials stores; 78 Size 5-7-9 shops featuring feminine clothing for sizes one through nine; 113 Jeans West stores offering jeans, tops, and outerwear for young adults; and 30 United sporting goods stores offering a complete line of sports equipment and apparel.

Melville Shoe operates 717 Meldisco shoe departments, all in K-Mart stores; three shoe chains (Thom McAn, Miles, and Vanguard); cvs, a chain of health and beauty aids stores; Foxmoor Casuals, a chain of fashion apparel stores directed at the 15 to 24-year-old, middle-income woman; Chess King, a fashion apparel chain targeted at young men; Clothes Bin, a chain of discount women's apparel stores; and 19 shoe and men's apparel manufacturing facilities.

As consumer markets become more segmented and as life styles become more diverse, an increasing number of retailers will probably diversify their operations, despite the managerial problems and risks involved.

High Performance Strategies in Wholesaling

Some wholesalers increased both their growth and their profits in the early 1970s. Data on the firms pursuing the strategies discussed here are given in Appendixes C and D. Seven kinds of strategic thrusts were particularly important.

VOLUNTARY GROUP PROGRAMS

The voluntary group movement picked up momentum in the early 1970s as wholesalers either expanded existing programs or developed new programs for affiliated stores. In the grocery field, for example, Wetterau, Super Valu, and other voluntaries steadily increased their market share between 1970 and 1974. More important, however, is the rapid growth of voluntaries in other lines of trade. As shown in table 7–7, voluntaries have become a major force in both the drug and hardware fields, with most of this expansion occurring in the early 1970s. Voluntaries are also expanding rapidly in the automotive, automatic vending, and variety store fields. In short, voluntary groups continue to be an important mechanism for rationalizing the distribution process.

Genuine Parts and The McLain Grocery Company illustrate the results that can be achieved by aggressive voluntary wholesalers. Genuine Parts, with annual sales of almost $600 million, is a charter member of NAPA, the largest voluntary group in the automotive field. The company provides a full range of services to affiliated jobbers, including a comprehensive inventory protection program.

McLain is a large IGA wholesaler operating in Ohio, Pennsylvania, and

Table 7-7

Leading Voluntary Groups in the Drug and Hardware Fields, 1974

Voluntary Groups In the Drug Field	Number of Affiliated Stores	Voluntary Groups In the Hardware Field	Number of Affiliated Stores
Economost	5,000	Western Auto	4,230
Good Neighbor Pharmacies	1,400	Sentry	4,200
Associated Druggists	1,132	Pro	2,650
United Systems Stores	744	Ace	2,500
Family Service Drug Stores	350	Gamble-Skogmo	1,200
Triple A	300	Coast-To-Coast	1,040
Velocity	250	Trustworthy	800
Community Shield Pharmacies	200	Stratton & Terstegge	550
FIP	200	Farwell, Ozman, Kirk & Co.	495
Sell-Thru Guild	200	American Wholesale Hardware	175
Total	9,776	Total	17,840

Sources: Chain Store Age and Hardware Age.

West Virginia. Like many other voluntary wholesalers, McLain has steadily diversified its inventories and expanded the scope of its services in recent years. As a result, the company is rapidly evolving into a total capability supplier, providing its customers with a high proportion of the merchandise and services they need to operate effectively in increasingly competitive markets.

INVENTORY DIVERSIFICATION

For many wholesalers, inventory diversification has proved to be an effective growth strategy. The logic of inventory diversification is fairly self-evident. By adding product lines, wholesalers can simultaneously increase their sales and strengthen their relationship with customers. Furthermore, wholesalers with highly diversified inventories have the option of positioning themselves as single-source suppliers, which partially insulates them from transactional competition.

Despite the complexities involved in inventory diversification programs, many wholesalers began to broaden their product lines in the early 1970s, particularly in the hardware, building materials, and grocery fields. Hughes and Rykoff are two high-performance companies that have increased their growth through inventory diversification programs.

Hughes, originally a plumbing supply wholesaler, began to diversify its inventories in the early 1970s. By 1974, the company had evolved into a *full-line* distributor of electrical, industrial, plumbing, and utility supplies. In the process, Hughes increased its rate of return on net worth from 5.2 percent in 1970 to 15.0 percent in 1974.

Rykoff has used a similar strategy. Originally an institutional food distributor, Rykoff has emerged as a full-line supplier in the food service field. The company currently distributes a broad range of nonfood products, including dinnerware, glassware, silverware, restaurant equipment, and supplies, which represent an increasing proportion of its sales.

WHOLESALE DIVERSIFICATION

Some wholesalers have gone beyond inventory diversification to establish separate profit centers in totally unrelated lines of trade. In wholesaling, as in retailing, however, the trend toward corporate diversification has tended to produce mixed results, largely because of the problems involved in managing multiple businesses. Some companies, however, have been conspicuously successful with their diversification programs. Bluefield Supply, Premier Industrial, and J. M. Tull are among the most successful of the diversified wholesalers.

Bluefield Supply is a highly diversified distributor with sales divided as follows: heavy construction and industrial equipment, 67.1 percent; hardware and industrial supplies, 17.8 percent; household appliances and home entertainment products, 10.5 percent; and hospital supplies, 4.6

percent. The company currently operates 28 distribution centers in six states and is rapidly expanding its operations for the future.

Premier Industrial is also highly diversified, as is J. M. Tull. The former, for example, operates separate profit centers in four unrelated fields: industrial maintenance, specialty chemicals, fire-fighting equipment, and electronic parts and supplies; while the latter operates nine metal service centers, an automotive parts distributorship, and an industrial supplies division. In short, these companies demonstrate that diversification programs can be used to generate unusually attractive returns.

RETAIL DIVERSIFICATION

In the early 1970s, numerous wholesalers began to operate retailing outlets. This trend was particularly apparent among grocery wholesalers.

Malone & Hyde, for example, currently operates 35 conventional supermarkets, 30 super drugstores, and 10 tonnage supermarkets. The company presently obtains 24.1 percent of its volume from its retail operations. Nash Finch, a Minneapolis-based grocery wholesaler, also operates a wide range of retail outlets, including 30 warehouse supermarkets and 25 family centers.

As profitability pressures intensify, more wholesalers will probably enter the retail field. Multi-level merchandisers like Malone & Hyde and Nash Finch will become increasingly common.

PRODUCT AND MARKET SPECIALIZATION

Specialized wholesalers have become a *major* competitive force in many product categories. As a group, specialists carry broader assortments of merchandise and maintain higher service levels than their general-line competitors. They maintain massive inventory investments and tend to offer more frequent deliveries and provide a higher level of technical support. As a result of these and other competitive advantages, specialists have steadily increased their market share over the past four years.

The range of specialization defies easy description. The following companies are among the leading specialists in their product lines: Bearings, Inc. (antifriction bearings and power transmission equipment and supplies); Farmer Bros. (coffee, condiments, and coffee brewing equipment); Kar Products (automotive and industrial maintenance supplies); Lawson Products (maintenance, repair, and operating supplies); and D. L. Saslow (dental equipment and supplies).

NATIONAL BRAND PROGRAMS

Wholesalers are becoming ever more involved in the total marketing process. Already, an increasing number of firms have the capability to design and develop complete marketing programs.

Ehrenreich Photo-Optical, for example, markets 19 brands of cameras on a national basis, including Nikon, Mamiya, and Bronica. S. Riekes is another national marketer of branded merchandise. The company designs and distributes a broad range of glassware products manufactured to its specifications. Heavy emphasis is placed on the firm's proprietary lines, including Riekes Crisa, Riekes Chalet, and The John Riekes Kristaluxus Collection.

Telecor and Waxman Industries are other wholesalers who provide complete marketing services. Telecor is the exclusive distributor of Panasonic products in California and 13 contiguous states. Waxman Industries markets its own lines of plumbing and electrical supplies, largely through home improvement centers. The company supports each of its lines with a comprehensive range of merchandising services.

All of these companies have enjoyed extraordinary success because of their ability to develop and execute complete marketing programs, a further indication that wholesalers have gone well beyond their traditional redistribution function.

FORWARD OR BACKWARD INTEGRATION INTO MANUFACTURING

Wholesalers steadily increased their manufacturing capability between 1970 and 1974, many of them evolving into self-supply organizations that also provide processing services to their customers.

Bristol Products and Superscope, for example, are totally committed to self-manufacturing programs. W. W. Grainger, Earle M. Jorgensen, and Pioneer Standard Electronics are other wholesalers who have made a major commitment to their manufacturing divisions.

The rise of manufacturing wholesalers dramatizes the shift in market power that has occurred in many product categories. Large wholesalers are becoming a dominant force in the marketplace.

Concluding Remarks

The "case studies" cited underscore the importance of developing high-performance strategies in the field of distribution. To an increasing extent, strategic rather than tactical decisions will determine corporate success in the 1970s. Distribution companies interested in improving their performance over the decade ahead should, therefore, make a major commitment to the strategic planning process.

Appendix A

Strategic Profit Model Ratios and Compound Annual Growth Rates for 19 Leading Retailers, 1970–71/1974–75

Strategic Thrust	Company (Annual Sales In Millions of Dollars)	Strategic Profit Model Ratios[a] (1974–75)					Compound Annual Growth Rates (1970–71/1974–75)	
		Net Profits to Net Sales (Percent)	Net Sales to Total Assets (Times)	Net Profits to Total Assets (Percent)	Total Assets to Net Worth (Times)	Net Profits to Net Worth (Percent)	Net Sales	Net Profits
	Long's Drug Stores, Inc. ($340.2)	3.5	4.1	14.7	1.4	19.9	19.1	19.4
Supermarket Retailing	Oshman's Sporting Goods, Inc. ($49.6)	4.1	2.0	8.2	1.5	12.0	22.8	17.1
	Standard Brands Paint Co. ($96.2)	7.9	1.8	14.0	1.3	18.1	19.5	21.9
Store Positioning	The Limited Stores, Inc. ($26.0)	5.9	2.1	12.6	2.8	35.2	77.4	87.0
	Mervyn's ($134.5)	3.7	2.7	10.0	2.0	19.7	38.6	45.6

Appendix A—continued

Strategic Thrust	Company (Annual Sales In Millions of Dollars)	Strategic Profit Model Ratios[a] (1974–75)					Compound Annual Growth Rates (1970–71/1974–75)	
		Net Profits to Net Sales (Percent)	Net Sales to Total Assets (Times)	Net Profits to Total Assets (Percent)	Total Assets to Net Worth (Times)	Net Profits to Net Worth (Percent)	Net Sales	Net Profits
Non-Store Retailing	G.R.I. Corporation ($60.3)	9.4	2.1	19.4	1.5	29.1	35.0	44.5
	Mary Kay Cosmetics, Inc. ($31.8)	14.0	1.3	18.0	1.2	22.0	39.6	42.9
	Unity Buying Service Co., Inc. ($56.9)	4.1	3.3	13.3	1.9	25.2	25.9	44.5
Expansion into Secondary Markets	Bi-Lo, Inc. ($302.6)	1.8	8.7	15.8	1.9	29.5	34.8	42.6
	Pamida, Inc. ($202.2)	3.2	2.6	8.5	1.5	13.1	25.4	15.3
	Wal-Mart Stores, Inc. ($238.7)	2.7	3.2	8.4	2.0	17.2	52.0	40.0

Market Intensification							
Caldor, Inc. ($195.4)	2.7	3.1	8.4	1.8	15.1	18.6	8.9
Lowe's Companies, Inc. ($362.5)	4.0	2.4	9.7	2.2	21.7	29.6	31.6
Weis Markets, Inc. ($313.5)	4.2	3.5	14.7	1.2	17.4	12.1	10.7
Product Specialization							
Aaron Brothers Corporation ($10.2)	4.4	1.9	8.3	1.9	15.4	28.6	22.4
Child World, Inc. ($59.3)	3.7	2.9	10.7	1.3	13.5	34.9	35.0
Jerrico, Inc. ($48.8)	4.7	1.8	8.5	2.2	18.4	51.3	67.7
Retail Diversification							
Edison Brothers Stores, Inc. ($420.5)	4.0	2.5	10.0	1.6	16.2	13.2	18.1
Melville Shoe Corp. ($765.1)	3.5	2.6	9.3	1.7	15.5	13.1	5.6
Median	4.0	2.6	10.0	1.7	18.1	28.6	31.6

aThe strategic profit model ratios may not multiply to the totals indicated because of rounding.

Source: Company annual reports and authors' calculations.

Appendix B

Liquidity and Growth Potential Ratios for 19 Leading Retailers, 1970–71/1974–75

Strategic Thrust	Company (Annual Sales In Millions of Dollars)	Liquidity Ratios (1974–75)			Growth Potential Ratios (1974–75)	
		Current Assets to Current Liabilities (Times)	Cash[a] to Current Liabilities (Percent)	Net Profits (Before Interest and Taxes) to Interest (Times)	Net Profits (Before Interest and Taxes) to Total Assets (Percent)	Net Profits (After Dividends) to Net Worth (Percent)
	Long's Drug Stores, Inc. ($340.2)	2.2	49.0	b	b	15.9
Supermarket Retailing	Oshman's Sporting Goods, Inc. ($49.6)	3.6	9.2	b	b	12.0
	Standard Brands Paint Co. ($96.2)	3.2	23.8	37.3	29.3	14.8
	The Limited Stores, Inc. ($26.0)	1.8	68.4	13.0	26.6	33.3
Store Positioning	Mervyn's ($134.5)	1.9	4.8	25.5	20.1	19.7

Non-Store Retailing	G.R.I. Corporation ($60.3)	2.9	38.3	b	b	26.5
	Mary Kay Cosmetics, Inc. ($31.8)	2.4	88.3	155.7	34.3	17.0
	Unity Buying Service Co., Inc. ($56.9)	2.2	46.7	51.1	27.8	25.2
Expansion into Secondary Markets	Bi-Low, Inc. ($302.6)	1.8	21.7	62.5	31.7	28.3
	Pamida, Inc. ($202.2)	3.2	9.7	10.6	18.5	13.1
	Wal-Mart Stores, Inc. ($238.7)	2.1	12.1	7.8	18.6	15.4
Market Intensification	Caldor, Inc. ($195.4)	2.2	40.4	29.3	17.2	13.6
	Lowe's Companies, Inc. ($362.5)	2.2	25.9	11.7	21.3	20.2
	Weis Markets, Inc. ($313.5)	3.8	195.5	b	b	13.2

Appendix B—continued

Strategic Thrust	Company (Annual Sales In Millions of Dollars)	Liquidity Ratios (1974–75)		Net Profits (Before Interest and Taxes) to Interest (Times)	Growth Potential Ratios (1974–75)	
		Current Assets to Current Liabilities (Times)	Cash^a to Current Liabilities (Percent)		Net Profits (Before Interest and Taxes) to Total Assets (Percent)	Net Profits (After Dividends) to Net Worth (Percent)
Product Specialization	Aaron Brothers Corporation ($10.2)	2.9	55.0	18.8	17.9	15.4
	Child World, Inc. ($59.3)	3.7	127.9	b	b	13.5
	Jerrico, Inc. ($48.8)	1.2	36.9	11.0	21.9	18.4
Retail Diversification	Edison Brothers Stores, Inc. ($420.5)	2.7	48.1	14.6	20.5	11.0
	Melville Shoe Corp. ($765.1)	3.5	51.6	8.9	17.8	7.7
Median		2.4	40.4	16.7	20.9	15.4

aIncludes marketable securities.
bInterest expenses not shown separately in the company's annual report.
Source: Company annual reports and authors' calculations.

Appendix C

Strategic Profit Model Ratios and Compound Annual Growth Rates for 23 Leading Wholesalers, 1970–71/1974–75

Strategic Thrust	Company (Annual Sales In Millions of Dollars)	Strategic Profit Model Ratios[a] (1974–75)					Compound Annual Growth Rates (1970–71/1974–75)	
		Net Profits to Net Sales (Percent)	Net Sales to Total Assets (Times)	Net Profits to Total Assets (Percent)	Total Assets to Net Worth (Times)	Net Profits to Net Worth (Percent)	Net Sales	Net Profits
Voluntary Group Programs	Genuine Parts Company ($572.8)	4.2	2.8	11.7	1.5	17.5	13.2	15.6
	The McClain Grocery Company ($148.3)	.8	10.5	8.2	2.1	17.3	13.8	22.0
Inventory Diversification	Hughes Supply, Inc. ($100.8)	3.0	2.8	8.4	1.8	15.0	27.0	35.6
	S. E. Rykoff & Co. ($123.9)	2.2	3.8	8.5	1.7	14.4	18.9	25.3

Appendix C—continued

Strategic Thrust	Company (Annual Sales In Millions of Dollars)	Strategic Profit Model Ratios[a] (1974–75)					Compound Annual Growth Rates (1970–71/1974–75)	
		Net Profits to Net Sales (Percent)	Net Sales to Total Assets (Times)	Net Profits to Total Assets (Percent)	Total Assets to Net Worth (Times)	Net Profits to Net Worth (Percent)	Net Sales	Net Profits
	Bluefield Supply Company ($105.4)	4.8	2.1	10.2	1.9	19.0	12.7	27.8
Wholesale Diversification	Premier Industrial Corp. ($151.7)	6.2	1.7	10.4	1.5	16.1	10.0	9.5
	J. M. Tull Industries, Inc. ($114.3)	5.4	2.7	14.5	2.0	28.6	22.7	56.3
	Malone & Hyde, Inc. ($718.6)	1.3	6.5	8.2	2.0	16.2	14.2	15.5
Retail Diversification	Nash-Finch Company ($470.8)	1.6	5.7	9.0	2.1	18.6	17.4	26.4

Bearings, Inc. ($156.5)	4.8	2.2	10.6	1.5	16.0	13.8	16.4
Farmer Bros. Co. ($66.8)	4.0	2.1	8.3	1.4	11.2	15.7	25.7
Kar Products, Inc. ($26.1)	8.6	2.2	18.8	1.3	24.8	21.3	29.4
Product and Market Specialization Lawson Products, Inc. ($33.4)	9.6	2.0	19.1	1.4	26.4	29.7	38.0
D. L. Saslow Co., Inc. ($24.7)	4.6	1.8	8.1	2.2	17.5	43.9	36.6
Enrenreich Photo-Optical Industries, Inc. ($76.5)	5.1	1.6	8.0	2.0	16.2	17.4	50.0
National Brand Programs S. Riekes & Sons, Inc. ($57.7)	3.8	3.1	11.8	1.9	22.9	21.3	37.9
Telecor, Inc. ($64.1)	5.0	1.8	8.9	2.1	18.9	16.8	21.1
Waxman Industries, Inc. ($19.7)	5.4	1.8	9.8	2.6	25.1	33.2	34.1

Appendix C—continued

Strategic Thrust	Company (Annual Sales In Millions of Dollars)	Strategic Profit Model Ratios[a] (1974–75)					Compound Annual Growth Rates (1970–71/1974–75)	
		Net Profits to Net Sales (Percent)	Net Sales to Total Assets (Times)	Net Profits to Total Assets (Percent)	Total Assets to Net Worth (Times)	Net Profits to Net Worth (Percent)	Net Sales	Net Profits
	Bristol Products, Inc. ($27.0)	5.1	2.2	11.1	1.3	14.3	14.4	63.0
	W. W. Grainger, Inc. ($315.2)	5.3	1.9	10.3	1.6	16.8	21.1	19.1
Forward or Backward Integration into Manufacturing	Earle M. Jorgensen Co. ($232.0)	6.1	2.0	12.1	1.7	21.1	20.1	45.2
	Pioneer Standard Electronics, Inc. ($33.0)	4.1	2.5	10.3	1.7	17.3	21.6	26.2
	Superscope, Inc. ($157.2)	6.3	1.3	8.1	2.3	18.5	28.8	33.6
Median		4.8	2.2	10.2	1.8	17.5	18.9	27.8

[a]The strategic profit model ratios may not multiply to the totals indicated because of rounding.

Source: Company annual reports and authors' calculations.

Appendix D

Liquidity and Growth Potential Ratios for 23 Leading Wholesalers, 1970–71/1974–75

Strategic Thrust	Company (Annual Sales In Millions of Dollars)	Liquidity Ratios (1974–75)			Growth Potential Ratios (1974–75)	
		Current Assets to Current Liabilities (Times)	Cash^a to Current Liabilities (Percent)	Net Profits (Before Interest and Taxes) to Interest (Times)	Net Profits (Before Interest and Taxes) to Total Assets (Percent)	Net Profits (After Dividends) to Net Worth (Percent)
Voluntary Group Programs	Genuine Parts Company ($572.8)	2.7	21.7	b	b	11.2
	The McClain Grocery Company ($148.3)	1.8	31.8	12.9	15.3	13.7
Inventory Diversification	Hughes Supply, Inc. ($100.8)	2.2	3.0	26.3	17.2	15.0
	S. E. Rykoff & Co. ($123.9)	2.2	2.6	25.0	18.2	12.6

Appendix D—continued

Strategic Thrust	Company (Annual Sales In Millions of Dollars)	Liquidity Ratios (1974–75)			Growth Potential Ratios (1974–75)	
		Current Assets to Current Liabilities (Times)	Cash[a] to Current Liabilities (Percent)	Net Profits (Before Interest and Taxes) to Interest (Times)	Net Profits (Before Interest and Taxes) to Total Assets (Percent)	Net Profits (After Dividends) to Net Worth (Percent)
	Bluefield Supply Company ($105.4)	3.5	28.0	11.4	21.0	15.3
Wholesale Diversification	Premier Industrial Corp. ($151.7)	3.9	13.3	15.4	21.3	10.6
	J. M. Tull Industries, Inc. ($114.3)	2.9	7.5	11.6	31.6	25.8
Retail Diversification	Malone & Hyde, Inc. ($718.6)	2.1	21.4	13.4	17.2	12.4
	Nash-Finch Company ($470.8)	1.7	6.4	26.3	19.2	13.5

Bearings, Inc. ($156.5)	2.6	7.4	22.3	22.7	13.3
Farmer Bros. Co. ($66.8)	3.0	23.7	b	b	9.0
Kar Products, Inc. ($26.1)	3.7	50.1	b	b	23.5
Lawson Products, Inc. ($33.4)	3.7	7.1	b	b	23.3
D. L. Saslow Co., Inc. ($24.7)	2.8	17.2	b	b	17.5
Product and Market Specialization					
Enrenreich Photo-Optical Industries, Inc. ($76.5)	2.0	6.0	12.9	17.4	14.4
S. Riekes & Sons, Inc. ($57.7)	2.0	8.1	65.5	23.6	20.4
Telecor, Inc. ($64.1)	1.7	38.9	25.4	18.3	14.8
Waxman Industries, Inc. ($19.7)	2.2	19.5	b	b	23.5
National Brand Programs					

Appendix D—continued

Strategic Thrust	Company (Annual Sales In Millions of Dollars)	Liquidity Ratios (1974–75)			Growth Potential Ratios (1974–75)	
		Current Assets to Current Liabilities (Times)	Cash^a to Current Liabilities (Percent)	Net Profits (Before Interest and Taxes) to Interest (Times)	Net Profits (Before Interest and Taxes) to Total Assets (Percent)	Net Profits (After Dividends) to Net Worth (Percent)
	Bristol Products, Inc. ($27.0)	3.0	1.0	21.0	22.3	14.3
	W. W. Grainger, Inc. ($315.2)	3.4	5.9	10.4	23.0	13.3
Forward or Backward Integration into Manufacturing	Earle M. Jorgensen Co. ($232.0)	2.3	5.1	26.3	24.9	17.7
	Pioneer Standard Electronics, Inc. ($33.0)	2.3	2.1	12.9	21.8	15.5
	Superscope, Inc. ($157.2)	1.5	5.3	4.7	18.2	18.5
Median		2.3	7.5	15.4	21.0	14.8

^{a}Includes marketable securities.
^{b}Interest expenses not shown separately in the company's annual report.
Source: Company annual reports and authors' calculations.

PART THREE

Industry Structure,
Strategy, and Performance

8

Market Structure and Industry Influence on Profitability

FRANK M. BASS, PHILLIPPE J. CATTIN,
AND DICK R. WITTINK

Despite its crucial significance, an assumption underlying all empirical studies of market structure-profitability relationships has received very little attention. Every such study has assumed that the long-run equilibrium relationships may be appropriately estimated by analyzing data from a cross section of firms or industries. If, however, the relationships are not homogeneous across the sample, i.e., if factors peculiar to an industry or class of goods are not accounted for in the model, then the estimates will be biased. Moreover, if different kinds of relationships exist for various subsets of the data, then estimates based on data pooled over these subsets may result in grossly misleading conclusions. Despite the rather obvious possibility of variation in relationships by industry or by classes of goods, very few studies have tested the hypothesis of homogeneous relationships —the foundation upon which their analysis rests.

Bain (1970), in reviewing the early development of industrial organization theory, touched upon fundamental issues. Mason (1939) argued that there was something like a deterministic association between market structure and performance. Nourse (1938), on the other hand, believed that influences specific to the firm (i.e., "management") were the major determinants of performance. Bain points out that if Nourse's views are correct, statistical analysis of structure-performance would be pointless since every firm or industry would be unique. However, Bain notes, the empirical evidence supports neither view since, although statistically significant relationships have emerged in most studies, the unexplained variance is ordinarily quite large. One possible reason for the large unexplained variance is the uncritical pooling of data over nonhomogeneous relationships.

This paper focuses on the homogeneity issue. In our study of the influence on profitability of market structure variables (e.g., concentration, industry advertising-to-sales ratio, and industry growth) as well as firm-related variables (e.g., market share, firm size, and firm diversification), we shall use data from a sample of firms producing frequently purchased consumer products.

Industry Variation in Relationships

The basic rationale that underlies cross-sectional studies of the influence of market structure variables upon profitability is that the inter-industry variation in market structure variables "explains" the interindustry variation in profitability, i.e., a change in one or more of the market structure variables in an industry would cause a change in the profitability of the industry. Moreover, there is an implicit assumption that the relationships are homogeneous for each of the industries represented in the cross section. For example, a given change in the concentration ratio is assumed to influence profitability in exactly the same way in one industry as in another. In some studies an attempt has been made to account for variation in the relationships by including interaction terms. Gale (1972), for example, estimated equations in which there was interaction between market share and concentration, growth, and the size of firms. Nevertheless, unless the interaction terms account for the variation in relationships across industry groups, estimates based on data pooled over heterogeneous relationships will be biased.

Porter (1974) hypothesized that the influence of product differentiation, as reflected by the industry advertising-to-sales ratio, would vary according to whether the products of an industry were sold predominantly in convenience retail outlets or nonconvenience retail outlets. He showed that advertising-to-sales was statistically significant when estimated on data pooled over 19 convenience goods industries, but was not significant when estimated across 23 nonconvenience goods industries. However, when estimated on the basis of data pooled over the entire sample of 42 industries, advertising-to-sales was significantly related to profitability. Thus, Porter's results strongly suggest the existence of heterogeneous relationships within the entire sample. Is it not reasonable to suggest that further testing might have revealed yet other subsets of the data for which the relationships would vary according to the pooling scheme?

The Federal Trade Commission (1969) studied the relationship between market structure and firm-related variables and profitability for 97 firms in the food industry. In the FTC study the most significant variable was the advertising-to-sales ratio. Bass (1974), however, reanalyzed the data employed in the FTC study and tested the homogeneity hypothesis. The hypothesis was overwhelmingly rejected both for slope coefficients and for intercept dummies representing the industries in which the firms were operating. The data were further analyzed by clustering firms into three groups so that homogeneous relations could be assumed within each group, but not across groups. For two of the three groups, advertising-to-sales ratio was not significant in relation to profitability.

The evidence strongly suggests that market structure-profitability relationships vary according to the industry groups included in the analysis. Moreover, the variation is not just a matter of degree but of kind. Variables significant when estimated over one sample are not significant, or have opposite sign, when estimated with a different sample. Thus, since a fundamental premise of the statistical method employed in all of the studies in the literature seems to be highly questionable, from a scientific viewpoint it would appear that generalizations about relationships between market structure variables and profitability are not justified. To put it more strongly, there is good reason to question the validity of conclusions that have been developed from a very large body of literature on industrial organization.

It is one thing to assert that a certain methodology is inappropriate. It is quite another to suggest an appropriate alternative. In the framework used in the remainder of this paper, it is assumed that the apparent heterogeneity in market structure-profitability relationships is to be accounted for by variation in these relations by industry.

There are two possibilities: (1) each industry has a unique structure-profitability relationship; and (2) sets of industries have such relationships that estimates based on data pooled over industries in a homogeneous set would adequately describe the relationships for industries in the set. If the relationships are uniquely defined for each industry, then the only conceivable basis for estimating the relationship would lie in the analysis of data from a cross section of firms in a single industry. Even here, it might be argued that the measures of structure variables should be constant for each firm in the industry so that the only basis for explaining the within-industry profit rate would be firm-specific variables such as market share, firm size, and diversification. Nevertheless, if the data consist of a cross section of firms in different industries, it is possible to test for the appropriateness of pooling data for firms in all industries or groups of industries by examining the homogeneity of firm-related influences on profitability. The rejection of the homogeneity hypothesis implies that unrestricted pooling is inappropriate. Most studies utilizing data from a cross section of firms, such as those by Imel and Helmberger (1971), Vernon and Nourse (1972), and the Federal Trade Commission (1969), have not examined the most fundamental of issues. On the other hand, when the issue has been examined, as it was in studies by Bass (1974) and Cattin (1974), as well as in the study reported here, the hypothesis of unrestricted homogeneity has been clearly rejected.

In the many studies of market structure and profitability based on statistics for separate industries, there exists no basis for testing for industry-by-industry variation. If there were some rationale for clustering the data from different industries into groups of industries, it would then be possible to compare the estimated relationships among the different groups. A somewhat similar situation applies when the data consist of measurements from firms in different industries except that in this case it is possible to examine the intraindustry variation as well as the interindustry variation. A key issue is the criteria for assigning industries to groups. Besides the rather obvious distinction based on the type of product (e.g., producer or consumer products), other potential causes of variation might lie in the differences in managerial response of firms in different industries to the structural constraints imposed on profitability within industries. For example, firms in industries with slow growth rates may be more inclined to diversify than firms in industries with rapid growth. One might not expect the effects of diversification to be the same in the two groups.

Given the limited theoretical foundation for distinguishing industry variation in relationships, our analysis of variation must be largely exploratory. The exploratory character of the appropriate basis for pooling data into homogeneous sets in no sense lessens the force of our nonexploratory conclusion that it is inappropriate to pool data over heterogeneous relationships.

The Model and the Data

In this study we shall analyze data from a sample of firms selling consumer products that are frequently purchased and low in price. As in other studies of this type utilizing data from firms, some of the independent variables are intended to account for the effects on profitability of firm-specific influences while other independent variables are intended to account for the effects of market structure influences. The model used for this study is as follows:

$$P = \beta_0 + \beta_1 AS + \beta_2 C + \beta_3 G + \beta_4 MS + \beta_5 S + \beta_6 D + u$$

where:

$P =$ profitability of the firm;
$AS =$ weighted average of industry advertising-to-sales ratios in the firm's product markets;

> $C =$ weighted average of the four-firm concentration ratios in the firm's product markets;
>
> $G =$ weighted average of changes in industry demand in the firm's product markets;
>
> $MS =$ weighted average of the firm's market share in its product markets;
>
> $S =$ size of the firm, measured by the reciprocal of the logarithm of firm assets;
>
> $D =$ firm diversification.

For a precise definition of the variable measurements, see appendix A. The first three independent variables are market structure variables and the last three are firm-specific variables.

The criteria for selecting firms for analysis and the data sources are briefly discussed in appendix B. After eliminating those firms that failed to satisfy the constraints, a total of 181 observations on 63 firms remained. The data include three time-series observations (1957, 1963, and 1970) for most of the firms.

The 63 firms in the sample were classified into ten industries (see table 8–1). Since the interest is in market structure relationships, it is meaningful to analyze observations within these industries. The hypothesis that the market structure-profitability relationship is the same across all industries can then be tested. If this hypothesis of overall homogeneity is rejected, we can then investigate whether this is due to a difference in slope coefficients or in intercepts. Rejecting the hypothesis of equality of slope coefficients implies that it is meaningless to pool all observations either with or without dummy variables. The dummy variables would allow estimation of separate intercepts for the different industries.

Pooling, Testing, and Estimation

The first step in the analysis of the data is a determination of the appropriateness of pooling data from all of the 63 firms in all ten industries. The test of the homogeneity hypothesis is well known and straightforward. The hypothesis of overall homogeneity of relationships (slopes and intercepts) was rejected since the calculated $F = 3.55$ exceeds $F_{.01,63,111} = 1.66$. Similarly, the hypothesis of equality of slope coefficients was also rejected since $F = 3.85$ while $F_{.01,54,111} = 1.70$. $F_{p, x, y}$ indicates the fraction of the time p that the statistic this large or larger could be expected due to chance when the degrees of freedom of the numerator are x and the degrees of freedom of the dominator are y. We conclude that it is inappropriate to pool all observations with or without a dummy intercept for each industry.

Table 8–1

The Ten Industries and Their Composition

Industry	Firms
1. Packaged food companies (21 observations)	General Foods General Mills Kellogg Quaker Oats Keebler Nabisco Standard Brands
2. Meat packers (16 observations)	Hormel Hygrade Mayer Rath Swift Tobin
3. Dairy companies (18 observations)	Beatrice Foods Borden Carnation Fairmont Kraft Co. Pet
4. Food canners (18 observations)	Campbell Del Monte Gerber Green Giant Libby McNeil Libby Stokely Van Camp
5. Bakeries (15 observations)	American Bakeries General Host Interstate Bakeries Tasty Baking Ward Foods
6. Confection companies (11 observations)	Hershey Peter Paul Tootsie Roll Wrigley

Table 8–1—continued

Industry	Firms
7. Breweries (29 observations)	Anheuser-Busch Falstaff Grain Belt Heileman Lone Star Olympia Pabst Pittsburgh Schlitz R.C. Cola
8. Liquor companies (11 observations)	American Distilling Barton Brands Brown-Ferman Heublein
9. Tobacco companies (24 observations)	American Brands Ligget and Myers Philip Morris Reynolds Bayuk General Cigar Helme U.S. Tobacco
10. Cosmetic companies (18 observations)	Alberto-Culver Avon Faberge Helena Rubinstein Helene Curtis Revlon Procter and Gamble

The inappropriateness of pooling all observations does not preclude pooling observations for some industries. There exist many possible schemes and rationales for pooling subsets of the data. We have chosen a pooling scheme here that derives from the notion that a substantial portion of the variation in industry relationships can be accounted for by the heterogeneity of the firm-specific influences across the different industries. The firms in each industry will respond strategically to the external environment of that industry and the profit effects of that response will in turn

Table 8–2

Means and Standard Deviations of Variables by Industry Group

Industry	Profitability Mean	S.D.	Concentration Mean	S.D.	Industry Growth Mean	S.D.
1. Packaged foods	.139	.052	62.81	9.08	1.190	.061
2. Meat packers	.073	.051	59.25	1.69	1.155	.053
3. Dairy companies	.106	.028	41.56	2.41	1.141	.070
4. Food canners	.095	.049	56.17	5.49	1.180	.038
5. Bakeries	.076	.090	53.60	0.83	1.084	.034
6. Confection companies	.148	.026	73.82	9.21	1.174	.074
7. Breweries	.136	.064	78.34	7.43	1.215	.120
8. Liquor companies	.123	.043	55.64	5.90	1.250	.114
9. Tobacco companies	.121	.042	67.67	10.03	1.124	.075
10. Cosmetic companies	.181	.101	38.67	8.65	1.337	.072

vary with the environment. In some industries firms may profitably pursue a policy of diversification because the industry environment has caused them to develop managerial, marketing, and organizational skills that can be exploited outside the primary product categories of the industry. In other industries, on the other hand, organizational skills required for success in that industry may not be so easily exported to other product categories. Estimates based on data pooled over heterogeneous relationships with respect to firm-related variables will reflect not only this bias, but will also confound the bias in the estimates of market structure influences.

Table 8–2 shows the means and standard deviations of the dependent and independent variables computed by industry. We shall use the diversification ratio as a basis for pooling. An examination of the means of the diversification ratio by industry in table 8–2 indicates that industries 6, 7, and 8 (confection, breweries, and liquor) have very little diversification, while 1, 3, and 9 (packaged food, dairy, and tobacco) have substantial diversification. The remaining industries are moderately diversified. Thus, the diversification ratio provides a basis for sharply classifying industries to form subsets of the data. This approach is, to be sure, exploratory; but it is interesting to observe that the degree of diversification appears to reflect product development potential and growth rate of an industry. It is reasonable to expect that the influence of structural variables would vary with these factors. A test of the hypothesis of homogeneity between industries in each of the subsets is accepted, but a test of the hypothesis of homogeneity between the subsets is rejected. The remaining subsets are developed so that homogeneity between industries in a subset can be accepted but homogeneity between subsets, pairwise or in combination, is rejected.

Industry Adv. | Sales		Firm Size 1/Log Assets		Market Share		Diversification	
Mean	S.D.	Mean	S.D.	Mean	S.D.	Mean	S.D.
6.16	4.25	.185	.029	23.78	14.56	0.37	0.26
0.44	0.27	.234	.051	3.68	3.91	0.14	0.18
1.73	0.68	.189	.040	8.34	5.50	0.50	0.17
3.67	1.76	.199	.032	8.31	5.76	0.14	0.15
0.97	0.06	.274	.081	3.30	1.65	0.10	0.20
4.33	4.83	.282	.097	18.67	24.09	0.02	0.06
3.84	0.54	.312	.108	4.33	4.48	0.02	0.08
7.25	1.11	.245	.038	3.07	1.34	0.06	0.07
6.08	2.93	.214	.067	16.57	13.36	0.30	0.24
21.06	6.18	.264	.132	10.69	11.71	0.11	0.18

The result, shown in table 8–3, is five subsets for which it is possible to accept homogeneity within each subset.

The means and standard deviations of the variables for subsets and for the entire sample are shown in table 8–4. It is interesting to note that the industries with the greatest diversification are those with the least industry growth. Conversely, those industries with the greatest growth are the

Table 8–3

Subsets of Industries Defined by the F-Statistic Algorithm

Subset Number	Industry Numbers	Industry Description
1	1	Packaged food companies
	3	Dairy companies
	9	Tobacco companies
2	6	Confection companies
	7	Breweries
	8	Liquor companies
3	2	Meat packers
	4	Food canners
4	5	Bakeries
5	10	Cosmetic companies

Table 8–4

Means and Standard Deviations of Variables in Industry Subsets

Industry Subset	Profitability		Concentration		Industry Growth	
	Mean	S.D.	Mean	S.D.	Mean	S.D.
1. Industries 1,3,9	.123	.044	58.59	13.70	1.151	.074
2. Industries 6,7,8	.136	.054	72.47	11.73	1.213	.111
3. Industries 2,4	.085	.054	57.62	4.39	1.168	.046
All industries	.121	.066	59.92	14.43	1.185	.101

least diversified. This tends to confirm the view that the strategic variable, diversification, at least partially reflects the response of firms to structural conditions.

In estimating the relationships for each of the subsets, we have discovered, not unlike the results of other studies, that the residuals are correlated with the size of the firm. It is well known that OLS (ordinary least squares) provides unbiased but inefficient estimates in the case of heteroskedasticity. By making an appropriate transformation, we obtain consistent and asymptotically efficient estimates. The transformation used in previous studies—multiplying all variables by the fourth root of assets—was empirically verified in this study. Table 8–5 shows the results obtained by using WLS (weighted least squares) for each of the five subsets as well as for all observations pooled.

When a subset consists of more than one industry (i.e., subsets 1, 2, and 3), it could be argued that the most appropriate method for estimation is a variance components model. In this method, the disturbance term is decomposed into an industry-effect component and a firm-effect component. Using GLS (generalized least squares) by incorporating ρ, the ratio of the variance of the industry disturbance to the sum of the variances of the industry and firm disturbances, we obtain an unbiased and efficient estimation method. The ratio is, in general, unknown. Hence, we have used a method suggested by Nerlove (1971) called $2RC\ A$ for estimating ρ. In the first step, ρ is estimated by performing a least squares regression with dummy variables (one per industry). In the second step, the estimate of ρ is used to obtain consistent and asymptotically more efficient estimates of the parameters in the model.

Table 8–6 shows the GLS estimates (on the data corrected for heteroskedasticity) for subsets 1, 2, and 3, as well as for all observations pooled. The estimates obtained are similar to the corresponding estimates obtained by WLS. Both tables 8–5 and 8–6 clearly show that the relationship between the advertising-to-sales ratio and profitability is positive and significant if all observations are pooled. However, since we rejected the null

Industry Adv. / Sales		Firm Size 1/Log Assets		Market Share		Diversification	
Mean	S.D.	Mean	S.D.	Mean	S.D.	Mean	S.D.
4.86	3.63	.197	.051	16.62	13.42	.38	.24
4.68	2.64	.291	.097	7.15	12.85	.03	.07
2.15	2.07	.216	.051	6.13	5.44	.14	.16
5.59	6.26	.240	.088	10.29	12.27	.19	.23

hypothesis of homogeneity across industries, pooling leads to biased estimates. Thus, the statistical estimates derived from data pooled over the entire sample lack meaning. In fact, the estimates of the parameters for each of the subsets differ markedly. In the subset with highly diversified firms the diversification variable has a highly significant and positive influence on profitability, while industry growth rate is not statistically significant in this subset. In the second subset, however, growth is significant but diversification is not. In both subsets the market share variable is significant and has a positive sign. All of this suggests the rather obvious conclusion that in industries where demand is growing the firms that participate in this growth, either because of their own efforts or because of the growth in primary demand, achieve profitability benefits in proportion to their participation. On the other hand, slow-growth industries achieve profits in proportion to the degree of diversification. This is not to suggest that all firms can profitably diversify, rather that when industry structure implies the availability of exportable organizational assets, firms exporting the assets to a greater degree achieve profits to a greater degree.

The firm-related variable market share is statistically significant in both the high-growth and the low-growth industry groups. The positive and significant influence of market share on profitability is found in the estimates for both of the two major subsets as well as in the estimates derived from data pooled over all of the observations. The rather pervasive finding in the several cross-sectional studies of data from firms of a positive influence of market share on profitability tends to confirm the reality of the relationship since the statistical results do not appear to depend strongly on the data set or the pooling scheme. On the other hand, the influence of other variables does appear to vary significantly according to the data base and pooling scheme. When estimated from data pooled over all of the observations, diversification is not statistically significant, but the coefficient for the industry advertising-to-sales ratio is highly significant. The usefulness of these estimates, however, is greatly suspect since the assumption of homogeneity on which they are based has been shown to be false.

Table 8–5
WLS Regression Results (OLS on Data Corrected for Heteroskedasticity)

Subset	Sample Size	$\sqrt[4]{}Assets$	AS	C	G	MS	SIZ	D	R^2
1	63	−.032 (.063)[a]	−.0004 (.0018)	.0009[b] (.0004)	.021 (.046)	.0023[c] (.0003)	−.025 (.093)	.111[c] (.019)	.902
2	51	.055 (.107)	−.008 (.003)	−.001 (.001)	.126[b] (.063)	.0018[c] (.0007)	.141 (.105)	−.033 (.089)	.452
3	34	.099 (.197)	.005 (.005)	.005 (.003)	−.017 (.136)	.0005 (.0033)	−.353 (.308)	−.104 (.056)	.641
4	15	−7.68[c] (1.15)	2.01[c] (.62)	.111[c] (.016)	.823 (.596)	−.065 (.028)	4.17[b] (2.19)	−.855[b] (.364)	.935
5	18	.671 (.549)	.018 (.019)	−.003 (.011)	−.246 (.546)	.001 (.006)	.811 (.768)	−.184 (.145)	.920
All industries	181	−.110 (.065)	.004[c] (.001)	.0002 (.0003)	.145[c] (.049)	.0013[c] (.0004)	.034 (.083)	.019 (.020)	.614

[a]Figures in parentheses are standard deviations.
[b]Significant at .05 level.
[c]Significant at .01 level.

Table 8-6

GLS Regression Results (On Data Corrected for Heteroskedasticity)

Subset	Sample Size	$\sqrt[4]{Assets}$	AS	C	G	MS	SIZ	D	R^2
1	63	−.078 (.074)[a]	−.001 (.002)	.0013[b] (.0006)	.036 (.048)	.0024[c] (.0003)	.023 (.110)	.115[c] (.019)	.899
2	51	.055 (.110)	−.008 (.003)	.0012 (.0007)	.126[b] (.064)	.0018[b] (.0008)	.141 (.107)	−.033 (.091)	.452
3	34	−.157 (.219)	.003 (.007)	.0065 (.0040)	−.036 (.141)	−.0002 (.0035)	−.389 (.329)	−.086 (.064)	.618
All industries	181	−.012 (.080)	.006[c] (.001)	−.0007 (.0005)	.119[b] (.053)	.0012[c] (.0004)	−.059 (.106)	.004 (.022)	.577

[a]Figures in parentheses are standard deviations.
[b]Significant at .05 level.
[c]Significant at .01 level.

We have shown here that unrestricted pooling of data for the purpose of estimating the influence of market structure on profitability is inappropriate. The conclusions of much of the literature on this relationship should be seriously questioned since, in the absence of rigorous examination of the underlying basis for the studies, we must assume that the statistical estimates may be grossly misleading.

Conclusions and Speculations

The statistical issues touched upon in this paper are not unrelated to the distinctions between the views of Mason and Nourse in the formative stages of the development of the field of industrial organization. Mason's view of a strongly deterministic relationship between market structure and performance implies that comparisons across industries would be valid. On the other hand, Nourse's hypothesis that "management" is the major determinant of performance would tend to support the notion of heterogeneity. The available statistical evidence strongly rejects the hypothesis of complete homogeneity. A substantial body of empirical literature has been developed on the basis of an assumption that is not supported by the evidence. Thus, there are strong scientific grounds for rejecting the entire body of empirical literature. As to the true strength of "management" vis-à-vis structure, one can only speculate, but it does seem likely that both are important and that their relationship is complex.

Our exploratory analysis of relationships within homogeneous subsets suggests that strategic firm-related variables reflect, in part, a response to structural variables. The notion that guides empirical studies of cross-sectional firm data has been that the firm-related variables remove the effects of firm differences so that structural variables can account for the remaining differences in profitability. If, however, the effects of the firm-related variables vary with the structural variables, then the analysis can give only jumbled representations of the relationships. Moreover, it is not unlikely that at least some of the variables that have been taken as measures of structure may be, in fact, results more than causes of profitability. Industry advertising, for example, can be shown, under profit-optimizing behavior, to increase with profits. The tortured rationale frequently given, that advertising is a measure of "product differentiation" and a "barrier to entry," represents one of the more flagrant oversimplifications to be found in the literature on structure and performance.

Were it not for the fact that policymakers are taking the empirical studies seriously, one could regard the structure-strategy-performance literature with some amusement. It is very important that the work in this area progress, but it is even more important that future work proceed on a more rigorous scientific basis than has been characterisic of the previous work in this emerging field.

APPENDIX A

Mathematical Derivations of Variables

The variables used in the mathematical derivations are defined first. They are as follows:

V_{ij} = the value of shipments of firm i in product j,
m_{ij} = the % of sales of firm i in product j,
S_i = the sales of firm i,
A_j = the advertising expenditures of product j,
V_j = the value of shipments (plus imports and minus exports) of product j,
P = the ratio of net income after taxes to shareholders' equity,
AS_i = the weighted average of industry advertising-to-sales ratios in firm i's product markets,
C_j = the 4-firm concentration ratio of product j,
C_i = the weighted average of the 4-firm concentration ratios in firm i's product markets,
MS_i = the weighted average of firm i's relative market share in its product markets,
G_j = the ratio of demand for product j (value of shipments plus imports and minus exports) in year $t+2$ to demand for product j in year $t-2$ (all previous variables are defined for year t),
G_i = the weighted average changes in industry demand in firm i's product markets,
D_i = the 3-digit SIC diversification of firm i.

Then,

$$m_{ij} = \frac{V_{ij}}{S_i}$$

$$AS_i = \sum_j M_{ij} \frac{A_j}{V_j}$$

$$C_i = \sum_j m_{ij} C_j$$

$$MS_i = \sum_j m_{ij} \frac{V_{ij}}{V_j} = \sum_j m_{ij} \frac{m_{ij} S_i}{V_j}$$

$$MS_i = S_i \sum_j \frac{m_{ij}^2}{V_j}$$

$$G_i = \sum_j m_{ij} G_j$$

$$D_i = 1 - \sum_j m_{ij}^2$$

The above definition of MS_i is believed to be the proper mathematical expression for the weighted average of firm i's relative market share in its product markets. (The mathematical expression of Market Share in the FTC study is

$$\sum_j V_{ij} \left[(V_{ij}/V_j)/C_j \right] \Big/ \sum_j V_{ij}$$

Thus, the weights used in developing weighted market share in the FTC study reflect the four-firm concentration ratio of each industry and this, it would seem, mixes firm-specific effects and structural effects.)[1] In the case of diversification, m_{ij} corresponds to the percentage of sales of firm i in 3-digit SIC industries instead of the basic product markets (which are 4-digit SIC industries with a few changes).

1. Federal Trade Commission, *"Economic Report on the Influence of Market Structure on the Profit Performance of Food Manufacturing Companies,"* September 1969, p.49.

APPENDIX B

Firm Selection: Criteria and Data Sources

To be included in the observations for analysis, a firm must
a. derive at least 75 percent of its revenues from the selected industries;
b. derive at least 75 percent of its revenues from the United States;
c. be relatively large (only the firms included in "Compustat," prepared by the Standard Statistical Service of Standard and Poor's Corporation were considered).

The advertising data were obtained from:
—"National Advertising Investments," Leading National Advertisers, Inc. (network, television, and magazine expenditures);
—"Expenditures of National Advertisers in Newspapers," Bureau of Advertising of the American Newspaper Publishers Association (newspaper expenditures);
—"Spot TV Expenditures," Television Bureau of Advertising, Inc. (spot television expenditures).

Other data were compiled from:
—"Compustat," containing company reports data for twenty years;
—"Annual Survey of Manufacturers" and "Census of Manufacturers," containing 4-digit SIC industry value of shipments and 4-firm concentration ratios.

REFERENCES

1. Bain, Joe S. "The Comparative Stability of Market Structures," in *Industrial Organization and Economic Development In Honor of E. S. Mason,* edited by Markham, J. W., and Papanek, G. F. Boston: Houghton Mifflin, 1970.

2. Bass, Frank M. "Profit and the A/s Ratio," *Journal of Advertising Research*, Vol. 14, No. 6, December 1974, pp.9–19.
3. Cattin, Phillippe. "An Econometric Analysis of Advertising and Profitability." Unpublished Ph.D. dissertation, Purdue University, May 1974.
4. Federal Trade Commission. *Economic Report on the Influence of Market Structure on the Profit Performance of Food Manufacturing Companies.* Washington, D.C., 1969.
5. Gale, Bradley T. "Market Share and the Rate of Return," *The Review of Economics and Statistics*, Vol. 54, November 1972, pp.412–23.
6. Imel, J. Blake, and Helmberger, Peter G. "Estimation of Structure-Profit Relationships with Application to the Food Processing Sector," *American Economic Review*, Vol. 61, September 1971, pp.614–27.
7. Mason, E. S. "Price and Production Policies of Large-Scale Enterprise," *American Economic Review*, Vol. 29, No. 1, March 1939 Suppl., pp. 61–74.
8. Nerlove, M. "Further Evidence on the Estimation of Dynamic Economic Relations from a Time Series of Cross Sections," *Econometrica*, Vol. 39, No. 2, March 1971, pp.359–96.
9. Nourse, E. G., and Drury, H. B. *Industrial Price Policies and Economic Progress.* Washington, D.C., 1938.
10. Porter, Michael E. "Consumer Behavior, Retailer Power and Market Performance in Consumer Goods Industries," *The Review of Economics and Statistics*, Vol. 56, November 1974, pp.419–36.
11. Vernon, John M., and Nourse, E. M. "Profitability and Market Structure: An Analysis of Major Manufacturers of Non-Durable Consumer Products." Marketing Science Institute working paper, April 1972.

COMMENTS ON THE ESSAY
BY BASS, CATTIN, AND WITTINK

F. M. Scherer

The paper by Bass et al. correctly points out the dangers of pooling data from numerous industries without an adequate theoretical rationale concerning advertising-profitability relationships both within and between industries. But the sword cuts both ways. Depooling can also be hazardous if done without proper a priori justification.

I faced similar problems in earlier work on Schumpeterian hypotheses concerning technological innovation.[1] Schumpeter argued in effect that innovation flourished best in a monopolistic environment. When I related an index of scientific and engineering (S & E) employment per thousand employees to the four-firm concentration ratios for 56 industry groups, the simple correlation was + 0.46, supporting Schumpeter rather strongly. However, it seemed obvious that the intensity of an industry's S & E effort is related at least as much to the richness of its science base as to market structure. Following a careful qualitative analysis, I therefore divided the industry sample into four classes: those with traditional, general and mechanical, chemical, and electrical technologies. Given this depooling, the S & E employment-concentration correlations deteriorated sharply for all but the traditional technology group, and for chemicals the relationship actually turned negative. What had happened was that the industries enjoying the richest science bases also happened to be the most concentrated on average, so that when the science base was taken into account, the apparent Schumpeterian relationships faded. "Happened," however, may suggest too simple a relationship. A highly plausible chain of causation runs from the enjoyment of rich technological opportunities to superior innovativeness and/or the acquisition of basic patents by some firms to

198

rapid market share growth to high concentration—a sequence quite different from what Schumpeter had in mind.

In this story there is a moral for one's evaluation of the Bass paper. My depooling was based upon two compelling a priori hypotheses: that the science base matters, and that causality may flow from the science base to concentration. I find no such a priori rationale for depooling the advertising-profitability data. Indeed, Professor Bass indicated in his oral presentation that his depooling was "algorithmic," which I interpret to mean, "try alternative industry groupings and see what happens." That, I believe, is not good scientific method. Moreover, it can be argued quite plausibly that it is inter*industry* differences in advertising that primarily matter if high advertising acts as a barrier to entry leading in turn to high profitability. If so, algorithmic depooling could obscure what is in fact a valid causal relationship. And to the extent that there are economics of scale in advertising,[2] it is reasonable to expect a *negative* relationship between advertising intensity and profitability *within* industries, since firms that enjoy those economies more fully will have lower advertising costs per dollar of sales and hence, all else being equal, higher unit profits. The more one depools to the individual industry level, therefore, the more any positive relationship reflecting interindustry entry barrier differences is likely to be obscured.

The really important question, it seems to me, is why entry barriers might be high in industries that exhibit high average advertising-to-sales ratios. Is the causation related to intensive advertising per se, or to some set of product characteristics that happen also to induce intensive advertising, or to some interaction between special product characteristics and advertising? Or might the causal flow be in the opposite direction, from high profit margins to high advertising via the Dorfman-Steiner theorem?[3] To explore these structure-performance link possibilities, one needs a model much more richly specified than that of Bass et al. And to settle the outstanding questions conclusively, it is important that the model's specification have a firm basis in a priori theory. Heuristic depooling or other analysis of the data will not suffice.

NOTES

1. Scherer, F. M. "Market Structure and the Employment of Scientists and Engineers," *American Economic Review,* June 1967, pp.524–31.

2. See Scherer, F. M.; Beckenstein, Alan; Kaufer, Erich; and Murphy, Dennis. *The Economics of Multi-Plant Operation: An International Comparisons Study.* Cambridge, Mass.: Harvard University Press, 1975, pp.245–52.

3. Dorfman, Robert, and Steiner, Peter O. "Optimal Advertising and Optimal Quality," *American Economic Review,* December 1954, pp.834–35.

REJOINDER TO SCHERER'S COMMENTS

Frank M. Bass

Scherer's comments on my paper reflect the attitudes, biases, and non-scientific orientation typical of a large number of industrial organization economists. If the data support the theory, Scherer and his colleagues point to the data; but if the data do not support the theory, they then argue that the data, or the analysis, must be defective. In this way theories are never rejected. Only the data may be brought into question. For example, in Scherer's book[1] the literature of empirical studies of the relationship between advertising and concentration is examined and the statistical association between these two variables is found to be very weak. Nevertheless, Scherer concludes: "It does not seem too farfetched to conclude tentatively that intensive advertising sets into motion forces which tend to increase market concentration, though many other forces are simultaneously at work, so that the net observed effect of advertising on concentration is a weak one, surrounded by considerable variance." In other words, the theory might still be true even though it is not supported by the evidence.

My paper shows that the purported strong relationship between advertising and profitability is based on defective statistical analysis, Thus, as Scherer confesses, it is not possible to argue that the evidence supports the theory. True to his orientation, however, he argues that the theory might still be true.

Scherer argues that his study of innovation by industries used a strong a priori basis for identifying industries: the type of science base. My basis for defining subsets is the degree of diversification. Readers may judge for themselves which basis is stronger. In any case, I made it clear that my analysis was exploratory. "The exploratory character of the appropriate basis for pooling data into homogeneous sets in no sense lessens the force of our nonexploratory conclusion that it is inappropriate to pool data over heterogeneous relationships." Thus, I did not argue that my analysis of homogeneous subsets was, as suggested by Scherer, the final work on advertising-profitability relationships.

Scherer obviously is convinced of the merits of proceeding from strong a priori theories. He asks "why entry barriers might be high in industries that exhibit high average advertising-to-sales ratios." Is this an example of an a priori theory or an a priori bias? Why did Scherer not ask why it might be true that entry barriers were average or low in these industries? The value of strong a priori theories becomes clear in this context. After all, if one's a priori views are strong enough, one can dispense with the objective evidence altogether.

NOTE

1. Scherer, F. M. *Industrial Market Structure and Economic Performance.* Chicago: Rand McNally, 1970, p.343.

9

Structure and Strategy in the Gasoline Industry [1]

JAMES M. PATTERSON

Structure governs strategy! This is an intriguing idea that has had a long and important role in the theory of industrial organization. However, its use as an important analytical approach in marketing is of more recent origin. In the process of borrowing the idea, marketing analysts have tended to include within it factors not usually considered by the industrial organization economist. In one sense this is an improvement. In another sense it is a regression, since the more elements seen to be relevant to explaining a strategy after the fact, the more difficult it is to predict a strategy beforehand. And unless one's ability to predict a particular strategy from a given structure is increased, it is only a semantic exercise to add to the list of structural variables.

One way to test whether the enlarged concept of structure coming to be used in marketing is a net gain or not is to examine its predictive ability in a radically changing situation. The gasoline industry is such a situation. Few industries have faced such radical structural change in such a short period. Surely, if structural analysis is of any value at all in predicting strategic response, it should show up here.

Evolution of Marketing Strategies in the Gasoline Industry [2]

The dominant strategy in the marketing of gasoline that reached its zenith in the late 1960s first began to develop in the early thirties. Before World War I gasoline was sold by livery stables and garages and by hardware, grocery, and general stores. However, by the mid-1920s, there emerged a clear need for a new type of outlet as a consequence of the dramatic growth of automobile registrations. The result was the development of the retail gasoline service station that was soon to dominate the retailing of gasoline.

The initial demand for service stations was quickly met by thousands of independent businessmen eager to capitalize on the profit opportunity in this important new venture. The result was intense competition between the major oil companies for exclusive representation by these outlets.

There were two consequences of this competition. The first was that the price of quality representation became quite high. The other was that the frequent brand switching by the independently owned outlets often disrupted a brand's representation in an area. For both these reasons and others, the major oil companies began to integrate forward to control their key marketing facilities, either by outright ownership or through long-term leases. Forward integration assured that the outlets would sell only the brand of the supplying company. It also permitted greater control over station operation and appearance. Such control was obviously very important in the development of a favorable brand image for a fungible product.

While the ownership or control of retail properties permits employee operation, until recently most major gasoline marketers have chosen to use independent dealers to operate their service stations. This was not always so. Initially it was quite common for the major marketers to operate their stations with company employees. But by the mid-1930s most majors had moved away from direct operation in favor of dealer operation. Low retail returns, chain store taxes, and the threat of union organization influenced this decision. As the marketing strategy shifted to the single brand, dealer-operated, supplier-controlled service station, other elements of the majors' marketing strategy also began to take shape.

First, price competition had to be de-emphasized. With only a few major sellers in any given local market, price cuts were self-defeating. If one seller on a corner or major traffic artery cut price, others had to follow suit or else lose market share. And since the motorist does not necessarily buy much more gasoline as the price falls, the only effect is a loss of profit by each seller.

With price competition minimized, the burden of competition was shifted to other measures. For example, the intensity of market coverage became an important basis for competition. Other factors being equal, market share and even average volume per outlet is closely related to station share. Brand image and product differentiation also assume a primary role in the major's marketing strategy. The reason is obvious. If price is not to be the basis for consumer preference, other bases must be developed. Many elements enter into the "image" the motorist forms of a particular brand. Some are psychological while others are more nearly aesthetic, e.g., station design, color schemes, and logo symbolism.

Brand image and accompanying brand preference are importantly shaped by advertising, especially television advertising. When a product is as difficult for a motorist to assess as is gasoline, slogans and symbols play a key role in the development of customer preferences. "Texaco is Working to Keep Your Trust" or "You Expect More From Standard— And You Get It" have been extremely successful image builders. Note that these campaigns say nothing about gasoline as such. Other marketers have sought to build a favorable brand image around a technical aspect of the product. Shell's special mileage ingredient "Platformate" or Mobil's "detergent" gasoline are good examples of this approach.

The major marketers have also found that the retail setting within which gasoline is sold becomes a basis for forming an image about the unseen product. Uniformly clean, well-run, modern, quality-controlled outlets imply that the gasoline sold by such outlets is of a uniformly good quality, and motorists form a brand preference on this basis. For this reason, the major companies have spent a considerable part of their marketing budget on modernizing old stations and building aesthetically appealing new ones. Considerable attention is also given to the supervision of station operation and appearance in order to foster a favorable brand image.

As important as brand image is in the major marketer's marketing strategy, strong preferences for a single brand are uncommon. In any given market, most motorists would regard the top half-dozen major brands as close substitutes for each other. When price dare not be used, and when several competing brands have developed equally good images, other patronage techniques are required. Credit cards, service bays, trading stamps, short-term continuity premiums, and games were widely used by major gasoline marketeers until recently.

A Search for Structural Explanations

The conveniently located, modern, aesthetically appealing, supplier-controlled, dealer-operated, retail service stations offering a single nationally advertised brand of gasoline and a host of continuity promotions, including gasoline credit cards, became the normal way for major oil companies to market their gasoline by the late 1960s. In part, this approach represented a calculated decision by each major oil company to gain some measure of control over the demand for their most important product—gasoline. But it also represented a predictable response to key structural features of the industry—namely, vertical integration, crude oil tax treatment, and other government policies related to imports and pro-rationing.

Vertical integration is important in explaining why a marketing strategy need not be profitable in its own right. When firms are vertically integrated, transfer prices and, hence, gross margins at each level are set by managerial action rather than by market forces. The result is that profit at a particular level can be manipulated as the logic of the total integrated operation dictates. In the case of the marketing of gasoline, vertical integration permitted a top-heavy, expensive, and often inefficient marketing structure to be maintained by profits from the crude production level.

At first blush, a strategy of subsidizing operations at one level with profits from another sounds foolish. But if profits at a particular level are not competitively determined, and if not all competitors are vertically integrated, subsidization makes good competitive sense from the point of view of system-wide profits. The advantage of shifting profits from one level to another is increased because special tax advantages accrue to crude oil profits and not to marketing or refining profits. Profit shifting also permits the integrated firm to regulate the competition and growth of its nonintegrated rivals.

In addition, the fact that the price of crude oil could be administered heavily influenced the way the majors operated their vertically integrated systems. From the mid-thirties until recently, the price of crude was set by monopsonistic refiners (who were also the major crude producers) in conjunction with state regulatory authorities. The institutional arrangement that allowed crude prices to be rigged was "demand pro-rationing." This practice kept crude oil production balanced with the amount of crude oil demanded at the administered price.

In the name of conservation, individual producers of crude were denied the right to increase their output to their maximum efficient rate and thereby bid the price down. The one big loophole was the threat of abundant supplies of low-priced foreign crude. However, this loophole was effectively closed by the import quota system, which was imposed in 1959 and remained in effect until mid-1973.

The operating logic of the vertically integrated system and the way this structural feature affects marketing is as follows: For the total system to maximize profits, high crude prices must be set and as much crude as possible produced at that price in order to exploit the crude tax preferences. (See the appendix for the arithmetic of this argument.) In order to protect these tax-sheltered profits, the large crude producer now needs to control its crude market. This means it must have adequate refining capacity so that it has a guaranteed, high-priced market for its crude. If most refiners were independent of crude production, they would have an interest in lower crude prices and hence would bid down the high administered crude oil price. Controlled refining is thus essential to support high crude profits.

The same is true of the need for controlled marketing. Unless a major producer/refiner can sell a large share of its gasoline through controlled branded outlets, it will be required to sell its gasoline to independent marketers who would play refiners off against each other and thereby weaken the price structure all the way back to crude.

Controlled refining and controlled marketing is thus essential to the maintenance of high crude profits. Further, by holding refining and marketing margins low relative to crude margins, the growth and behavior of the nonintegrated and partially integrated refiners and marketers can be carefully controlled. Thus does structure affect strategy! Vertical integration in the context of an imperfectly competitive, tax-favored crude oil market places marketing in a supportive role. Marketing's role is to dispose of crude. Inefficient, costly marketing arrangements and practices such as those described earlier make sense only because they sustain and enlarge high, tax-sheltered, crude profits. They would not otherwise persist.

The End of the Old Order

Possibly beginning with the Tax Reform Act of 1970, but most certainly with Libya's move to increase production payments in the fall of 1970, a sequence of events was set in motion that left the oil industry with a marketing strategy ill-suited for the new structural realities. For the last couple of years, the industry has been frozen into past arrangements and practices by government regulation, but as controls are removed, new marketing strategies are sure to emerge.

More than anything else, the debilitation of the crude oil profit center represents a major structural change that strikes at the very foundation of the former marketing strategy. Under the old system the name of the game was to move as much crude oil as possible, irrespective of cost. The emphasis of marketing was primarily on sales volume and not upon return on investment.

A host of factors have contributed to the need to re-evaluate the old game plan of subsidizing downstream operations with high crude profits. Not the least of these is the loss of control by the international oil companies over crude oil production in the major exporting nations. With increased equity participation amounting to complete nationalization in several cases, the profitability of increased foreign crude flows no longer accrues primarily to the major oil companies. The days of high profits from increased foreign crude production are probably gone forever. The loss in cash flow to the industry is staggering, amounting to perhaps as much as $2 billion per year.

Coincident with the end of oil colonialism and high profits from international crude production, domestic crude production peaked in 1970, then began to decline. Pro-rationing had ceased to function to hold domestic crude in the ground after Texas and Louisiana went to 100 percent maximum efficient rates of production in May 1972. From this point on, increments in volume had to be met by increased imports, and as already noted, the profits from imports were no longer the exclusive property of the international majors. International crude profits are now shared. As a result the motivation for volume at any cost has come to an end. And a marketing system designed primarily to generate volume has ceased to be functional.

Not only have increases in crude consumption ceased to be the best way to maximize profits for the integrated major oil companies, they have even become undesirable from the standpoint of national policy. As a result of the oil embargo and attendant shortages in 1973–74, petroleum conservation has become an important national objective. The ball game has completely changed.

Other factors also have radically changed the structure of the industry. During the last year the crude oil tax shelters have been generally emasculated. Import quotas were lifted in May 1973 and replaced by a license-fee system. Environmental factors importantly affect the product and its marketing and manufacture. The doubling of price and periodic product shortages have made the motorist more sensitive to price differences and less responsive to brand images. Government involvement in every aspect of the industry continues to be a fact of life. Unbridled growth in demand has come to an end. Low rates of growth will be compelled by public action. All these factors and others have an important bearing on the way strategies for marketing gasoline will evolve during the next ten years.

The Rise of New Marketing Strategies

The basic problem facing the oil companies during the balance of the decade will be to develop a new marketing strategy that adequately reflects the realities of the new marketing structure. How are profits to be generated in a near static market? Numerous authoritative projections see a 2 percent growth rate as about all that will be allowed. Some additional profits will come from the de-control of regulated crude and from increases in crude prices now administered by OPEC. But these are very likely to be subjected to windfall taxes. Consequently, as the profit-generating role of crude changes, and with increases in crude consumption generally opposed by public policies, profit growth must increasingly come from refining and marketing—from more efficient operations, and from higher prices and margins. Some changes in refining will take place, but the major shifts will come in marketing. Marketing must now make money on its own.

Some of the expected changes were already under way before the embargo. Others are just now beginning to emerge. Still others can be inferred from the changing structure. The most obvious change will be a radical decline in station population. The number has already fallen to less than 190,000 from the 1972 high of 226,000 branded outlets. Because market share was closely correlated with station share in any given geographic market, overbuilding was inevitable so long as marketing's role was to move the almighty crude. The obvious consequence of this strategy was to reduce average station volume and hence to raise the retailing cost per gallon. The practice has its parallel in the parable about the tragedy of the commons. In the parable, each herdsman knows that the benefits of adding an additional animal to a bounded commons accrue exclusively to him while the negative effects of overgrazing are shared by all. As a consequence, each individual herdsman is compelled to add animals to the meadow even though the collective consequence of these individual decisions is ruin for all.

So long as gasoline marketing was subservient to crude sales, the ruin was postponed. Now that marketing must make money on its own, the day of reckoning has arrived. Low volume stations are not only a drag in their own right, they are a drag on all other stations. On the assumption that the average station will be selling 60–70 thousand gallons per month by 1980, the total number of stations should have declined to 160,000 by then.[3] Furthermore, in the search for marketing profits, we should see even more geographic concentration of marketing activities as suppliers continue to withdraw from thin markets and concentrate on those markets where they can achieve good market share and consequently will have effective marketing impact.[4]

One of the consequences of this increase in average station volume will be a re-thinking of the way stations are operated. When gasoline retailing was treated as a break-even operation, the heavy reliance on lessee-dealers made good sense. Now, serious questions arise. Many high-volume stations are just too profitable for dealer operations. Given the relatively high margins of the recent past and the significant volume that is now moving through a great many branded dealer stations, the rewards to the dealer are way out of line with his contribution.[5]

Increasingly, these prime, potentially high-volume stations will be converted to other forms of operation as the law and circumstances permit. Several companies have already begun to shift to employee-operated gas-and-go, or self-serve operations.[6]

Adding to this growing disaffection with the lessee-dealer system of retailing is the trouble many suppliers have had in trying to get dealer-run stations to be competitive.[7] Many dealers are staying open shorter hours and clinging to their newly won margins.[8] Old methods of controlling dealer marketing practices are either no longer appropriate or too disruptive of marketing profits to be used. The growing militancy of dealers and the rise of "dealer rights" laws in the Congress and in the state legislatures will make it even harder to order dealers around in the future.

Certain companies have been experimenting with incentive plans involving rent adjustments, but the big move is going to be in the direction of selective direct operation. With 25 to 50 key direct operations, suppliers will again be able to call the tune on the way dealers in any given metropolitan market operate and price.[9] Direct operations also becomes an alternative to temporary competitive allowance off tankwagon price as a method of meeting local price competition.[10]

Along with the rise in direct operations in profitable key locations will come a radical shift in the mix of retail operations. Specifically, there will be considerably less emphasis on the traditional full-service operations, and much greater emphasis given to the fast-serve, less-service, and self-service type of operation. The profit potential of such operations has already been amply demonstrated by the private branders over the last decade.

Tie-in operations with convenience stores, dairy stores, car-care centers, tire stores, car washes, and the like will also grow as new forms of retail synergy are sought to justify high-priced locations and quality management.[11]

Basically, the gasoline market will become much more segmented, with major brand participation in all segments. Full-service, conveniently located operations will not disappear by any means. They will remain an important segment, but no longer the dominant one. My guess is that before 1990 the market will be divided as in figure 9–1.

Figure 9–1
Gasoline Market Segments, 1975–1990

Method of Operation	Assortment	
	Gasoline only	Gasoline plus
Full service	5% to 20%	70% to 10%
Less service	5% to 10%	5% to 10%
Self service	10% to 25%	5% to 25%

As the major suppliers move aggressively to participate in all market segments, new forms of retailing are bound to emerge. For example, one can expect that the traditional price appeal of the discount marketer will soon come to be augmented much as the purchase proposition of the early discount department store evolved from an exclusive price emphasis. New definitions of convenience are also bound to emerge. For example, the ultimate convenience would be to bring the gasoline to the car, rather than to take the car to the gasoline. On the whole, the retailing of gasoline will become much more complex. Consequently, one can expect to see a much bigger role being played by non-gasoline retailers as new forms of gasoline retailing evolve. Food marketers, general merchandise firms, and others will assume important new roles in gasoline retailing.[12]

In the case of many of the minor majors—the Marathons and the Phillips and the Continentals[13]—they will perforce become primarily discounters. As this trend progresses, the other majors will have to respond. When this happens, the dominance of the classic gasoline service station, which reached its zenith in the late 1960s, will fade into history. And, as the traditional service station begins to diminish in importance, we can expect to see the integration into retailing by the refiner-supplier diminish. The discrepancy of assortments will be too great to sustain integration. The residual integration will be very selective. In a sense this will represent a form of voluntary marketing divestiture by the oil companies.

As the retail structure begins to shift, so too will the ways of relating to that structure. For example, we can expect a decline in the importance of the jobber.[14] So too can we expect to see the dealer tankwagon method of pricing be replaced by some form of origin pricing with add-ons for branding, credit, etc.[15] Brand has already become much less important and price much more important than in the past. Credit, continuity premiums, and other promotions will diminish in importance.[16]

A multiplicity of patronage inducements beyond price or location or brand image will come to be used. Successful gasoline marketers operating under this new structure will continue to present new purchase combinations to new segments. Consequently, they will need to be both more diversified and more focused on their target segments. In short, the change will represent a shift from a homogeneous strategy to a heterogeneous strategy.

Conclusion

Structure has clearly influenced strategy in the marketing of gasoline. Vertical integration, crude oil tax preferences, demand pro-rationing, and import quotas all worked to produce a marketing strategy designed to maximize crude oil profits.

This is all beginning to change. The justification for old strategy no longer exists. A new strategy, profitable in its own right, is bound to emerge. The insistent pressures for increased retail productivity can no longer be denied. The economies of volume operation are too important to be ignored. The old system is ill suited for exploiting the profit potential of high volume operations.

The full-blown emergence of a price-conscious discount segment, the desire for the convenience of one-stop shopping, and the economies of increased transaction size means the margin and assortment strategies of the past will change. New retail forms are bound to emerge.

Whether these structural changes will produce the specific strategies outlined in this paper remains to be seen. The fact that many of the projected changes have already begun, however, does suggest that the structure-strategy paradigm has analytical value.

APPENDIX

For a strategy of shifting profits to the crude level to be profitable, the gain from higher prices at the captive crude level in the integrated firm must be greater than the loss in profits due to the higher cost of crude inputs at the refining level.

Given the following assumptions, an integrated firm that is 81% self-sufficient would find it profitable to take its profits at the crude level.

a. Corporate income tax = 52%
b. Depletion allowance = 22%
c. Severance tax and typical royalty payment = 15%
d. Import quota = 12%

A. *Refining Loss from a Crude Price Increase*

a. Given a federal corporate income tax rate of 52%, the refining operation only has to absorb 48% of the price increase. The federal government absorbs the balance.

b. Since refiners were entitled to a 12.2% import quota from 1959 to 1973, only 88% of the captive refiner's crude requirements are affected by a domestic crude price increase. (If the entire crude input is affected by the price increase, then the integrated firm's world-wide self-sufficiency rather than its domestic self-sufficiency is the relevant figure for calculating profitability.) With only 88% of the refiner's crude requirements affected by the crude price increase and only 48% of this being absorbed by the refiner, his loss is only 42.24% of the price increase.

$$.88 \times .48 = .4224$$

This means that for each penny increase in the price paid for domestic crude, the integrated refinery operation will lose .4224 cents. This now needs to be compared with the gain from integrated crude sales due to the increased crude price.

B. *Crude Gain from a Crude Price Increase*

For each penny increase in the price of domestic crude, the integrated crude operation would subtract .22 cents for the depletion allowance and .15 cents for severance tax and royalty payment or .37 cents total. They would then owe 52% federal income tax on the remainder. This amounts to .3276 cents. This leaves a net profit after tax of .3024 cents for each penny of crude price increase. Add back in the depletion allowance of .22 cents and this means the net gain is .5224 cents for each penny increase on each barrel of domestic crude the integrated crude operator produces. If the integrated firm were .8086 percent self-sufficient, the crude oil gain would just equal the refining profit loss. This 52.24% gain from each penny increase on the 81% of the refinery input the integrated company supplies itself will just equal the 42.24% loss the refining operation suffers as a result of the crude price increase. Anything above this is sheer profit.

Before 1970, the depletion allowance was 27.5% not 22%. With this rate, the break-even self-sufficiency level is 76.66%. In 1971 under the 22% rate, the following firms would have found it profitable to shift profits upstream:

	Percent Self-sufficient
Getty	162.4
Gulf	88.0
Kerr McGee	80.1
Marathon	85.6
Exxon	95.5
Texaco	94.5
Skelly	124.2

Note: Domestic self-sufficiency is here defined as the ratio of net domestic crude production to domestic refinery crude runs.

NOTES AND REFERENCES

1. The author wishes to acknowledge the influence of Professor Fred Allvine on his thinking about gasoline marketing. Collaboration on two books and a dozen years of close association have blurred the origins of many ideas.

2. This section is drawn from chapters 2 and 3 of Allvine, Fred C., and Patterson, James M., *Competition Ltd.: The Marketing of Gasoline.* Bloomington, Ind.: Indiana University Press, 1972; and chapter 2 of Allvine, Fred C., and Patterson, James M., *Highway Robbery: An Analysis of the Gasoline Crisis.* Bloomington, Ind.: Indiana University Press, 1974.

3. Recent FEA figures show the average gallonage to be 28,000 gallons per month. This ranges from an average for company-operated stations of 61,000 gallons to 21,000 gallons per month for open account stations. *National Petroleum News,* October 1975, p.11.

4. This geographic concentration was already in full bloom before the October 1973 embargo, but has been temporarily slowed by the Emergency Petroleum Allocation Act, which froze 1972 supply relations. Nevertheless, Arco, American, Phillips, Gulf, Sun, and Continental all began plans for reconcentration in 1972. See "If a Major Can't Make it in a Market," *National Petroleum News,* February 1972, p.43.

5. Dealer figures are hard to come by, but the steady increases in margins

since early 1973 lifted the income of many dealers above the $20,000 mark with a substantial percentage above the $25,000 level by mid-1974. Many earned more than the oil company executives who supervised them. *National Petroleum News,* April 1974, p.9.

6. For example, Gulf has converted more than 250 service stations to Gulf-operated self-serve units and plans to expand the trend in 1975 according to its annual report. *The Oil Daily,* May 19, 1975, p.18.

7. It was reported that Crown Central may take over its retail outlets because many lessee dealers are reluctant to cut price and compete. *National Petroleum News,* October 1975, p.13.

8. See "Long 'Spreads' and Frantic Pricing Stir New Problems," *National Petroleum News,* May 1975, p.50.

9. Dan Usner of the Louisiana Retail Gasoline Dealers Association testified that Exxon is able to regulate its dealers in New Orleans with 25 key direct operations. Testimony before the U.S. House of Representatives, Committee on the Judiciary, Subcommittee on Monopolies and Commercial Law, July 31, 1975.

10. In the past, when a price cutter began to make inroads into a nearby major station's volume, that station's supplier would subsidize the dealer's price competition on a 70/30 or 80/20 basis by means of a temporary cut in tankwagon price. In order to avoid Robinson-Patman problems, this temporary allowance would have to be "feathered" out to a large number of surrounding stations. This could prove to be quite costly.

On the other hand, direct operation permits the refiner to meet the competition of the price cutter without the need to grant an allowance to his nearby dealers. It is thus a more efficient and economical way of focusing price cuts from the standpoint of the major refiner.

11. Of the 10,000 convenience stores surveyed in a recent study, 21 percent sell gasoline. They are able to operate profitably on a 3-cent gross margin as opposed to 5 cents for self-service and 7 cents for full-service stations.

12. It will probably be easier for firms already in other lines of business to market gasoline than the reverse. Joint ventures are also possible. Nevertheless, the Sears, Food Fairs, and K-Marts of the world will play an increasing role in gasoline retailing.

13. This trend has already begun. For example, Marathon has recently purchased 208 Bonded stations and has converted some 230 more of its Marathon stations to the Speedway brand. This is in addition to its other secondary brands. Conoco, in the fall of 1973, began converting selected markets to discount operations under the Fasgas operation. They already had substantial operations under the Kayo and Douglas brands.

14. The jobber will continue to play a key roll in thin markets, but the relative volume moving through jobbers will decline as the majors increase direct operations and as other types of gasoline retailers grow. The surviving jobber 15 years from now will be more of a branded chain operator than a middleman in the conventional sense.

15. Within the last month or two several sweeping proposals have been made that support this thesis. In a major speech in September, Mr. T. W. Sigler proposed that gasoline sales by refiners be separated from the sale of

other commodities or services and offered to any prospective buyer without franchise or lease requirements. Similarly, the sale of a brand franchise would be separated from the purchase of gasoline and leasing of service stations. *The Wall Street Journal*, "Broad Changes in Gasoline Marketing Practices are Proposed," September 18, 1975, p.10.

In addition, Sunoco has introduced a new franchise program that while retaining the tankwagon price approach charges separately for other franchise services. *National Petroleum News*, October 1975, p.46.

16.   Recent figures suggest that the cost of credit is 2 cents per gallon. *National Petroleum News*, March 1975, p.18. Credit is often forecasted to be one of the early casualties of de-regulation since its value in promoting patronage continuity has declined relative to its cost since the shortage.

COMMENTS ON JAMES PATTERSON'S ESSAY

Willard H. Burnap

I am in fundamental agreement with Mr. Patterson's description of the gasoline marketing structure and strategy of the past. While I could disagree with certain minor points, I believe he is correct in outlining the structure and strategy that have evolved over many years in gasoline marketing. I want to emphasize the word *evolved,* because that is what happened over time in response to federal and state tax laws and the various regulations affecting crude oil production.

I do want to make one observation about Mr. Patterson's description of the strategy of the past. He pointed out that a wasteful aspect of that strategy was the overbuilding and overcosting of service stations in this country. While that was an additional cost that the consumer ultimately paid, I think it is important to note that the consumer got a much greater benefit from the vertical integration of oil companies in a competitive market.

He is correct in saying that there has been no pure free market in the past in crude oil because of state proration and import quotas. Given this situation, which Mr. Patterson describes as a price-administered environment, one would expect the benefits of the depletion allowance to have resulted in excessively high returns on investment for oil companies. The facts are that the market competition and relative subsidization of refining and marketing operations had the effect of returning to the consumer the benefits of the depletion allowance. I believe the proof of this statement is shown in the fact that integrated oil companies have for many years earned a lower return on assets than the average of all manufacturers. The Chase Manhattan Bank reported that in the United States the rate of return on invested capital for oil companies was 11 percent in 1969, 12.2 percent in 1968, and 12.5 percent in 1967, below the return for manufacturing industries, which had a lower degree of risk. Thus competition and vertical integration converted the depletion allowance on crude oil production into a subsidy of the consumer by the taxpayer at the gasoline pump. If the industry had not been vertically integrated, this situation could not and would not have developed.

Need for Change

Certainly to us in Conoco it has been apparent for more than five years that past strategies needed to be changed. We saw that the existing practices—which to some degree locked everyone into the same strategy whether he liked it or not—were not in the best interests of either the consumer or the industry.

In October of 1970 one of my colleagues, Tom Sigler, who is our vice-president of marketing, gave a speech suggesting that the existing gasoline pricing system and the practices of subsidization were in no one's best interests—not even the consumer's. He concluded that marketing objectives aimed only at increasing sales volume and subsidizing obsolete retail outlets would have to go.

In July of 1971, I got on my soapbox to suggest that suppliers should consider three different kinds of pricing for three commodities or services. One would be a price for gasoline which would be available to any and all buyers at any refinery or terminal. The second would be a brand franchise charge available to anyone who wanted to buy it, which would include credit cards, advertising and other benefits. The third would be a charge for the use of supplier-owned outlets to the retailers' profits.

It is apparent from these statements that we agree to a large extent with Mr. Patterson's predictions of future marketing strategies. It obviously would not be in the best interests of our shareholders to divulge in any detail our marketing strategy plans, but I do believe the natural evolution of industry marketing lies in the direction Mr. Patterson describes.

However, we believe the most critical determining factor of future strategy will not be the natural economic evolution in the marketplace; rather, it will be state and federal government actions affecting the market structure.

Political Problems

Since the crisis of 1973, Congress has failed to decide on a national energy policy. In two years, our domestic oil production has declined steadily while our oil imports have risen to about 40 percent of our needs —more than at the time of the 1973 oil embargo—and increased coal production and nuclear plants have been delayed by a variety of legal and legislative tactics. Despite this erosion of our energy base, we still have no national energy bill from the 535 members of Congress—most of whom do not seem to understand the economics or technologies involved, and some of whom are using the problems for their own political motives.

During the fall of 1975 the House actually attached an amendment involving school busing to energy legislation. Another House amendment would have allowed the government to regulate refinery output to force conservation by creating an artificial gasoline shortage. Two presidential candidates announced they would campaign against big oil companies. And the Senate, without holding one committee meeting or one public hearing, came within six votes of divesting oil companies of their marketing, refining, and transportation operations.

These actions, it seems to me, reflect efforts by many in Congress to make short-term political gains by appealing to that segment of the public that is angry at the oil industry and doesn't trust it. But short-term political gains are not compatible with planning our long-term energy strategy.

Within the industry itself there is disagreement over the desirability of ending price and allocation controls that were created during a shortage to spread the misery. There is no longer a shortage of crude oil in the world, refining capacity is adequate, and projected refinery expansion will be adequate to handle increased demand for at least the next five years. In spite of these facts, various dealer organizations and private retail brand organizations oppose decontrol. The jobber organizations have swung back and forth between support for decontrol and opposition to it, and certain medium-sized refiners have voiced their concern about the effect of decontrol on them.

In my opinion, the reluctance of some of these organizations to get free of these government controls reflects their concern that certain practices of the past will continue and will hurt them. For these reasons, we recently proposed (in a speech given by Tom Sigler at Fort Wayne, Indiana) a legislative compromise designed to prevent both perpetual regulation and vertical divestiture.

Price and Allocation Controls

Vertical divestiture is still a proposal in the Congress, but one form of divestiture is a law in at least one state—Maryland—and was passed but declared unconstitutional in Florida. The Maryland law, which would prohibit oil companies that have production and refining operations from operating service stations in the state, is being challenged in the courts. That two states passed divestiture laws, that others are considering them, that the Senate almost voted for such a law—all cause concern among many in the downstream end of our business that their future could be adversely affected by the possible changing strategies of major oil companies.

However, in my judgment any national or state vertical divestiture legislation would create far more problems than it would solve for all concerned. The consumer would be the first victim. The head of the American Petroleum Institute recently pointed out that divestiture was the surest way to raise the price of gasoline to one dollar a gallon because it would interpose several layers of middlemen between the producers and the customers.

Another strongly possible result might be the acquisition or takeover of the resulting refining or marketing/refining firms by the OPEC member nations. If and when the OPEC cartel weakens significantly, it is not illogical to assume that there would be a rapid struggle among the producing nations to acquire marketing and refining outlets around the world. Vertical divestiture would leave financially weak refining and marketing companies trying to stand alone and make them prime targets for such takeover efforts.

In summary, while I concur in general with Mr. Patterson's description of the past strategies and predictions of future strategies, I do not believe the present political situation will permit the time necessary for normal economic forces to bring about the logical evolutionary developments he described. Rather I believe that political forces are going to determine future strategies. And right now I can see only three possible choices: perpetual regulation, or vertical divestiture, or acceptable legislative compromise within the industry.

I favor the last; a competitive market that relies on the consumer's voice at the pump is better for the industry than a regulated market restricted by bureaucratic rules and cluttered by subsidies and special deals.

10

Structure, Conduct, and Productivity in Distribution

LOUIS P. BUCKLIN

Introduction

Discussions of the relative advantage of large-scale, integrated distribution systems are frequently found in the marketing literature.[1] The list of reasons why these new systems are superior is a long and familiar one, requiring no repetition here. But what is infrequently provided are empirical tests of the validity of the hypothesized advantages. Supporting evidence is confined, at best, to engineering specifications or comparative profits. More typically a rising market share under the new system is taken as proof of its superiority.

What these evaluations lack, however, is any formal demonstration of greater efficiency in field operations. Comparisons of alternative systems are seldom made. Indeed, concepts of efficiency and of system characteristics are usually so weakly developed that empirical tests are not feasible.

This paper explores associations between the types of distribution systems and their performance. Performance is, of course, a multidimensional construct, but it will be limited here to productivity, an aspect infrequently studied. The level of productivity of various distribution institutions will be evaluated with regard to both the structural conditions of the marketplace and conduct as reflected in the degree of vertical channel control. Data are derived from published sources and from two surveys with which the author was associated.

Before consideration of these relations, some general concepts concerning productivity will be developed. These provide the base for the exposition of a model of productivity in distribution and for the empirical work that follows. An appraisal of the findings concludes the paper.

The Concept of Productivity

Productivity is a construct emerging from the theory of the production function.[2] In this theory, physical resources—land, labor, and capital—are characterized as the basic inputs necessary to create goods. Given the available technology, increasing quantities of goods—output—are obtained as more resource units are added. The mathematical relationship between the quantity of resources and the resulting quantity of output is the production function.

Productivity is the ratio of outputs produced to inputs used. Estimates may be derived directly from the mathematical expression of the production function or from empirical observations of output and input usage. Both estimates are sensitive to changes in the level of output if economies or diseconomies of scale exist. Productivity will also change over time as improved technology in machinery and management permit a greater number of output units to be squeezed from a given quantity of inputs.

These elementary definitions are stressed to reinforce the point that productivity deals with physical quantities, not monetary units. Thus, it provides an invaluable and unique measure of performance. It yields insight into resource utilization and efficiency in a way that profitability measures cannot. (It also provides the researcher with innumerable headaches in trying to derive the desired quantities accurately.)

This distinctive aspect of the productivity ratio may be shown as follows. The level of sales of a firm is determined by the quantity of output produced times the average price at which it is sold, i.e., $S = O \times P_o$. Costs incurred are similarly determined by the quantity of resources used multiplied by their purchase price, $C = I \times P_i$. Dividing the first expression by the second, we have:

$$S/C = O/I \times P_o/P_i. \tag{1}$$

The profit margin of the firm is determined by S/C, or $(S/C) - 1$. O/I is the productivity ratio, and P_o/P_i is the ratio of output to input prices.

This analysis shows that the profitability of a firm depends upon two conditions. The first is the efficiency with which it employs its resources—its productivity. The second is the ratio of output to input prices—its terms of trade. Under competitive pressures, the second condition cannot be appreciably influenced by the individual firm. Hence, with respect to this factor, the firm may prosper or fail because of circumstances it can do relatively little to alter, especially in the short run.

On the other hand, management of the firm is directly responsible for productivity. The ability to extract as much as possible from a given set of resources, and to improve upon that technology through time, is the mark of excellent management. Failure to keep pace with even average achievement is an indicator of eventual distress and possible exit from the industry.

Consequently, the concept of productivity is a measure of particular importance for evaluating performance. It focuses directly upon the facet of a business that is usually most controllable by management. If new distribution systems are presumed to improve performance, this should be verified by measuring, not profitability alone, but productivity as well.

Against all of the desirable attributes of the productivity measure lies the difficulty in deriving accurate measures of quantity. There are many stumbling blocks. On the output side, there are obstacles to deriving the appropriate index of prices for purposes of properly deflating S to obtain O. Indices reflecting the product mix of industries, let alone of firms within industries, are notoriously difficult to obtain. A particularly troublesome subissue is the identification and adjustment for qualitative difference in output units, e.g., style or horsepower in automobiles or personal services in retailing or wholesaling.

There are equally difficult problems on the input side. Trouble almost always appears when making estimates for inputs of capital and land. Data are recorded on the basis of cost, but depreciation rates are more frequently related to tax considerations than to the actual utilization of assets. In the labor category, there are vexatious issues over the actual number of hours worked and whether proportions of the total provided by different components of the labor supply have changed. Finally, because few firms, if any, use only labor, land, and capital as inputs, we must take account of intermediary goods supplied by other industries. Ideally, these should either be established as a separate input or be subtracted from output to form a value-added measure of the goods provided.

Because of the problems involved in deriving capital inputs, many studies deal only with an index termed "the partial productivity of labor." This is the ratio of real output divided by labor units of input only. Although such measures have substantial value, judgments about differences in comparative studies must be tempered by the realization that the differences may be caused by unknown, but unequal, capital/labor ratios. In that event, variations in labor productivity may only reflect the distinctive location of institutions upon the same production function (economies of scale, etc.), not differences in distribution technology.

The Productivity Model

It is apparent from the foregoing discussion of productivity that if the effect of structure and conduct upon this measure of performance is to be evaluated, the role of resource input level will have to be held constant. The components of the model, therefore, must include those representing productivity constructs, as well as those of structure and conduct.

PRODUCTIVITY COMPONENTS

The model will include several types of productivity components. As mentioned, representation of the level of various inputs will be required. This would involve labor, capital, and intermediary goods, where possible.

Where gross output measures are used and no information on intermediary inputs is available, information on the degree of vertical integration will be useful. Where firms or systems differ in vertical integration, comparative measures of productivity based upon gross output will reflect this dimension—not differences in efficiency—unless this system characteristic is properly controlled.

Measures relative to the effect of different types of outputs may similarly be appropriate. For example, where service levels across the systems being studied vary, productivity ratios will show differences unrelated to technological superiority. Similarly, where transaction size is different in distribution organizations, disparities in productivity may be expected to arise. All types of firms are sensitive to transaction-size issues, but distribution agencies are particularly sensitive, since a large proportion of inputs is devoted to exchange.

STRUCTURE COMPONENTS

The term *structure* in industrial organization theory refers to certain features of a market hypothesized to be determinant of the intensity of competition. The three principal features measured are the degree of concentration, the height of entry barriers, and the extent of product differentiation—all defined with respect to the seller level of the market. These are occasionally joined by additional characteristics such as concentration at the buyer level, degree of integration across buyer and seller levels, and degree of horizontal integration into other related industries or products.

Conceptually, the link between the state of competition and productivity is clear. The greater the intensity of competition, the more likely firms are to eliminate inefficiencies, operate at optimal scales, and introduce new technologies. Hence, it would be appropriate to introduce all factors developed by industrial organization theory into a model of productivity.

However, the variables traditionally used by industrial organization theorists exhaust neither the set of all identifiable characteristics of a market (such a set being more properly labeled as the structure) nor the subset of features that might in some way or other have a major impact upon competition and productivity. The problem of developing a general taxonomic approach to the classification of markets has been considered by some authors in marketing,[3] but neither conceptual nor empirical work has proceeded very far.

This issue is particularly acute because the traditional set of variables has some limitations that impede the study of competition in distribution. For one thing, the competitive stresses of trade markets tend to be local, and national statistics of the type usually employed with manufacturing have little relevance. Similarly, because of the small capital typically required for trade establishments, and the minor and easily imitated distinctions in product services provided, traditional industrial organization theory variables are not sensitive to differences in competition between regions. Besides this, empirical representations of these variables are difficult to obtain.

Fortunately, an alternative approach may be derived from studies of the evolution of distributive institutions.[4] These studies show that competitive pressures are intensified by the appearance of new forms of trade firms, e.g., the department store, supermarket, discount house, etc. These break up the "solidarity" of the nonprice tactics of the existing set of retailers, forcing prices to lower levels.

Other studies suggest some of the structural conditions of the environment that are likely to facilitate the introduction of these new firms.[5] First, there is the development of densely populated urban areas, markets in which consumers can readily reach a number of alternative trade firms, causing price elasticities at the firm level to rise. Second, there is the general expansion of the market. Where markets are growing, entry of new institutions is both more feasible and desirable from a managerial point of view. Areas where demand is dormant tend to stagnate.

Data representing this dimension of market structure are readily available on a regional basis. Variables based on these data will be applied here to reflect competitive intensity in trade industries.

CONDUCT COMPONENTS

The dimension of conduct to be studied is the degree of control exercised by one firm over others in the same market. This type of control may be most formally exercised by means of vertical integration, as where a chain store initiates the operation of its own warehouse. In this vein, the distinction between this act and that of vertical integration as an element of market structure is blurred.

For present purposes, however, two kinds of integration may be distinguished. The first occurs when an action alters fundamentally the activity set of the integrated establishment by incorporating or deleting functions usually performed by independent (nonintegrated) establishments. For example, in the case of department stores, vertical integration occurs when buyers purchase directly from manufacturers instead of from wholesalers and have goods delivered directly from the factory to the store.

In the second kind of integration, the activity set of the integrated establishment is not dramatically altered. Instead, several jointly owned and vertically articulated establishments (e.g., a chain store-warehouse system) coordinate their flow of activities.

It is this second kind of integration, distribution system control, that is the object of this study. Such control may be exercised both in integrated firms and in nonintegrated organizations. In the latter, contractual relationships, as in the case of franchising systems, are the vehicles through which the formal authority involved in coordination is developed. Variables representing different degrees of system control may range from direct measures of the mode and effectiveness of coordination to dichotomous representations of systems of different types. Since we are concerned here with the relative merits of different systems, the latter types of variables will be employed.

Structural Application of the Model

To evaluate the role of structure, comparisons should ideally be developed between marketing systems that differ markedly in terms of their basic characteristics. Hence, for this purpose, a macroevaluation of the determinants of productivity in the retail trades of Japan and the United States will be introduced. Necessary data for this study were derived from *Censuses of Business* from the two countries and from related social and economic statistics. The unit of analysis was the region: the state for the United States, the prefecture for Japan. Comparability in census statistics for both countries facilitated the analysis greatly. Data from both countries for two census years in the 1960s were prepared.

Output was measured by retail sales deflated by consumer price indices appropriate to each country. Predictor variables were from the productivity and structure group.

PRODUCTIVITY VARIABLES

Five variables were developed to represent the several dimensions of the production function. The first of these was employees of retail establishments plus all proprietors. The second was two proxies for the resources invested in retail establishments: the number of establishments per capita (in thousands) and trade wages per month. The use of these is admittedly controversial and warrants explanation.

Perhaps the chief reason for their use is that census statistics in the United States have no information on capital invested in retail facilities. Hence, to represent this dimension without extensive primary survey evaluation, it was necessary to resort to proxies. Parenthetically, however, it might be noted that the most recent Japanese census did have information on store size. Attempts to employ this in the regression studies proved fruitless—too little variation between square footage and employment existed among prefectures to permit the independent effects of each to be shown.

The number of establishments per capita is an alternative expression of store scale. Where there are more establishments per capita, and personal income is held constant, retailing is conducted on a smaller scale and is probably more specialized with respect to product. An increase in the number of establishments per capita should act to reduce productivity levels. This variable, however, does not fully represent the extent of capital in the individual establishment. It was hypothesized that this would be related to wage levels. Higher wages would force shop managers to utilize proportionately more capital, reducing the necessary quantity of labor. Higher wages, therefore, should be associated with greater productivity of labor.

Two measures were introduced to adjust for deficiencies in the gross output measure of retail trade. These were income per capita and the market share of department stores in retailing. Income per capita was employed to represent the effect of greater purchasing power upon productivity, especially upon transaction size. With greater incomes, purchases at retail may be expected to be made in larger aggregates, requiring retailers to use fewer resources to provide a given level of output. Income per capita, then, should be positively associated with productivity.

The percentage of department store sales was used to control for the different degrees of vertical integration in trade. As noted earlier, department stores—especially in the United States—typically tend to bypass the wholesaler establishments. The greater vertical integration of department stores should influence the productivity measure negatively in areas where they have a greater market share.

STRUCTURAL VARIABLES

Although, in the broader sense, the variables discussed above in terms of establishments and income per capita, department store market share, and trade wages are elements of market structure, they were not introduced to reflect the degree of competitive pressure. For this purpose, two other variables were employed.

The first was urban density, a combination variable reflecting both the proportion of a state or prefecture population located in urban areas and the population density of each state or prefecture. It was hypothesized that both of these factors would create an environment conducive to the development of more competitive types of retail institutions.

The second variable was rate of population growth between the two census years for each state or prefecture. Again, it was hypothesized that this would stimulate the development of more competitive institutions, resulting in a positive relationship with productivity.

THE STATISTICAL MODEL

The resulting model included the seven structural and production function variables plus a dummy variable to reflect any technological change between the two census years. Tests on the coefficients for each census year showed no statistical difference in either country. This permitted the pooling of the data for both years in each country, thus providing more degrees of freedom for the analysis.

The regression model employed was log-linear as follows:

$$O = (a + b_1 X_1) \prod_{i=2}^{8} X_i^{b_i} , \qquad (2)$$

where O is retail output, a the constant term, b_1 the coefficient of the time dummy variable, X_1, for the census year (0 for the first year, 1 for the second), and b_i the exponential coefficients for the seven structural and production function variables labeled X_i. The exponential coefficients in this model represent elasticities, reflecting the proportionate change in output derived from a given increase (or decrease) in the explanatory variable.

This form of the model does not reflect productivity directly. That is, no explicit output/input ratios are produced. However, the impact of changes in variables upon partial productivities can be readily discerned. For example, if the coefficient for per capita income is positive and statistically significant, then higher per capita income will create a greater level of output if labor is held constant. Such development results, in effect, in a more efficient use of labor; productivity has thereby been improved.

RESULTS OF THE ANALYSIS

Results from the regression analysis applied to the Japanese and American data are shown in table 10–1. The coefficient columns for the two countries represent separate runs deriving the a and b_i values of equation (2). The t-scores beside the coefficients reflect the probabilities that they are different from zero. The final column of t-scores provides a means to assess whether the coefficients of the two runs are significantly different from each other.

Coefficients of determination for both the United States and Japanese equations are almost equal to one, a result of the typically close association between retail employment and retail sales. Also of interest is that all the coefficients, with the exception of urban-density for the United States, are likely to be greater than zero, with a probability of 90 percent or better. The model, as a consequence, appears to provide important in-

Table 10–1

Pooled Cross Section, Log-Linear Regression Coefficients for Retail Outlets, Japan[a] and the United States[b]

Explanatory Variables	United States		Japan		t-Score Differences U.S.–Japan
	Coefficient	t-Score	Coefficient	t-Score	
a Constant term (antilog)	.30	2.8c	.14	3.0c	.8
b_1 Time dummy (antilog)	.01	3.7c	−.02	2.6c	3.7c
Production Function					
b_2 Employment	.99	210.4c	1.09	58.6c	−5.8c
b_3 Establishments per capita	−.07	−1.9d	−.24	−2.1d	1.6
b_4 Trade wages	.36	4.8c	.23	3.3c	1.0
b_5 Income per capita	.07	1.7d	.65	6.9c	−6.1c
b_6 Department store market share	−.08	−4.6c	.04	2.7c	−4.1c
Structure					
b_7 Urban × density	.00	.4	−.04	−3.6c	3.9c
b_8 Population growth	.18	3.8c	.17	1.7d	.1
	$R^2 = .9992$		$R^2 = .9955$		
	$\bar{R}^2 = .9912$		$\bar{R}^2 = .9951$		
	$n = 96$		$n = 92$		

[a]Census years 1964 and 1968.
[b]Census years 1963 and 1967.
cP $\geq$ .99.
dP $\geq$ .90.
n = number of observations.

sights into the operation of retailing, and the independent variables selected appear to be important despite cultural differences.

The role of labor is the dominant element in the equations for both countries. Similarly, both the reduction in the number of establishments per capita and an increase in income per capita suggest higher levels of sales. Increases in trade wages also appear to spur output, other factors being held constant. Finally, output in both countries appears responsive to population growth.

Major interest here, however, lies in the comparison of the coefficients between the two countries. Of particular significance is that expansion of the scale of the system is likely to produce proportionately higher outputs in Japan than in the United States. This is reflected in the higher coefficient for employment and establishments per capita for Japan. Although the latter barely misses being statistically significant at 90 percent, the two taken together suggest that the Japanese system, generally consisting of smaller and more specialized establishments, possessed a greater opportunity for future improvements in productivity through scale expansion than did the United States retail trade. Conceivably, the latter may already have exhausted many of the benefits from that source.

The sharpest difference between the two countries appeared in the effect of increased purchasing power. This is interpreted to mean that while higher income (and the probable higher retail transaction size that accompanies this) stimulates productivity, the degree of stimulation is sharply higher for Japan. The implication again is that as a retail system adjusts to higher levels of consumption, the benefits from transaction-size expansion are highest during the early stages of development and diminish with system maturity.

Although the difference between the two countries in the trade wages variable was not significant, it is of interest to note in passing that the direction of difference seems plausible. With the proportion of paid labor in American stores being higher, because of relatively fewer unpaid family members, one might reasonably expect American retail store managers to be more sensitive to pressures for higher wages. The lesser effect of this variable in Japan may further reflect the small-scale establishment characteristic of the system and its impact upon productivity.

The final production function variable is the role of the department store. The different signs for the coefficients for the two countries indicate that department stores are less vertically integrated in Japan. Hence, in that country, their greater scale of operation (and, presumably, the economies that flow from it) would contribute directly to higher productivity. Because U.S. department stores have a far greater tendency to bypass wholesalers, they need proportionately more employees to support their sales floors than other retail types do.

With regard to the structural or competitive-intensity variables, retail sales in both countries reacted in a similar way to the growth of population. Evidently, in regions where population is growing, the introduction of new, more efficient retail facilities is more likely to occur. Growth and efficiency, in this manner, move together.

A disparity developed, on the other hand, with respect to the urban-density variable. Here, the U.S. coefficient was zero, while the Japanese coefficient was opposite in sign to that hypothesized. No reasons for this could be derived from the data. However, it is conceivable that where growth and retail stores per capita are held constant, higher densities do not contribute to efficiency. Possibly the urban conditions in Japan have become so crowded, and land so valuable, that large-scale institutions have great difficulty in obtaining the space necessary for their operations.

A final comment is warranted with regard to the dummy variable for time. As shown in table 10–1, the coefficient for Japan is negative, implying that, over time, other factors held constant, output has declined. That such a negative technological gain has occurred seems unlikely. It may reflect flaws in the specification of the model, the data, or both. Data for more years need to be considered.

In sum, the results indicate that productivity can be reasonably well reflected in the framework proposed. The production function variables contributed most importantly to the determination of output. However, the character of this condition was altered by the specific environmental context of each country. More specifically, the opportunity for gain with rationalization of the retail system and economic development seemed greater for Japan because the system is in an earlier stage of development. The opportunity to expand through population growth seemed vital as a structural variable for both countries. Contrary to what was hypothesized, however, high population densities may deter improvements in efficiency.

Control Applications of the Model

The second phase of the empirical work focuses upon the control element of the productivity model. Here, because of the need to make comparisons between institutions that vary primarily in terms of the type of channel-control mechanism, the study design calls for more highly disaggregate data. The unit of analysis becomes the firm or a group of similar firms. In such a micro setting, the pressures of competition are presumed to operate uniformly, hence this factor is not included in the design. Three sets of data will be examined. The first is for supermarkets, the second for fast-food restaurants, and the third for insurance.

SUPERMARKETS

Both the potential and frustration involved in the use of secondary data are to be seen in this analysis of a study made by the National Commission on Food Marketing on the relative performance of different supermarket organizations.[6] Forty-nine operators of supermarkets in two cities, one in the Midwest and the other in the East, provided information on the activities of almost 100 establishments. The data included the sizes of the stores, wages and pay scales, gross margins, input and output prices, and estimates of service quality. The data were disaggregated by type of system, reflecting the level of system control, i.e., national chain organizations, local chain organizations, affiliated retailers of wholesalers, discount supermarket operators, and unaffiliated food-store operators.

As with most published data, the disappointing dimension is the absence of sufficient disaggregation, usually as a result of requirements to protect the identity of the individual establishments. Hence, data on only the five classes were provided. Consequently, the analysis conducted on the data can only be regarded as indicative of the type of approach that would have been followed had more detailed statistics been available. But, even with this proviso, the results are worth a cursory examination.

The productivity function derived by regression analysis again took the log-linear format. Output of each of the groups was measured by the difference between deflated sales and deflated cost of goods sold, i.e., double-deflated dollar gross margins. Three independent variables were employed: total employment hours, scale of establishment (in square feet of building space), and the subjective service rating. The output and employment data were estimated from the information provided and were not directly supplied in the commission's report. The coefficients and t-scores (in parentheses) from the regression are:

$$O = 2.81L^{1.09}K^{.46}S^{-1.08}$$
$$(.7) \ (8.1) \ (2.8) \ (-2.6) \tag{3}$$

$$R^2 = .9994 \qquad t \geq 3.1, p \geq .9$$
$$\bar{R}^2 = .9976 \qquad n = 5$$

where L is the class average labor hours per store, K is class average store size, and S is class average service. As in the structural equations of table 10–1, the major determinant of output was employment, with store size of lesser consequence (and questionable significance). The sum of the coefficients of employment and store size suggest significant scale economies, although insufficient degrees of freedom remain in this model to test this condition.

The service score, again of questionable significance, is both high and negative. It implies that if services are increased while labor and store size are held constant, total output must diminish. This is the direction one would expect, although the proportion appears high.

To evaluate the impact of vertical control upon productivity, two measures of this construct were created. The first was partial labor productivity, based upon output divided by employment. The second, total factor productivity, is an estimate derived from the regression residuals. Where actual output exceeded predicted output from the regression equation, productivity was regarded as greater than the average, and vice versa.

These ratings are shown in table 10–2. Partial labor productivity, in index form, is closely associated with scale of store (not shown in table). They are clearly unassociated with the total factor productivity scores, which suggests that they are poor proxies for this important dimension.

Table 10–2

Productivity in Different Types of Food Distribution Systems

Type of System	Partial Productivity Index—Labor (1)	Total Factor Productivity (2)	Degree of Vertical Control (3)
National chain	.87	1.01	1
Local chain	1.04	.99	2
Affiliated independent	.81	1.02	3
Discount supermarket	1.14	1.00	4
Unaffiliated independent	.69	.98	5

$$R_{12}^2 = .004$$
$$\overline{R}_{23}^2 = .25$$

Source: National Commission on Food Marketing, *Organization and Competition in Food Retailing.* Washington: U.S. Government Printing Office, 1966, pp. 305–34.

Evaluation of whether there was any vertical control effect was made by correlating the total factor productivity rankings with the hypothesized order of degree of control. The resulting R^2 is in the hypothesized direction, but represents no more than an 80 percent chance of being statistically significant. Hence, with the limited number of data points, the test fails to provide support for the thesis that vertical control improves productivity.

CASUALTY AND PROPERTY INSURANCE AGENTS

Derivation of the data for this study of productivity was the work of Michael Etgar as part of his doctoral dissertation on the distribution of insurance.[7] A long questionnaire was sent to a random sample of agents selling casualty and property insurance in the state of California. The questionnaire inquired into the status of the agent's business and the relationships between the agent and his insurers. The response rate for usable replies was approximately 20 percent.

Two major types of agents were especially studied: so-called independent agents and direct-writing agents. The first group was made up of middlemen who represent several insurers on a commission basis; they are free to form or sever relationships with any insurer and to shift their clients among insurers as they see fit. The direct writers, on the other hand, represent a single company and are usually captive to it. If they were to break relationships, they would probably lose most or all of their clients, as the latter tend to identify and be tied more closely with the insurer. In some instances, the direct-writing agents may actually be employees of their insurers, not middlemen in the true sense of the word.

The direct writers, therefore, operate in a distribution system in which the degree of vertical control may be expected to be significantly greater than that of the independent agents. If the degree of control has an impact upon performance, productivity should be higher for the direct writers than for the independents.

Examination of the data showed output per agent, as measured by annual premiums, to be larger for the average independent agency than for the direct writer.[8] This appears to show that the channel with the least vertical control was more productive. However, when input factors were added to the relationship, the impact of the system type declined.

This may be seen from regression equation (4). Here, O is agency premium volume, E the number of agency employees and managers, K the capital employed, Y the number of years in business, and V the dummy variable representing distribution system type. In this instance, $V = 1$ for independent agencies and 0 for direct writers. As can be seen, when employment, capital, and age are held constant, system type no longer contributes any statistically significant reduction to the variance of the output O.

$$O = (63.74 - 7.44V)E^{.73} K^{.05} Y^{.23} \qquad (4)$$
$$(25.6)(-.18)(7.0)(1.8)(3.5)$$

$$R^2 = .62 \qquad\qquad t \geq 2.3, p \geq .99$$
$$\bar{R}^2 = .60 \qquad\qquad n = 91$$

Interestingly, other data from the survey, not represented in equation (4), imply a higher level of coordination in the direct-writing system. There was, for example, less duplication to be found in claims handling, underwriting, renewals, and billing activity between direct-writing agents and their insurers. Accounting procedures had been more unified and less time was required for homeowner policies to be completed and endorsements made. Sensitivity of insurers to agent suggestions concerning underwriting procedures, new products, and promotion was rated also as higher in direct-writer systems. Insurers also provided more training and more financial and budgetary tools to direct writers. It seems reasonable to suppose, therefore, that direct writers are indeed more productive. Conceivably, the roughness of the data received from a mail survey, as indicated by the relatively low coefficient of determination for this type equation, prevents system type from being statistically significant.

FAST-FOOD RESTAURANTS

Another study, this one involving productivity of individual fast-food restaurants, has been completed by Jeffrey Doutt as part of the work for his doctoral dissertation. Here, operators of 50 randomly selected fast-food restaurants in California were personally interviewed on a wide range of topics related to their businesses. Data on sales, employee and proprietor hours, and facilities employed were also gathered. Approximately 30 of the restaurants were operated by independent businessmen; the remainder were franchises, e.g., McDonald's, Kentucky Fried Chicken.

The objective was to determine the extent to which the planning of restaurant operations and the coordination of contracts with supply sources resulted in savings of time at the retail level. Regression analysis of the data produced the following log-linear equation:

$$O = (.24 - .01V)L^{.88} \; K^{.19} \; D^{.05}$$
$$(2.9)\,(.3)\,(9.3)\,(2.8)\,(1.6) \tag{5}$$

$$R^2 = .80 \qquad t \geq 2.3, p \geq .99$$
$$\bar{R}^2 = .78 \qquad n = 50$$

where O is output in terms of restaurant gross margin, L is hours worked, K is capital invested in the restaurant building and equipment, D is parking space or land, and V is the dummy variable for system type. Coding for the latter, however, is the reverse of that used for insurance. Here, franchises (the more highly controlled systems) are represented by 1.

As in the supermarket equation, the largest part of the variance and the largest input exponent were generated by labor. The role of capital invested appeared to be second in importance and degree of significance. The lack of meaningful contribution from parking is surprising but may relate to an absence of sufficient variation in inputs among the data, e.g., parking was correlated with hours of employment and with capital, although not beyond a simple coefficient of .5.

As in the insurance case, the interesting result was the absence of any significant independent effect upon output by the degree of system control, V. The coefficient, as well as the associated t-score of .3, was minuscule, despite a simple correlation of .22 between V and the level of output. However, as before, when labor and capital investment were introduced into the regression equation, no separate effect from system type remained.

In the fast-food example, the largest stores were operated by the controlled system type, the franchisees. This was the opposite of the insurance case where the direct-writers were smaller than the independents on the average. In both instances, however, increased output could be traced to higher inputs, not to better coordination, despite evidence, in both insurance and fast foods, that better coordination did indeed exist in the systems with more vertical control.

Conclusions

This study of the retail trades has sought to evaluate through empirical studies at both macro and micro levels the effects of structure and conduct, in the form of vertical channel control, on productivity. The results suggest that of the two, structural conditions are likely to be the more important. Indeed, the results raise some doubt whether vertical channel coordination has any meaningful impact on productivity at the retail level.

In the macro study of retailing in Japan and the United States, the effect of the competitive structure on productivity was examined. In the absence of data for more traditional structural measures, two measures believed to show the degree of opportunity for new types of retailing to appear were devised. One was a measure of population growth and the other a measure of population density. It was anticipated that both growth and population density would foster the type of competitive conditions that improve efficiency.

Of these two measures, only population growth produced statistical results in the hypothesized direction. The implications of this are profound for the United States and other countries now contemplating a zero population growth rate. Some of the improved productivity in retail trade has undoubtedly come from the lower barriers to entry of large-scale retail firms in rapidly growing regions. Without this growth, it may well be more difficult for new establishments to find market room.

In Japan the population density variable produced an effect exactly the opposite of that expected. There was no effect in the United States. The implication is that very densely populated areas may be less capable of accommodating change because the high cost of land inhibits the kind of rebuilding necessary for newer, more efficient retail organizations to emerge. Countries where land is at a great premium may have substantial difficulties in duplicating the United States experience in the evolution and diffusion of new retailing systems.

At a somewhat deeper level, the macro study suggested that the stage of evolution of the retail system may play a role in the opportunity to improve productivity. The Japanese system, being at an earlier period in its development and principally small-scale in nature, seems poised for the opportunity to make significant improvements in productivity. The opportunity for the more mature United States system appeared to be significantly less.

An important component of this phenomenon was the role of transaction size. This was measured by per capita income. In Japan, with household income below that in the United States, the expansion of purchasing patterns through larger transactions would have a very substantial impact upon productivity. In effect, the process of growth itself makes available opportunities for greater efficiency at no cost. These opportunities appear to be sharply higher in the earlier stages than in the later.

In the micro studies, several different sets of data on productivity of retail operations subject to varying levels of vertical control were examined. It was hypothesized that those retailers whose activities were more coordinated with supplying agencies would show evidence of greater productivity. This did not appear. In all three cases—supermarkets, insurance agencies, and fast-food restaurants—no significant differences between retail types could be discovered. While evidence of better coordination was to be found, this did not affect output in any measurable way.

In effect, the dominant determinant for the level of output was the quantity of inputs provided. Large-scale units were more productive regardless of whether they were controlled or independent. Hence, when the role of inputs was introduced into the equations, the effect of system type disappeared.

This finding is perhaps the most surprising of the study. Given the contrary logic, and the admittedly rough and limited data bases from which it was derived, it *must be* regarded as highly speculative at this juncture. It also does not take into account the effect of efficiencies at the supplier level. However, it should be regarded seriously despite the poor quality of the data because it seems likely that if the level of control actually does have a powerful effect upon retail productivity, this would have appeared in the analysis.

If the finding proves true, its implications for public policy are substantial. It suggests that public action to reduce vertical control in distribution systems may not entail a loss of retail efficiency. Hence, fear of retail economic penalties need not be a deterrent to the undertaking of such policies.

NOTES AND REFERENCES

1. For a critical review of the literature, see Mattson, Lars-Gunnar. *Integration and Efficiency in Marketing Systems*. Stockholm: The Economic Research Institute at the Stockholm School of Economics, 1969, chapter 7.
2. The concept of the production function is well elaborated in Brown,

Murray. *On the Theory and Measurement of Technological Change.* Cambridge, England: University Press, 1966, chapter 1.

3.   Revzan, David A. *Wholesaling in Marketing Organizations.* New York: John Wiley, 1961, chapter 4.

4.   Grether, E. T. *Price Control Under Fair Trade Legislation.* New York: Oxford University Press, 1939; and Palamountain, Jr., J. C. *The Politics of Distribution.* Cambridge, Mass.: Harvard University Press, 1955.

5.   Hall, Lady Margaret; Knapp, John; and Winsten, Christopher. *Distribution in Great Britain and North America.* London: Oxford University Press, 1961, chapter 4.

6.   National Commission on Food Marketing. *Organization and Competition in Food Retailing.* Technical Study No. 7. Washington: U.S. Government Printing Office, 1966, chapter 16.

7.   Etgar, Michael. "An Empirical Analysis of the Motivation for the Development of Centrally Coordinated Vertical Marketing Systems: The Case of the Property and Casualty Insurance Industry." Doctoral Dissertation, University of California, Berkeley, 1974.

8.   Etgar, p.144.

11

Exploring Relationships between Market Structure and Performance in Retailing

JOHAN ARNDT

Introduction

The retailing literature is dominated by descriptive material on the structure in various industry groups and down-to-earth "how-to" publications for managers. Analytical or theoretical contributions attempting to explain structural changes in retailing are few in number. Notable exceptions are the well-known notion of the "wheel of retailing" proposed by McNair (1958), the in-depth study of the distributive trades by Bucklin (1972), and the book of readings on the economics of retailing by Tucker and Yamey (1973).

This paper reports an attempt to apply the theoretical framework of the so-called industrial organization or market structure approach to retailing. Since the work in this research tradition is well described and evaluated in Caves (1967), Bain (1968), and Scherer (1971), it may suffice for the purpose of this article to summarize: the essence of the approach is that an industry's *market structure* or organization (for instance, as measured by the degree of concentration) determines the *market conduct* or behavior of the firms in the industry. The conduct in turn determines the *performance* or efficiency of the industry. While this approach has revitalized empirical research in the microeconomic area, the analytical framework has so far mainly been applied to manufacturing industries and not to retailing and other distributive trades. Part

237

of the explanation for this neglect lies probably in the economists' general lack of interest in the distributive sector.

The Present Study

The present study was carried out as a part of a larger research project (see Arndt, 1972). The purpose of the study was to explain differences in performance between industry groups (or kind of activity classes) within Norwegian retailing.

The study covers the period 1963 to 1968, a time of substantial changes in retailing in Norway. Until 1963, changes in retailing structure seemed to be small and gradual. After 1963, the introduction and diffusion of new institutions such as supermarkets and department store chains upset the equilibrium and brought about pronounced structural changes.

On the basis of the logic of the structure-conduct-performance scheme, a high degree of seller concentration in an industry group was expected to make for less emphasis on low prices in the marketing mix and more emphasis on nonprice variables such as service. Next, such market conduct was believed to result in less efficiency in the industry. Hence, more seller concentration in an industry group was hypothesized to result in a poorer economic performance from a societal point of view (in this case reflected in higher percentage gross margins and lower increases in labor productivity). In turn, performance was expected to have a feedback effect on structure, in that high margins and smaller pressures for increasing labor productivity would, in the absence of high barriers to entry, attract new establishments into the industry group and/or decrease store mortality.

The postulated relationships are summarized in figure 11–1.

Method

As is often the case in empirical research, it was necessary to make a series of assumptions in order to apply the analytical framework to the available data. Hence, the data base influenced not only the operationalization of the indicators of structure and performance, but also the choice of indicators. The data on retailing were obtained from the following two publications of the Norwegian Central Bureau of Statistics: *Census of Establishments 1963, Volume II. Wholesale and Retail Trade* (1963 is the last year for which data from a complete census of distribution are available) and *Wholesale and Retail Trade Statistics 1968*. In these publications, the basic unit of analysis is the individual *establishment* (or the specific place where business is conducted) rather than the firm. The Central Bureau of Statistics is also the source of the population data.

An important set of assumptions relates to the boundaries of the retail markets to be analyzed. First, building on the thoughts of Caves (1967,

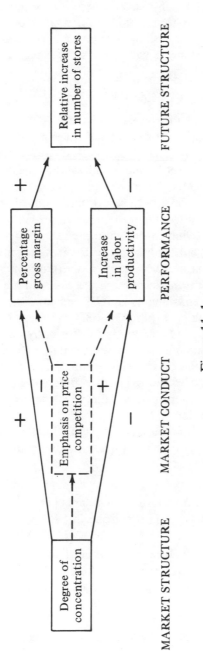

Figure 11-1
Postulated Relationships among the Variables

12), we view the market for a retailing establishment as being spatially defined by the population cluster where the establishment is located. A second assumption is that within each population cluster, competition occurs only among establishments offering fairly close substitute outputs, in this case, establishments within the same main industry group.

DEVELOPMENT OF THE MARKET CONCENTRATION MEASURE

A frequently used measure of structure is the market concentration ratio or the percentage of total industry sales made by the leading four or eight firms. (See Caves, 1967; Bain, 1968; and Scherer, 1971.) In this case, there was no access to data on the sales by the largest retail establishments in the different local markets.

It was therefore necessary to resort to the following indirect procedure. Our substitute measure of degree of concentration was the estimated share of the population living in population clusters large enough to provide room for enough retail establishments to meet the criteria for low concentration. Generalizing rather heroically from empirical findings from American manufacturing industries, the assumed critical point was when the eight largest establishments had 70 percent of the market. (See Caves, 1967, 107, and Bain, 1968, 430–68.) Needless to say, applying this criterion to retailing in Norway may be seriously questioned. It may well be argued that the minimum number of retailers to ensure workable competition would depend on industry group, size of population cluster, consumer buying habits, extent of product differentiation, and other factors. Nevertheless, this criterion was believed to be a rough indicator of the degree of concentration.

The estimation of the share of the population living in competitive areas was carried out in two steps. First, the minimum size of a population cluster was estimated as follows:

$$\text{Average number of inhabitants per establishment in the group in 1963} \times 8 \times \frac{100}{70}$$

Since this formula is based on *average* size of establishments (in terms of number of inhabitants per establishment) instead of on the actual size of the largest establishments, the minimum size of the population clusters is systematically underrated. However, this error should not affect the rank order of the various groups.

Second, using the census data on the percentage of the population living in five different classes of population clusters (based on size of population), it was possible to develop a rough measure of the proportion of the population localized in markets large enough for low concentration.

Table 11–1

Share of Total Market Meeting Minimum Requirement for Low
Concentration in Norwegian Retailing Groups

Industry Group (or subgroup)	Estimated minimum size of the market: number of inhabitants in 1963	Share of population localized in markets of estimated minimum size in 1963 (In percent)
Food, beverages and tobacco (excluding the subgroups Groceries, General stores, and Wines and spirits)	4,700	49
Groceries	6,900	47
General stores	6,400	48
Wines and spirits	665,000	17
Textiles and clothing	8,600	45
Clocks, watches, optical articles, musical instruments, etc.	40,800	29
Medical instruments and pharmaceutical supplies	124,000	25
Books, paper, stationery	44,300	29
Gold and silver ware, leather goods, cosmetics	47,800	29
Furniture and furnishings	19,700	39
Hardware, paints, etc.	22,900	38
Motor vehicles and accessories	46,300	29
Fuel and lubricating oils	19,600	39

The results are shown in table 11–1. The largest and perhaps most heterogeneous group, Food, beverages and tobacco, was divided into four subgroups: Groceries, General stores, Wines and spirits, and the remainder of the main group. Owing to the questionable assumptions in arriving at this measure, the absolute size of the percentage figures in table 11–1 does not mean much. For instance, for Wines and spirits, only the Oslo area would technically meet the criterion for low concentration. Even in Oslo there would be little or no competition since all stores belong to the same state monopoly. Hence, what is of most importance in table 11–1 is the *rank order* of the numbers.

In table 11–2, column 1, the industry groups have been ranked by our rough measure of degree of concentration and classified into three categories. The category *Regulated groups* consists of groups characterized by limited competition either because of direct state ownership (Wines and spirits), direct state control (Medical instruments and pharmaceutical supplies) or direct or indirect control by manufacturers

Table 11-2
Structure and Performance of Industry Groups and Subgroups in Norwegian Retailing
(In percent)

Industry group (or subgroup)	Share of population localized in markets of estimated minimum size in 1963 1	Percentage gross margin in 1963 2	Relative increase in sales per person engaged from 1963 to 1968 3	Relative change in number of stores from 1963 to 1968 4
Low concentration groups		(17.8)	(13)	(– 8.2)
Food, beverages, and tobacco (excluding the subgroups Groceries, General stores, and Wines and spirits)	49	13.3	9	– 14.5
General stores	48	13.7	10	– 7.2
Groceries	47	15.1	25	– 7.1
Textiles and clothing	45	21.2	7	– 4.2
Furniture and furnishings	39	21.3	12	– .1
Hardware, paints, etc.	38	20.7	11	– 4.5
High concentration groups		(27.1)	(14)	(– 2.0)
Clocks, watches, optical articles, musical instruments, etc.	29	32.5	19	1.4
Gold and silver ware, leather goods, cosmetics	29	26.5	15	1.5
Books, paper and petty stationery	29	24.2	10	– 9.0

Regulated groups			
Wines and spirits	30	16.2	19	6.6
Medical instruments and pharmaceutical supplies				
Motor vehicles and accessories				
Fuel and lubricating oils				
All groups		18.0	15	— 6.5

Spearman rank coefficients:

Column 1 and 2	−.85	$p < .01$
Column 1 and 3	−.36	Not significant
Column 2 and 4	.53	$p < .10$
Column 3 and 4	.56	$p < .05$

(Motor vehicles and accessories and Fuel and lubricating oils). Since a ranking within this category would be meaningless, these groups have been represented in table 11–2 by average figures (weighted by sales).

The remaining nine groups were classified as *High concentration groups* if the proportion of the population living in large enough population clusters was less than 30 percent. If the percentage was 30 or higher, the groups were put in the *Low concentration groups* category. Incidentally, as the observant reader may have noted, the ranking in table 11–2, column 1, could have been developed in a more economic manner simply by using number of establishments as criterion. This procedure, however, would have less clear theoretical meaning.

PERFORMANCE MEASURES

The performance measures used were also much influenced by the data situation. Since our first measure, percentage gross margin (operationally defined as total receipts less costs of goods sold and indirect taxes taken as a percentage of total receipts less indirect taxes), includes not only operating costs but also *profits,* the percentage gross margin is a somewhat confounded measure of efficiency, as was pointed out by Hall and Knapp (1973). In order to have a check on the first measure, gains in labor productivity were also measured. The measure was the relative change in sales (in constant Norwegian kroner) per person engaged (owners, other persons in the owners' families working in the store, and employees) from 1963 to 1968.

FUTURE STRUCTURE

The operational definition of this variable was the relative change in number of establishments in the various industry groups (or subgroups) from 1963 to 1968.

Results

As table 11–2 shows, there was a clear tendency for percentage gross margins to increase with concentration. The average gross margin for the *Low concentration groups* category was 17.8 percent compared with 27.1 percent for *High concentration groups.* For the *Regulated groups,* however, the margin was only 16.1 percent. A reason may be the relatively strict public price control and high indirect taxes in these groups, which have not been allowed to take advantage of their monopolistic or oligopolistic positions in margin terms. A less friendly interpretation of the apparent efficiency is the lessened service in the state-controlled stores. The long waiting lines in Norwegian liquor stores are notorious! The Spearman rank correlation coefficient for the relationship between degree of concentration and percentage gross margin was $-.85$ ($p < .01$), which in this case means a positive relationship in apparent support of the hypothesis. However, it should be pointed out that the results may also be explained by the different nature of the "product" in the various industry groups. For instance, it is possible that the high margin groups tended to offer more service than the low margin ones.

For the other performance variable, the results failed to conform to the theoretical expectations as the computed r_s was even negative. Contrary to our hypothesis, the largest gains in labor productivity were found for the *Regulated groups.* A possible reason for this unexpected pattern may be that the demand for the products carried by the stores in this category expanded much more rapidly during this period than was the case for most other groups. Even so, it is clear that high barriers to entry did not result in slower growth in labor productivity.

Finally, the relative change in number of stores from 1963 to 1968 is shown in column 4 in table 11–2. In general, there was a tendency for the store population to decrease. The mortality was particularly important in the *Low concentration groups* (8.2 percent). In the *High concentration groups,* the figure was somewhat smaller. In the *Regulated groups,* however, there was a net increase. This store expansion may have been a response to the increase in the demand for the categories of goods in question. The correlation of this variable with percentage gross margin was .53, which was in the expected direction, without reaching the .05 level of significance. For the other performance variable, gain in labor productivity, the result was significant ($r_s = .56, p < .05$), though in the wrong direction.

Discussion

The study did discover some linkage between the degree of concentration in industry groups in retailing and performance, and between performance and future structure. While the results tended to be in harmony with the theoretical expectations when the performance variable was percentage gross margin, the tendencies uncovered were not consistently strong. Moreover, alternative explanations (that is, explanations not involving market structure variables) cannot be ruled out. For the other performance variable, increase in labor productivity, the results were contrary to the initial expectations.

The ambiguity of the results is no doubt partly a consequence of the somewhat "opportunistic" research strategy chosen. As the study had to be based on secondary data, theoretical adequacy of the indicators chosen and their operational definitions had to some extent to be sacrificed for accessibility of data.

In retrospect, our hypotheses also seem to be too naive and simplistic. The better-than-average performance of the *Regulated groups* category suggests that low concentration is neither a sufficient nor a necessary condition for a satisfactory productive and allocative efficiency. If we are to gain deeper insight into how firms respond to different forms of public regulation and control, there seems to be no alternative to making explicit measurement of conduct variables through in-depth studies of intrafirm decision processes to adapt to changes in their task environment. Such a "behavioristic" approach would mean a merging between the relevant part of organizational theory and traditional industrial organization theory.

REFERENCES

1. Arndt, Johan. *Norsk Detaljhandel Frem Til 1980*. Oslo: Johan Grundt Tanum Forlag, 1972.
2. Bain, Joe S. *Industrial Organization*. 2d ed. New York: John Wiley and Sons, 1968.
3. Bucklin, Louis P. *Competition and Evolution in the Distributive Trades*. Englewood Cliffs, New Jersey: Prentice-Hall, 1972.
4. Caves, Richard. *American Industry: Structure, Conduct, Performance*. 2d ed. Englewood Cliffs: Prentice-Hall, 1967.
5. Central Bureau of Statistics of Norway. *Census of Establishments 1963, Volume II. Wholesale and Retail Trade*. Oslo, 1967.
6. Central Bureau of Statistics of Norway. *Wholesale and Retail Trade Statistics 1968*. Oslo, 1972.
7. Hall, M., and Knapp, J. "Gross Margins and Efficiency Measurement in Retail Trade." In Tucker, K. A., and Yamey, B. S. (below), pp. 242–57.
8. McNair, Malcolm P. "Significant Trends and Developments in the Postwar Period." In Smith, A. B. (ed.) *Competitive Distribution in a Free, High-Level Economy and Its Implication for the University*. Pittsburgh: University of Pittsburgh Press, 1958, pp.1–25.
9. Scherer, F. M. *Industrial Market Structure and Economic Performance*. Chicago: Rand McNally and Company, 1971.
10. Tucker, K. A., and Yamey, B. S. (eds.). *Economics of Retailing*. Harmondsworth, Middlesex: Penguin Books, 1973.

PART FOUR

Organization and Interorganization
Structure, Strategy, and Performance

12

Saving an Organization from a Stagnating Environment

WILLIAM H. STARBUCK AND BO L. T. HEDBERG

Three central points summarize this paper. First, the fact that an organization finds itself in what it perceives to be a deteriorating, stagnating environment tells us a great deal about the organization but little about environmental potentialities. Second, an organization rarely, if ever, solves a realistic problem. Third, extracting an organization from a stagnating environment frequently requires replacing its leadership.

These conclusions are based on several case studies by Hedberg (1973, 1974) and by Miller and Mintzberg (1974), but a single case is used here for illustration.

Facit AB was formed in 1922 and grew into a large, profitable, multinational company. By 1970, Facit employed about 14,000 people in manufacturing and selling business machines, computers, and office furnishings. Although based primarily in Sweden, the organization manufactured products in 20 cities in five countries, operated sales companies in 15 countries, and owned six Swedish subsidiaries. Suddenly, profits became losses, and the stockholders' shares plunged to 30 percent of their former price. Technological changes had eroded Facit's competitive position; decreasing sales and mounting financial problems threatened thousands of jobs. Consultants were called in, and executives were reassigned again and again—all to no avail. Drastic cutbacks seemed the only recourse (Hedberg, 1974).

How Success Can Ruin an Organization

Many an organization finds itself in Facit's predicament: an environ-

249

ment the organization sees as benevolent unexpectedly and rapidly deteriorates into a morass of insurmountable problems. How and why this happens will only be outlined here, because two papers have already been written on the topic (Hedberg, Nystrom, and Starbuck, 1976; Nystrom, Hedberg, and Starbuck, 1976).

An organization's immediate environmental situation is far from being an immutable state of nature dictated by external forces. It is a habitat the organization partly creates by selecting geographic locations, technologies, product lines, legal structure, suppliers, and employees. It is also partly constructed through cooperative agreements, research, capital expenditures, advertising, education, and employment policies (Starbuck, 1976).

After the initial, creative selection and construction of the environment, interaction with it tends to become stylized; the organization sets up behavior programs that promote habitual responses to expected cues. Behavior programs enable an organization to act consistently in ways its members and its external associates expect; programs conserve creative resources by eliminating hunts for new responses to familiar situations. However, these programs can seduce an organization into misperceiving situations and acting inappropriately. Because situations appear equivalent as long as they can be handled by the same programs, programs remain in use after the situations they fit have faded away. When new situations are at last recognized, the first response is to try out programs already in the behavioral repertoire; efforts to invent new, appropriate behaviors do not start until the old behavioral repertoire has been clearly shown to be inadequate.

Moreover, because nearly all of the cues that trigger programs originate outside an organization, because reorientations nearly always derive from reassessing small parts of the behavioral repertoire, because superficial impressions and erroneous information can strongly influence unprogrammed choices, and because an organization has special difficulty in appraising its inadequacies and incompetences—for all these reasons, remedial efforts are often haphazard (Bell, 1974; Mintzberg, 1972; Normann, 1971; Starbuck, 1976; Wildavsky, 1972). Successive choices contradict one another, good alternatives are overlooked or rejected by mistake, pursued alternatives turn out to be undesirable or impractical.

Continued success incubates potential failure, by increasing an organization's dependence on its programs (Cyert and March, 1963; Miller and Mintzberg, 1974; Thompson, 1967). Ideologies spring up around programs' past efficacy, and today's activities are expected to conform to traditions (Clark, 1972). Plans are founded on programs' apparent capabilities, and planning becomes the dominant method for organizational coordination. Communication channels lose versatility, and the practices for observing environmental happenings grow insensitive to the unusual.

Thus, the successful organization gradually loses touch with present realities, gathers behavioral inertia, and risks disaster by inadvertently choosing or creating a future situation that verges on stagnation. Social and technological changes are not seen, are underestimated, or are interpreted as combatable threats; obsolescence accumulates, developing opportunities are not pursued, and no efforts are made to beget desirable opportunities.

Of course, opportunities can be created if not enough exist: a stagnating environment is a pathological illusion that an organization inflicts on itself. There are two reasons an organization finds itself in an environment that it perceives to be predominantly stagnating. Defective managerial practices make the organization somewhat more insensitive and lethargic than other organizations are—in part, because it has enjoyed success. It is also unlucky; many organizations are saved from stagnating environments by forces beyond their control.

When an organization first notices that environmental benevolence appears to have vanished, no serious thought is given to the idea that these changes might be permanent. Rather, the hard times are perceived as transient challenges that can be met by temporary expedients that will leave no long-run scars. The expedients emphasize cost cutting: marginal activities are excised, investments and postponable expenses stop, budgets tighten, and control is centralized. Moreover, the initial diagnoses describe what is wrong very superficially. Formal reports, such as accounting statements, become the primary sources of analytic information, and superficial analyses lead to superficial remedies. For example, cash shortages often induce an organization to sell its most readily marketable assets.

Temporary expedients usually succeed for a time, but this success creates long-run disadvantages. An organization in a stagnating environment ultimately cannot escape the fact that environmental benevolence will not return all by itself. Yet even after this fact has been acknowledged, the organization remains unable to generate appropriate, new behaviors, because old ways of behaving must be unlearned before new behavioral modes can be adopted.

Unlearning begins when temporary measures are taken to meet the supposedly transient challenge: subunits quarrel, people lose confidence in their leaders, opportunism undercuts long-run aspirations, and personally satisfying activities cease. Later, the threat of organizational failure accelerates unlearning. Job assignments and leaders are shifted around; there is no longer agreement about the organization's proper domain and its most effective strategies; and the organization's weak financial position fosters more conflict—only a few experiments can be tried, and they must come at the expense of existing activities.

Unfortunately, it is nearly impossible for an organization to boot-strap itself out of this situation. The organization accumulated enough defects so that it drifted unawares into a stagnating environment. Then, the responses to stagnation centralized control, emphasized reliance on the routine programs that had succeeded in the past, used up flexible resources, and drove away entrepreneurial, imaginative personnel. The stresses of unlearning bred hostilities and eroded the will to experiment.

Facit AB followed these typical patterns. The company succeeded consistently throughout the forties, fifties, and sixties. From 1962 to 1970 alone, employment rose 70 percent, and sales and profits more than doubled. New products, including a line of electronic computers, were launched, and mergers added more products and more sales locations.

However, an observer with hindsight can see that difficulties had begun to appear by 1967: a few hundred employees were laid off, and gross profits almost halved. Facit's 1967 annual report explained that currency devaluations and a "tough economic climate" had caused passing problems, but "Facit is well equipped to meet future competition. . . . Improvement is under way, but has not affected this year's outcome."

The annual reports through the late sixties spoke time and again of the fierceness of market competition, of the risks and uncertainties associated with new ventures, and of the company's satisfactory liquidity.

Facit appeared to do well in 1968 and 1969, more than regaining the ground lost in 1967. A performance peak, by statistical measures, was reached in 1969 or 1970. Then began three years of losses: employment and sales decreased each successive year, and gross profits were consistently negative. During 1970, the marketing organization was reorganized twice, the managing director was replaced, a ban was put on white-collar hiring, and a department was set up to do long-range planning. In 1971 layoffs began in earnest, and the managing director was replaced again. Each new managing director announced that the company's past performance had actually been worse than had been publicly portrayed; then he predicted a rosy future. Every Swedish operation except the typewriter division reported losses in 1971.

In 1972 Facit's director of engineering, who also directed the typewriter division, resigned. The production manager and marketing manager exchanged jobs. Several small plants were closed, the main plant making office furnishings was sold, and efforts to sell a mechanical-calculator subsidiary failed. The company stopped manufacturing voting machines after the Swedish government cancelled a large order because Facit's machines did not satisfy quality specifications. A 60 percent increase in the number of products was planned and announced. McKinsey & Company were hired, ostensibly to find a new managing director. The consultants actually advised extensive retrenchments: 2400 people should be fired, some operations should be closed, and costs should be cut. An executive from another firm was asked to become the managing director and to act on the consultants' report, but he refused the position.

In October 1972, Facit was sold to Electrolux AB.

Why an Organization Rarely Solves Real Problems

Facit, like other organizations in stagnating environments, could not solve its strategic problems with the people who were then in the organization. In fact, it is improbable that Facit could even state its problems realistically. Every organization in a stagnating environment suffers from unrealistic perceptions and from a deficiency of perceptual capacities. The organization sees its problems as arising from its environment, not from its own perceptions, methods, and people; and, at least at first, it sees the key problem as being merely a transient challenge. Facit's top management, for example, repeatedly announced that the firm was sound and an upturn was imminent. Indeed, the chairman of the board and the managing director issued such announcements only two days before Facit was sold; the top-management group probably believed these announcements voiced unrealistic hopes, but other personnel may have found the announcements credible.

The perceptions of an organization in a stagnating environment are unusual only in the degree of error, not in the kind. Almost every organization, nearly all of the time, fails to identify realistically the problems it confronts. An organization's top management develops a characteristic world view that is shared by many lower-level personnel: this world view dictates what phenomena the organization will try to perceive and what phenomena it will ignore; then when happenings are perceived, the world view determines how they are interpreted. In particular, the world view shapes top management's conceptions of environmental phenomena.

Because the world view grows out of past experiences, it is partly inconsistent with the present and future. Today's happenings are not perceived or are misinterpreted; projections into tomorrow are warped fantasies.

The misperceptions are increased and amplified when an organization relies more and more on its past successes. In an organization in a stagnating environment, top management's world view relies so heavily on past experiences that, ultimately, the top management group sees the environment as inexorably deteriorating: social and technological changes are seen only as threats to stability, new opportunities are neglected because they are not recognized, and the possibility of migration to new environmental niches is dismissed as impractical. But every organization overlooks most opportunities and resists most innovations, because events are seldom correctly interpreted and accommodated unless they have obvious precedents and they make sense in the context of top management's world view.

A more fundamental issue is how useful it is to analyze an organization as a problem-solving system. Admittedly, an organization does perceive some problems, and it does generate actions that it calls solutions to problems. However, it is extremely rare for an organization to start by stating a problem, then to generate potential actions solely because they might solve this problem, and finally to choose a course of action solely because it appears the best solution to the stated problem. An organization ordinarily generates potential actions without the stimulus of specific problems, just because an organization is designed to generate actions. Generated actions become potential solutions on the ground that they appear to be good actions—they are consistent with past behaviors, they resemble what other organizations are doing, they use underutilized capacities and talents, or they are fun. An organization then adopts potential solutions for multiple reasons—partly because they may solve a perceived problem, partly because they are good actions, and partly because they may solve more than one problem and may bring more than one kind of benefit. Problems may not be perceived until a potential solution suggests their existence (Cohen, March, and Olsen, 1972).

Perhaps an organization ought to be regarded as an action generator in which nearly all actions have little to do with actual problems. Most actions are generated by behavior programs that are quite loosely associated with the perceived situation, and the situation is erroneously perceived. Those situational elements that get labeled as problems strongly resemble the nonproblematic elements. Superficial and incomplete rationalizations mate problems with actions that are then called solutions.

Facit's behaviors illustrate how independent problem-perceiving processes are from action-generating processes. Technological changes were stimulating proposals for new actions early in the 1960s. Especially relevant, in view of later developments, were proposals that Facit gain expertise in electronics and adopt less labor-intensive manufacturing techniques. But these sensible proposals were not accepted. Undoubtedly, the rationale was that these proposals did not mate with perceived problems: Facit's top managers shared a world view that screened out many of the signals that new kinds of challenges and opportunities were arising. They evidently saw the business-machines industry as being based on slowly evolving production technologies and product lines, but marked by fierce price competition, and they acted on this mistaken perception by investing heavily in specialized capital equipment. For example, the 1969 annual report implied that Facit had already made enough major changes in product lines to carry the company into the 1980s, and it expressed confidence that sales of mechanical calculators would continue to increase.

One exception to this general lethargy was a 1965 agreement to develop electronic calculators and computers in cooperation with the Sharp Corporation; this venture was probably a less-than-enthusiastic hedge against unforeseen events. The year 1965 also brought a merger with Addo AB, a company with mechanical calculators as its major products. It is significant that this merger was primarily financial; not until after crises began developing in the early 1970s did Facit attempt to integrate Addo's management, production facilities, or marketing network with its own. This pattern typified Facit's handling of mergers and acquisitions: new components were appended to the existing organization but not integrated with it, so the top management's world view was no more than minimally disrupted.

This world view remained fundamentally unaltered through the turbulent early 1970s. Signs of technological change abounded, but were so inimical to Facit's established world view that top management could not sensibly interpret most of them.

Confusion, distrust, and indecision resulted. Official statements denying that Facit faced serious problems were interspersed with statements showing that extremely difficult problems would have to be solved. When an edition of the company newsletter was cancelled in December 1971, one of the executives publicly explained: "It is no use spending money on a newsletter that cannot give complete information anyhow." External interest groups and Facit's employees, including managers, grew skeptical of top management's credibility and judgment, and started depending instead on the pessimistic interpretations of Facit's situation being presented by the news media. As management's statements became increasingly erratic and were contradicted time and again by actual events, even the top managers began to doubt their own ability to perceive problems, and turned to outside sources, such as the news media and McKinsey & Company, for analyses of Facit's problems and prospects. The executives fought bitterly among themselves, lost confidence that they could generate successful actions, and finally, lost their willingness to act: despite numerous meetings, the board of directors could not decide whether Facit should carry out the retrenchments that McKinsey & Company had recommended. The board invited an executive from another firm to take over as the managing director and to decide whether Facit should retrench further.

Top management's incomprehension of events also turned Facit's environment into a hostile and burdensome place. Capital equipment bought in the mid-1960s had become obsolete by 1970. Because Facit was the major industrial firm in several communities, and virtually the only industry in the community where its headquarters were located, the top managers felt strongly committed to maintaining high levels of employment in these communities: they rejected actions that would make production less labor-intensive and avoided experiments that might turn out to be unemployment-producing mistakes. Community politicians, also recoiling from the spectre of mass unemployment, publicly criticized Facit's management and solicited an intervention by Sweden's Minister of Industry. The news media, both mass-circulation media and business and financial media, expressed increasing skepticism about the official statements of Facit's management and increasing doubts about the company's prospects. Had Facit executives been seeking outside capital, they would have found potential lenders suspicious. The top management were actually seeking new owners for Facit; after the company was sold, the chairman of the board admitted: "We would have sold Facit earlier if there had been a serious buyer."

Why Many Top-Management Heads Have To Roll

Within a week after Electrolux took full control, Facit's chief executives were evicted, and responsibilities for Facit's operations were distributed among the top management of Electrolux. Electrolux's managing director explained: "Facit means a 30 percent increase of Electrolux's sales volume. There is no need to add an extra management group just because a company grows 30 percent in one year."

These evictions were probably essential if Facit was to be turned around. When an organization is floundering ineffectually in a stagnating environment, sweeping replacement of top management frequently becomes a prerequisite for recovery.

The reasons top management has to be replaced follow almost automatically from the definition of a stagnating environment as a pathological illusion that is seen when managerial practices are riddled with extreme defects. A less defective organization would maintain more realism, would perceive sooner the need for strategic reorientations that are not merely temporary expedients, and would mend some of its own defects. In a less defective organization, the top management would take responsibility for identifying or constructing more viable environmental situations. However, in an organization in a stagnating environment, nearly all of the top-management group deny the existence of hope: messages are not comprehended if they describe opportunities or if they contradict major tenets of the generally held world view; centralized controls and the lack of flexible resources drive away entrepreneurs; repeated failures discourage optimists; conflicts over what is to be done multiply until they block action and reinforce the conviction that all actions will fail. Of course, actions are likely to fail if they are chosen by people who do not understand their world. When individuals are replaced in such a collegial group, the group being left largely intact, the newcomers obtain guidance from their experienced colleagues, and soon learn to think in the group's characteristic mode.

If it is to succeed, a turn-around must begin by destroying this atmosphere of hopelessness and discarding the world view that led to it. Since both are embodied in the organization's people, especially in its top management, the top management as a group must be replaced. The new group can safely retain only the deviant executives who did not accept their colleagues' world view.

The managing director of Electrolux immediately began speaking of

Facit's opportunities, and news media published the following quotations from the managing director during the first month after the sale. "I am optimistic. Electrolux grew 25 percent in 1971; the purchase opens new opportunities. Facit's excess capacity can be utilized for other purposes. ... We were attracted by Facit's know-how. A good bargain for both organizations. ... Fewer people will be fired than originally planned. ... We are going to move fast. McKinsey did a good job, but there is more to be gained. There are more opportunities. ... We have already studied Facit's organization abroad. The customers are coming back to us."

Because of their similarity to the optimistic pronouncements that Facit's top management made intermittently before the sale, the new managing director's statements must have been received skeptically. Actions —successful actions—were the only way to make the statements credible. But the new top management did deliver success. The parent company advanced 10 million kronor (roughly 2 million dollars) to finance new developments and to reduce the need to act solely out of financial exigency. Eight hundred employees were laid off initially; not only was this well below the 2400 lay-offs recommended by McKinsey & Company, but Facit started rehiring the laid-off employees within three months' time. A mechanical-calculator plant was converted to typewriters, other typewriter plants were expanded, and typewriter production tripled in six months. Sales of office furnishings also increased. Facit's research laboratories and the joint venture with the Sharp Corporation had developed electronic calculators, mini-computers, and computer terminals that now were put into production and aggressively marketed; the new Facit discovered substantial demands for these products. The Swedish government was persuaded to replace the withdrawn orders for voting machines.

Stories about Facit disappeared from the news media by the last quarter of 1973. A gross profit was reported for 1973, and the company had begun earning a net profit by September 1974, less than two years after the sale. During the last half of 1973 and the first half of 1974, employment increased 10 percent, and production rose 25 percent; exports increased from 20 percent of sales to 30 percent; sales of office furnishings exceeded the production capacity.

A newspaper story in September 1974 observed: "The surprised employees have witnessed how fresh money has been pumped into the operations. Although everything looks different today, the company is still more or less managed by the same people who were in charge of the company during the sequence of crises. It is now very difficult to find enough people to recruit to the factories. ... All the present products emanate from the former Facit organization, but still, the situation has changed drastically."

Although Facit had benefited from a general economic upturn, different attitudes were the main reasons the environmental situation had changed drastically. Facit's personnel had embraced a new world view that showed them a new world to explore, and this new world was filled with meetable challenges instead of frightening threats. Electrolux's managing director explained: "We have a more powerful hammer to hit on suppliers who fail to deliver. . . . There were many excess costs to cut down. . . . Hard competition is a challenge; there is no reason to withdraw."

However, it was a trade union official who best expressed the essence of Facit's attitudinal transformation. He said: "It is again fun to work."

REFERENCES

1. Bell, Gerald D. "Organizations and the External Environment." In McGuire, Joseph W. (ed.). *Contemporary Management: Issues and Viewpoints.* Englewood Cliffs, N.J.: Prentice-Hall, 1974, pp.259–82.
2. Clark, Burton R. "The Organizational Saga in Higher Education," *Administrative Science Quarterly,* Vol. 17, 1972, pp.178–84.
3. Cohen, Michael D.; March, James G.; and Olsen, Johan P. "A Garbage Can Model of Organizational Choice," *Administrative Science Quarterly,* Vol. 17, 1972, pp.1–25.
4. Cyert, Richard M., and March, James G. *A Behavioral Theory of the Firm.* Englewood Cliffs, N.J.: Prentice-Hall, 1963.
5. Hedberg, Bo L. T. *Organizational Stagnation and Choice of Strategy.* Working paper, International Institute of Management, Berlin, 1973.
6. Hedberg, Bo L. T. *Reframing as a Way to Cope with Organizational Stagnation: A Case Study.* Working paper, Preprint I/74–71, International Institute of Management, Berlin, 1974.
7. Hedberg, Bo L. T.; Nystrom, Paul C.; and Starbuck, William H. "Camping on Seesaws: Prescriptions for a Self-Designing Organization," *Administrative Science Quarterly,* Vol. 21, 1976, pp.41–65.
8. Miller, Danny, and Mintzberg, Henry. *Strategy Formulation in Context: Some Tentative Models.* Working paper, McGill University, 1974.
9. Mintzberg, Henry. *Research on Strategy-Making.* Working paper, McGill University, 1972.
10. Normann, Richard. "Organizational Innovativeness: Product Variation and Reorientation," *Administrative Science Quarterly,* Vol. 16, 1971, pp.203–15.
11. Nystrom, Paul C.; Hedberg, Bo L. T.; and Starbuck, William H. "Interacting Processes as Organizational Designs." Forthcoming in Kilmann, R. H.; Pondy, L. R.; and Slevin, D. P. (eds.). *The Management of Organization Design.* New York: American Elsevier, 1976.
12. Starbuck, William H. "Organizations and Their Environments." In Dunnette, Marvin D. (ed.). *Handbook of Industrial and Organizational Psychology.* Chicago: Rand McNally, 1976.
13. Thompson, James D. *Organizations in Action.* New York: McGraw-Hill, 1967.
14. Wildavsky, Aaron. "The Self-Evaluating Organization," *Public Administration Review,* Vol. 32, 1972, pp.509–20.

COMMENTS ON THE ESSAY
BY WILLIAM H. STARBUCK AND BO L. T. HEDBERG

Paul J. Gordon

Three points summarize this response. There is great merit in the proposition that in firms apparently troubled by stagnating environments the world view held by top managers is at fault. The proposition that organizations rarely solve realistic problems probably needs closer definition of the concepts of problem, reality, and objectivity. The proposition that extracting an organization from a stagnating environment requires replacing its leadership is more equivocal.

The first proposition might be further developed by considering the uses and the limits of a world view; studying companies that are more and less successful in restructuring their world view, their radar, and their strategy; and enlarging the sample for illustration beyond one case. The second proposition correctly points up both the institutional readiness to choose familiar action programs that "solve" other items at the same time, and the tendency to let opportunities and problems go either unrecognized or misapprehended. Perhaps it should have been noted that neither problems, nor reality, nor objectivity has any self-proclaiming signals or empirical referents to assure that one is on target.

As for the third proposition, the case is well argued that somehow the world view must be changed and that this cannot be done by sacking or rotating one or two top people. It is clearer, however, that the world view must be changed than that changing the leadership will do it.

The remaining question for the case illustration is whether both world view and environment were changed when the whole enterprise was re-potted. The continuing question is how to assure changing mental sets and radar screens for apparently successful companies while they are still enjoying success.

13

Structural Correlates of the Environment

JOHANNES M. PENNINGS

The research and debate on the environment-organization relationship has moved to a central place in organizational theory. It is commonly believed that organizations are influenced by their environments and that they must be tuned in to their environments to ensure their optimal effectiveness. The implication is that for a given type of environment a particular structure is appropriate. Thompson's (1967) widely quoted book heralded a new perspective in which organizations are viewed as open systems subject to environmental influences—a perspective rather different from the traditional practice of prescribing or endorsing an ideal universal type of organizational structure. It is the consonance between environmental and organizational structure that is crucial in explaining variance in organizational effectiveness.

In this paper some of the most relevant literature on the environment-organization research will be discussed. Whether it can be said that the goodness of fit between organizations and their environments influences effectiveness may depend on how effectiveness is defined. Therefore, this paper also examines the implications of the environment-organization research for understanding organizational effectiveness. The paper will report on selected investigations in order to highlight the present state of affairs.

Environment

Research on the environment-organization relationship is being conducted on two levels. Most of the research takes the organization as the focus and defines and examines the environment in relation to the focal organization. Empirical research conducted on this level usually involves having respondents rate the environment or its components on one or more attributes (e.g., Dill, 1958; Lawrence and Lorsch, 1967; and Duncan, 1971). Even when such subjective data are replaced or supplemented by objective data, there is still the tendency to define and to measure the environment from the perspective of individuals in the focal organization. A formal conceptualization is Evan's (1972) *organization set,* which is defined as all organizations with which the focal organization has some exchange of resources and information. Thorelli's *ecosystem* (1968, see chapter 14 of this volume) is a similar attempt to define the boundaries and content of the organizational environment. The ecosystem comprises the focal organization and its relevant environment; the relevant environment includes parent organizations (if any), suppliers, customers, competitors, and the general economic and social conditions of the society in which the focal organization is chartered.

More recently there have been attempts to define environment by moving from the level of the focal organization to the next higher level of aggregation. At this level we find such concepts as the population of organizations, or, more concretely, industry and market, or their noneconomic analogs (e.g., Hannon and Freeman, 1976; Pennings, 1976; Hirsch, 1975; and Aldrich, 1975). In studies on this level (e.g., Pfeffer, 1972; Hirsch, 1975) the population is part of the environment of each of its constitutive organizations and its characteristics can be used to describe part of the organizational environment from a different perspective. For any organization, inputs and outputs are interrelated (Mohr, 1973) although organizations that compete for inputs do not necessarily compete for outputs. Organizations acquire different kinds of resources (raw materials, capital, personnel, etc.) to make different products or services and thus may have several sets of competitors.

When dealing with the issue of structural correlates of the environment, it is important to distinguish two levels of analysis. If the information is gathered from the perspective of the focal organization, the environment can be construed *as a set of contingencies.* These contingencies are perceived by the firm and impinge on its behavior. The terms *organization set* and *ecosystem* are formal attempts to locate the origins of environmental contingencies with which the focal organization has to cope. These terms are good heuristic devices. It is our own view, however, that they cannot be viewed as "a system" since they do not have a collective structure.

On the second level of analysis—from the standpoint of the industry group instead of one firm—the environment can be seen as a *political economy.* Environment as a political economy is illustrated by a market/industry but also by bilateral oligopolies to which one could apply Leontief's input-output algorithm for describing interorganizational relationships. In such settings there does often exist a collective structure, a pattern of communication and coordination that is continuously reinforced by "political" devices such as self-regulation, interlocking directorates, and conspiracies—hence the label "political economy." This notion of environment is less pertinent for some organizations, for example, nonprofit organizations or firms in a market with very low entry barriers.

Environment and Uncertainty

Organizations depend on their environment for both resources and informational exchanges. In these exchange relationships organizations are confronted with various degrees of uncertainty. Uncertainty seems to be the most salient and all-encompassing attribute of the environment. The literature also recognizes other attributes such as complexity, turbulence or instability, resourcefulness, and competitiveness; but these can be subsumed under the more generic concept of uncertainty.

Uncertainty arises from incomplete information, randomness, or unpredictability of events. In markets where the degree of uncertainty is always high, the organization must be equipped structurally to cope with it. Lawrence and Lorsch (1967), Galbraith (1972), Duncan (1972), and Hunt (1970) are a few of the many authors who explicitly or implicitly have focused on uncertainty. Uncertainty, and other terms conveying a similar meaning (e.g., instability, variability), are used to point to those aspects of the environment that are considered essential in the explanation of structural differences between organizations. Hunt (1970), for example, sees in the work of Burns and Stalker (1961) and Woodward (1965) a parallel with the cybernetic models of Miller et al. (1960).

In Miller's frame of reference the notion of plan is central. The term *plan* defines a process that controls the sequence of a set of operations. Information (environmental signals) is received by the human performance system. If the information is compatible with an available plan, the plan is put in operation. If the performance feedback indicates satisfactory outcomes, the system continues to the next stage; if problems emerge a less routine search process is initiated. It is such reasoning that underlies most research and debate on interorganizational structural variations as a function of uncertainty. Within the present context environment can be construed as a set of stimuli having a certain configuration that must be matched (or has been matched) with plans of action.

The affinity of such a definition with the notion of uncertainty in information theory is evident. The environment is conceived as a source or a set of sources relaying messages with a certain probability of occurrence. The probability of occurrence is inversely related to the amount of information released. This approach toward environmental uncertainty is illustrated in the papers of Duncan (1971), Galbraith (1972), Pennings (1975), and Bernhardt and MacKenzie (1968). The first three deal with environment as a set of contingencies while the last describes environment as a political economy. Earlier we have defined these two levels of analysis. On the first level the uncertainty is operationalized in terms of number of types of customers, raw materials, distribution of different categories of transaction (e.g., Pennings, 1975), variety of inputs (Perrow, 1972), unpatterned variability in quality and quantity of inputs or outputs (Hinings et al., 1974), number of elements relevant for decision making (Galbraith, 1972), and randomness and clusteredness (Emery and Trist, 1965).

On the higher level of analysis Bernhardt and MacKenzie explicitly take information uncertainty to describe different types of political economy and mechanisms for uncertainty reduction (e.g., market segmentation and product differentiation). In this case customers and competitors constitute information messages.

We should caution, however, that there are environmental uncertainties that cannot be expressed as continuous probability distributions. Becker and Baloff (1969) tried to expand the uncertainty idea by creating and measuring environmental conditions that require both the identification of a number of plans of action and the choice among them of the most appropriate alternative (e.g., predicting food demands for variable football game crowds to purchase food quantities). March and Simon (1958) describe a somewhat similar thinking when they stress both the number of alternatives and their variable degrees of attractiveness. Such environments are ill-defined situations requiring unusual or novel uses of information and the flexibility to see things in different ways. Becker and Baloff found that such environmental uncertainty in combination with organizational structure has strong predictive power with respect to effectiveness. There is less predictive power if the uncertainty is merely information uncertainty.

In survey studies of individual organizations we have failed thus far to develop precise and valid definitions. Rather frequently, the uncertainty is imputed from questionnaire items asking, for example, the length of time to think through to solve a problem (Perrow, 1970), the specificity of feedback and the speed of feedback (Lawrence and Lorsch, 1967), and perceived environmental uncertainty (Duncan, 1972). Hickson et al. (1971) even go so far as to state that uncertainty can be imputed from the degree of bureaucratization, because of the preponderance of programmed activities in those organizations, which emphasize formal, standardized procedures and a rigid, hierarchical communication and authority structure. That is, the degree of bureaucratization has predictive validity for environmental uncertainty, since highly bureaucratic organizations tend to exist in environments with little unpatterned variability in input acquisition or output disposal. It seems more correct, however, to treat such aspects of bureaucratization as correlates of the environment, rather than as indicators of environment.

On the level of industry there have also been conceptualizations of uncertainty that deviate from the concept of information uncertainty. The concept of oligopoly or market structure is particularly useful. Pfeffer (1972) has proposed to take the deviation from "average" concentration as a measure of industry uncertainty. The previously mentioned entropy measure used by Bernhardt and MacKenzie (1968) suggests that the lower the degree of concentration the greater the uncertainty. However, if the number of competing organizations is large enough so that pure competition exists, the encounter between buyers and sellers acquires a probabilistic character. The parameters of market (industry or nonprofit analog) become constant and the environmental events have a stochastic nature. Therefore, Pfeffer argues, the relationship between concentration and uncertainty is U-shaped. Industries or markets with intermediate degrees of concentration belong to an environment that is more difficult to predict. The activities of firms have a volitional, potentially variable character. Knowledge about probable events is relatively deficient. For example, one of the competing organizations may secretly fail to conform to collusive agreements; an oligopolistic supplier may suddenly modify its sales policies, etc. Apart from concentration one should also observe the size distribution of organizations. The industry (market) uncertainty may be a function of the organization's relative size within a certain size distribution; it is at this point that disaggregation becomes essential.

Summarizing, two global ways of defining environment have been identified. In both frameworks the concept of uncertainty stands out. Organizations must cope with this uncertainty to ensure their effectiveness.

Environmental Uncertainty and Structure

While Miller et al. (1960) dealt with human problem solving, the very same thinking has been applied to organizational behavior. Burns and Stalker (1961) developed a crude dichotomy of organizational structure, distinguishing between mechanistic and organic structure. Hickson (1966) has shown that this typology shows a high degree of convergence with many others, even though they may employ different terms. He uses the term *role specificity;* roles are well specified in mechanistic structures but not in organic structures. Burns and Stalker claimed that changing environments require an organic structure while stable environments tend to be associated with mechanistic structures. Galbraith (1972) and Becker and Baloff (1969) were more explicit in viewing organizations as information-processing systems. They stress that uncertainty strongly impels an organization to decentralize and to de-emphasize rules and formal procedures.

Most of the research on environmental uncertainty and structure has been done at the single-organization level. Rigorous research on the higher level of market or industry has been relatively scarce (e.g., Pfeffer, 1972; Khandwalla, 1974), but a number of insightful case studies do exist. However, on both levels there is an inclination to adopt the theorizing with respect to environmental uncertainty and structure.

Some Empirical Results

I. This author has tried to investigate the structural correlates of the environment by studying 40 brokerage offices. The study tried to determine whether there are structural differences between these offices that are due to differences in their environments (Pennings, 1975). This study exemplifies the first level of analysis, examining environment from the focal organization's perspective.

The data for this research were collected in 40 widely dispersed offices of a U.S. brokerage firm dealing in securities and commodities. Each office had been assigned a sales territory; its performance was measured in terms of commission earned. The size of the offices varied from 34 to 141 employees.

Information collected from these offices included both subjective and objective data. Objective data were from company records and census information about standard metropolitan areas. Subjective data were obtained from questionnaires. The questionnaire measures of environmental and structural variables were aggregated to obtain means for each office.

The *environmental indicators* included the following:

Resourcefulness—the affluence of individuals living in the office's territory

Complexity—differentiation of the environment with respect to income sources

Quality of organizational intelligence

Environmental uncertainty as measured by four questionnaire items

Environmental turbulence as measured by four questionnaire items

Number of competing organizations

Demand volatility—fluctuations in transactions within each office

Feedback specificity about past performance

The *organization structure variables* included the following:

Horizontal and lateral communication

Participation in decision making

Frequency of formal meetings

Slope and total amount of power distribution (see Tannenbaum, 1968)

Specialization—dissimilarity in skill mixes among brokers

Cohesiveness—sense of harmony of interests
The reader is referred to Pennings (1975) for a complete description of these variables.

These variables were used to determine whether environment has structural correlates. The uncertainty or related environmental variables were scaled from low to high. All organizational variables were scaled so that a low score reflected strong bureaucratic, mechanistic meaning while a high score had a nonbureaucratic, "organic" meaning. For example, there was a moderately strong negative relationship ($r = -.28$, $p \leq .05$) between resourcefulness and total amount of power suggesting that a rich environment is associated with office personnel having little power in their office.

Most correlations between the two sets of indicators were negative and/or insignificant. Large positive correlations had been expected, but the average correlation coefficient was smaller than .2. Only the resourcefulness and complexity variables explained a significant proportion of the variance in the power and participativeness variables. In the case of resourcefulness the direction of that association was opposite to that expected. Altogether, this research showed that on the level of the focal organization there is little room for the contention that environment has structural correlates.

This correlational analysis was supplemented by a so-called typological approach in which the very same data were used to construct taxonomies of organizations and their environments (Pennings and Tripathi, 1976). Some of the pertinent literature has dealt with relating *types* of environments to *types* of organizations (e.g., Emery and Trist, 1965) rather than relating *variables* with each other. Although such an approach is rather common in botany and entomology, it has seldom been used by organizational theorists to examine whether certain types of organizations are more common in some "habitats" and not in others.

The data describing 40 brokerage offices were also used to create environmental and organizational taxonomies. The many measures of organizations and environment were reduced to two sets of nine factors. Four types of environment and four types of organizations could be obtained by stepwise multiple discriminant function analysis. This technique tries to group a set of elements into clusters. It minimizes the within sums of squares between environments (or organizations) belonging to a cluster (i.e., type) and maximizes the sums of squares between observations belonging to different clusters. Each of the types was characterized by a profile based on the environmental (or organizational) factors; none of the types resembled the many a priori or theoretical typologies abundant in the literature. It would require too much space to describe the taxonomies. The reader is referred to Pennings and Tripathi (1976).

Subsequently, an attempt was made to cross-classify those two sets of types. If organizations belonging to a certain type were more likely to prevail in one of the four environmental types, it might be concluded that environment has structural correlates. Table 13–1 highlights the major results of this attempt and shows the failure to detect a dominant type of organization in a particular environment.

Table 13–1

Frequency of Organizational Types in Four Organizational Environments Faced by the Brokerage Offices

Organizational Types	Environmental Types				
	I	II	III	IV	Total
I	1	4	5	4	14
II	3	4	2	1	10
III	3	3	2	2	10
IV	0	2	2	1	5
Total	7	13	11	8	39

It is evident from table 13–1 that most organizational types are equally well represented in the four empirically derived types of environment. Ideally, this cross-classification would have shown the preponderance of a particular type of organization in one and only one type of environment. Each pair of types represents an ecosystem (Thorelli, see chapter 14 of this volume) made up of the focal organization and its environment. The research reported here concludes that there is no association or, at most, a weak association between organizational structure and environment. It also corroborates the results of the correlational analysis.

II.   There has been surprisingly little research at the level of industry and market (or their nonprofit analogs) that focuses on the correspondence between environmental and structural variables. Only recently have there been attempts to relate market structure variables to interorganizational behavior or strategy: For example, Pfeffer (1972) and Pfeffer and Leblebici (1973) have examined merger frequency and executive recruitment as a function of market structure. Such inquiries used to be the exclusive concern of economists (e.g., Scherer, 1970). However, there has been little concern for relating market structure variables to variables descriptive of organizational structure or process. Some organization-environment studies have tried to measure market structure variables by relying on organizational respondents (e.g., Pfeffer and Leblebici, 1973;

Khandwalla, 1974). It is clear, however, that such perceptual measures may be at variance with objective indicators inherent in that next higher level. This applies especially to the concept of competition. The concept of competition may approximate market structure variables such as concentration ratio (and *ipso facto,* entry barriers, etc.). In the above mentioned studies, competition is defined in terms of the focal organization's perspective and is treated as one or multi-dimensional attribute of an undefined environment. At least in those studies the relationship between organizational structure and competition is examined. Pfeffer and Leblebici's results were ambiguous. That is, they did not show unequivocally that competition is related to organization structure. Khandwalla's extensive survey differentiated competition into price, market, and product competition as perceived by top managers. He found that the last kind of competition explained a small proportion of the variance of ratings on nine types of managerial controls (e.g., budgeting, auditing, cost variance analysis, etc.) and authority variables. Table 13–2 gives the major outcomes of his results.

Table 13–2

The Effect of Competition on Authority and Control Variables
(Standardized regression coefficients; $N = 96$) [a]

Dependent Variables	Price Competition	Promotion Competition	Product Competition
Delegation of authority by chief executive	−.10	.10	.19*
Use of management controls	−.05	.05	.36**

[a]From Khandwalla (1974)
* : $p \leq .05$
** : $p \leq .01$

Table 13–2 provides weak support for the hypothesis that competition as measured from the perspective of individual organizations is associated with decentralization and sophisticated management controls. It should be noted that these variables are primarily salient at the top of the organization hierarchy. Although the relationships between organizational and environmental variables are stronger than in the brokerage study, they cannot be seen as unequivocally supporting the hypothesis. Perhaps the estimates of the association could be improved by using a polynomial regression model, since some authors (e.g., Thorelli in this volume) have argued that the relationship between competition intensity and decentralization is nonlinear.

Some Implications

The intriguing question that arises from such studies concerns the complementary explanatory power of environment as contingencies and environment as political economy. To what extent, if at all, is the latter notion more useful in explaining interorganizational structure variations?

Khandwalla's results, as well as those from the study of brokerage offices, suggest that the organizations remain largely immune to environmental uncertainty. They are immune because they tend to create buffers, "boundary-spanning positions" (Thompson, 1967), to limit environmental influences on the organization. Occupants of such positions manage the interface between the organization and its environment.

An organization creates such buffering devices so that its core units can operate under conditions of certainty or near certainty; this may explain why general organizational variables seem so weakly correlated with environmental contingencies and/or industry/market structure variables. It may be more fruitful to focus on the boundary-spanning positions. Perhaps the structural context within which such units operate can be explained by environmental contingencies or uncertainties, while the remaining part of the organization's structure is not affected and cannot be explained by variations in environmental conditions.

Top management constitutes one of the most important subsets of boundary-spanning positions. These managers deal with external legitimization and support for the organization in its political economy. They are central in any major act of coordination between strategically interdependent organizations, both horizontally and vertically. These agents of interorganizational strategic behavior can be subsumed under the term *dominant coalition* (Thompson, 1967; Cyert and March, 1965).

Personnel in other groups of boundary-spanning positions operate under the constraints that are being defined by the "dominant coalition." Oligopolistic organizations create "strategic planning units" or "central intelligence units," whose primary function is to provide information to management. Supportive but less important boundary-spanning units are often found at lower levels, such as purchasing, marketing, public relations, R & D, and environmental protection units. Such units usually contribute little to the organization's strategic decision making. However, in novel, fast-growing markets with organizations of small, efficient size, a large part of the organization may be engaged in the management of the organization-environment interface. In such organizations there is probably a tendency toward decentralization. Each subunit may deal with its subenvironment and absorb or buffer what otherwise would be contingencies for other departments or top management (Hickson et al., 1971). The ability of the subunits to cope with the uncertainty reinforces decentralization since such coping creates quasi-certainty for management, which therefore becomes dependent on subordinate levels.

One may conjecture, however, that as markets move towards intermediate degrees of concentration, the organizations will move toward greater centralization—especially in the management of competition in purchasing and sales areas. This may be the case in the brokerage industry: the organization's headquarters define and modify the domain so that the individual offices have little additional coping behavior to perform. In fact, the brokers have become increasingly dependent on the head office for marketing and other services. This reinforces the tendency towards centralization. The offices are also subject to sophisticated management control systems, which further curtail their discretionary powers. Khandwalla's results show that competition tends to increase the reliance on management control systems. In so far as his results reflect the relationship between top management and the rest of the organization, they do not contradict the results of the brokerage study. There is obviously the need to interconnect the research on the two levels of aggregation to show whether they are complementary.

Perhaps the brokerage study may indicate how the two concepts—environment seen as a set of contingencies and environment seen as a political economy—are intertwined as far as their explanatory power for structural variations is concerned. When top management has successful strategic dealings with the environment, the tendency towards centralization will be reinforced. Decentralization would inhibit response readiness or adroitness. Furthermore, the local offices tend to have shorter horizons. Within the narrow limits of discretion there is little need for offices to deal with environmental contingencies. They operate under conditions of near certainty since top management largely defines, manipulates, and controls the environment in which the offices operate. Top management has been likely to have developed "niches" in the oligopolistic brokerage industry. Although no pertinent data are available that would relate political behavior among these oligopolists to their market structure, it is highly likely that the brokerage industry has relied on political devices to control its environment. The more successful the political devices are, the greater the likelihood that lower units in the organization have little power and autonomy.

In summary, environmental variables describing environment as contingencies may affect organizational structure if environmental variables at the level of industry or market are not relevant. This is the case with small organizations in fragmented industries. To the extent that the industry-level environment becomes increasingly important for organizational performance or survival, it is expected that the role of lower units in the organizations is less critical for dealing with the organization-environment interface. In contrast the strategic skills of top management become important. Such changes may account for oligarchical phenomena, if any, in more concentrated industries.

Environment, Structure, and Organizational Effectiveness

At the beginning of this paper it was stated that the environment-organization research may have implications for explaining organizational effectiveness. One could argue that the results reported here do not necessarily invalidate the hypothesis that environment has structural correlates. For example, the 40 brokerage offices included both effective and ineffective offices, and the ineffective ones may have distorted correlations based on the total sample. The implication of Burns and Stalker's (1961) research was that organizational effectiveness depends on the goodness of fit between structure and environment. There is little empirical evidence, however, to sustain such assertions.

It is often not clear what authors mean by effectiveness. Two different perspectives on organizational effectiveness are apparent: the so-called "goal approach" and the "systems approach." The goal approach defines effectiveness as the degree of goal achievement. The systems approach views organizational effectiveness as the degree to which the organization can preserve and maintain itself. While the goal approach has an economic bias, the systems approach incorporates both economic and psychological/sociological facets in its conceptualization of effectiveness.

The investigation of the brokerage study included data on organizational effectiveness. Some effectiveness criteria (e.g., production, change in production) could be called goal-oriented and others (e.g., turnover of personnel, job satisfaction) systems-oriented, although such a classification is not mutually exclusive. A factorial design was used to determine the effects of environment, organizational structure, and their interaction on a number of effectiveness indicators.

Virtually all the correlations between structural and environmental variables were not significant. This suggests that the goodness of fit between environmental and structural variables has little relevance for the effectiveness of the organization, no matter which approach we use in defining effectiveness (Pennings, 1975). A similar conclusion was arrived at in the attempt to cross-classify environmental and organizational types.

It was also found that the structural variables explain a considerable amount of the variance in effectiveness criteria. The decentralization measures (total amount of power and participativeness) appeared to be the strongest predictor of organizational effectiveness. In contrast the environmental variables did not explain variance in effectiveness. The results suggest that if the employees of the organization were left on their own, did not participate in decision making, did not communicate with each other or with their supervisors, effectiveness measured by any criterion would be below average.

Unfortunately, there are no studies at the level of industry or market that use the goodness of fit hypothesis to explain effectiveness. There is strong evidence, however, that environmental variables on this level are related to organizational effectiveness. For example, industry/market structure is related to return on investment (Hirsch, 1975; Comanor and Wilson, 1967; Lieberson and O'Connor, 1972; Weiss, 1962; Rumelt, 1974), growth (Comanor and Wilson, 1967), and price level (Esposito and Esposito, 1971). Organizational behavior that affects industry structure will probably alter performance. Examples of structure-altering behavior include collusive agreements, conspiracies, mergers, overlapping membership, regulations, product duplication, and market segmentation (Pennings, 1976). However, there is no evidence that within a certain range of industry structure organizations can improve their effectiveness by altering their own structure. It could be argued that the organizational structure is independent of the ability of top management to manage the vertical or horizontal interdependence with other organizations. That is, the coping strategies are developed by top decision makers and unfold primarily outside their internal organizational context.

Such reasoning has led Katz and Kahn (1966) to view organizational effectiveness as "political effectiveness," because the use of political devices (e.g., regulation and interlocking directorates) to alter market structure is the primary antecedent of increasing and maintaining returns to the organization and its members. Katz and Kahn distinguish political effectiveness from efficiency, which can be controlled by conditions internal to the organization.

This view may shed further light on the possible complementarity of the two approaches to the research on organizations and their environments. Research on the focal organization level may have implications for explaining *organizational efficiency,* while research on the industry/market level helps explain *organizational effectiveness.* In the present context, the differences in commission earned among the 40 brokerage offices could be described as differences in efficiency rather than effectiveness. The more "effective" offices are more *efficient;* that is, they accomplish higher production levels with the same amount of resources. While organizations in different industries expect different average returns on investment, great variations in returns among organizations in a particular industry/market indicate efficiency differences, except when such variations reflect differential use of political devices to exploit the environment. This distinction between effectiveness and efficiency is not merely a discourse on semantics. It is important to be able to identify the source of improvement or decrease in returns, to know whether such change is a function of internal organizational conditions or external environmental factors.

The distinction between efficiency and political effectiveness also helps resolves the seeming paradox that on the "lower" level organizational structure explains amount of returns while on the "higher" level environment explains returns to the organization. More research and theory development is needed to integrate these two levels of analysis, so that we are better able to explain why some organizations are more effective than other ones.

Conclusion

In this paper the relationship between organizations and environment has been examined on the level of focal organizations and on the level of industry or market. The concept of uncertainty was used to describe the environment from these two perspectives. Although the pertinent literature is rather unanimous in the assumptions or belief that organizational environments have structural correlates, there is not sufficient evidence to subscribe to this belief. The results reported in this paper indicate that most structural variables are not related to environmental variables. Furthermore, the so-called goodness of fit or consonance between structural and environmental variables failed to distinguish the low and high performers. It is striking, however, that on the focal organization level organizational structure explains performance and on the industry/market level environment explains performance. Much more research and conceptual development is needed, however, to integrate such outcomes and to arrive at suggestions for optimal forms of organizational designs.

It is unfortunate that organization theory in its research of organizations as open systems has been preoccupied with defining the environment from the focal organizational vantage point, as to explain structural aspects like communication and centralization. On the other hand, economists, market researchers, and other experts on market behavior have been rather ignorant as regards organization structure variables. Both categories of researchers are interested in finding optimal designs or strategies in order to improve organizational performance. There is a clear need for cross-fertilization or widening of research boundaries so as to integrate intra and interorganizational processes and to better account for organizational effectiveness.

REFERENCES

1. Aldrich, Howard. *Relations Between Local Employment Service Offices and Social Services Sector Organizations.* Mimeo. Ithaca, N.Y.: NYSSICR, Cornell University, 1975.
2. Becker, Selwyn W., and Baloff, N. "Organization Structure and Complex Problem Solving," *Administrative Science Quarterly,* Vol. 14, 1969, pp.260–71.
3. Bernhardt, Irvin, and MacKenzie, Kenneth D. "Measuring Seller Unconcentration, Segmentation and Product Differentiation," *Western Economic Journal,* Vol. 6, 1968, pp.395–403.
4. Burns, Tom, and Stalker, G. M. *The Management of Innovation.* London: Tavistock, 1961.
5. Comanor, William S., and Wilson, Thomas A. "Advertising, Market Structure and Performance," *The Review of Economics and Statistics,* Vol. 49, 1967, pp.423–40.
6. Cyert, Richard M., and March, James G. *A Behavioral Theory of the Firm.* Englewood Cliffs, N.J.: Prentice-Hall, 1963.
7. Dill, William. "Environment as an Influence on Managerial Autonomy," *Administrative Science Quarterly,* Vol. 2, 1958, pp.407–33.
8. Duncan, Robert B. "The Effects of Perceived Environmental Uncertainty on Organizational Decision Unit Structure." Doctoral dissertation, Yale University, 1971.
9. Duncan, Robert B. "Characteristics of Organizational Environments and Perceived Environmental Uncertainty," *Administrative Science Quarterly,* Vol. 17, 1972, pp.313–27.
10. Esposito, Louis, and Esposito, Frances F. "Foreign Competition and Domestic Industry Profitability," *Review of Economics and Statistics,* Vol. 53, 1971, pp.343–53.
11. Emery, Fred E., and Trist, Eric M. "The Causal Texture of Organizational Environments," *Human Relations,* Vol. 18, 1965, pp.21–31.
12. Evan, William M. "An Organization Set Model of Inter-organizational Relations." In Chisholm, R.; Tuite, M.; and Radnor, M. (eds.). *Interorganizational Decision Making.* Chicago: Aldine, 1976, pp.181–99.
13. Freeman, John H., and Hannan, Michael T. "Types of Organizations." In Starbuck, William H. (ed.). *Handbook of Organization Design.* New York: Elsevier, 1976.
14. Galbraith, Jay R. "Organizational Design: An Information Processing View." In Lorsch, Jay W., and Lawrence, Paul R. (eds.). *Organization Planning: Cases and Concepts.* Homewood, Ill.: Irwin, 1972.
15. Hickson, David J. "A Convergence in Organization Theory," *Administrative Science Quarterly,* Vol. 11, 1966, pp.224–37.
16. Hickson, David J.; Hinings, C. R.; Lee, C. A.; Schneck, R. E.; and Pennings, J. M. "A Strategic Contingencies Theory of Intraorganizational Power," *Administrative Science Quarterly,* Vol. 16, 1971, pp.216–29.
17. Hinings, C. R.; Hickson, D. J.; Pennings, J. M.; and Schneck, R. E.

"Structural Conditions of Interorganizational Power," *Administrative Science Quarterly,* Vol. 19, 1974, pp.22–44.

18. Hirsch, Paul M. "Organizational Effectiveness and the Institutional Environment," *Administrative Science Quarterly,* Vol. 20, No. 3, 1975, pp.327–44.

19. Hunt, Raymond G. "Technology and Organization," *Academy of Management Journal,* Vol. 13, 1970, pp.235–52.

20. Katz, Daniel, and Kahn, Robert L. *The Social Psychology of Organizations.* New York: Wiley, 1966.

21. Khandwalla, Pradip N. "Effect of Competition on the Structure of Management Control," *Academy of Management Journal,* Vol. 16, 1974, pp.285–95.

22. Lawrence, Paul R., and Lorsch, Jay W. *Organization and Environment: Managing Differentiation and Integration.* Boston: Graduate School of Business Administration, Harvard University, 1967.

23. Lieberson, Stanley E., and O'Connor, James F. "Leadership and Organizational Performance," *American Sociological Review,* Vol. 37, 1972, pp.117–30.

24. March, James G., and Simon, Herbert A. *Organizations.* New York: Wiley, 1958.

25. Miller, George A.; Galanter, E.; and Priban, K. H. *Plans and the Structure of Behavior.* New York: Holt, Rinehart and Winston, 1960.

26. Mohr, Lawrence B. "The Concept of Organizational Goal," *American Political Science Review,* Vol. 67, 1973, pp.470–81.

27. Pennings, Johannes M. "The Relevance of the Structural Contingency Model for Organizational Effectiveness," *Administrative Science Quarterly,* Vol. 20, No. 3, 1975, pp.393–410.

28. Pennings, Johannes M. "Coordination between Strategically Interdependent Organizations." In Starbuck, William H. (ed.). *Handbook of Organizational Design.* New York: Elsevier, 1976.

29. Pennings, Johannes M., and Tripathi, Rama C. "The Organization-Environment Relationship: Dimensional Versus Typological Viewpoints." In Karpik, Lucien (ed.). *Organizations and Their Environments.* New York: Russell Sage, 1976.

30. Perrow, Charles. "Departmental Power and Perspective in Industrial Firms." In Zald, Mayer N. (ed.). *Power in Organizations.* Nashville, Tenn.: Vanderbilt University Press, 1970.

31. Perrow, Charles. *Complex Organizations: A Critical Essay.* Glenview, Ill.: Scott, Foresman, 1972.

32. Pfeffer, Jeffrey. "Merger as a Response to Organizational Interdependence," *Administrative Science Quarterly,* Vol. 17, 1972, pp.382–94.

33. Pfeffer, Jeffrey, and Leblebici, Huseyin. "Executive Recruitment and the Development of Inter-firm Organizations," *Administrative Science Quarterly,* Vol. 18, 1973, pp.449–61.

34. Pfeffer, Jeffrey, and Leblebici, Huseyin. "The Effect of Competition on Dimensions of Organizational Structure," *Social Forces,* Vol. 52, 1973, pp.268–80.

35. Rumelt, Richard M. *Strategy, Structure, and Economic Performance.*

Boston: Division of Research, Graduate School of Business Administration, Harvard University, 1974.

36. Scherer, Frederick M. *Industrial Market Structure and Economic Performance.* Chicago: Rand McNally, 1970.

37. Tannenbaum, Arnold S. *Control in Organizations.* New York: McGraw-Hill, 1968.

38. Thompson, J. D. *Organizations in Action.* New York: McGraw-Hill, 1967.

39. Thorelli, Hans B. "Organizational Theory: An Ecological View," Academy of Management *Proceedings,* 27th Annual Meeting, Washington, D.C., December 27–29, 1967 (1968), p.84.

40. Weiss, Leonard W. "Average Concentration Ratios and Industrial Performance," *Journal of Industrial Economics,* Vol. 11, 1962, pp.237–54.

41. Woodward, Joan. *Industrial Organization: Theory and Practice.* London: Oxford, 1965.

14

Organizational Theory: An Ecological View

HANS B. THORELLI

The body of current organization theory is introspective, providing an inside view of leaders, groups, and internal communications, analyzing decision-making within the "black box," and so forth. Economics is obsessed with the environment but notoriously uninterested in what goes on inside the firm. This paper makes a case for the study of the interplay of organization and environment and predicts that ecological approaches will produce another vital strain in organization theory.

Ecology: A Trans-Disciplinary Focus

The term ecology originates with that branch of biology which deals with the mutual relations among organisms (or populations of plants or animals) and, especially, between organisms (or populations) and their environment. While the prime attention in biology as well as in the more recent field of "human ecology" generally has been on spatial, demographic, and physical aspects of the environment, there is an unmistakable tendency to broaden the concept to apply to the interrelations of an organism with its *total* setting. In this sense ecology stands not for a branch of biology or some other discipline but for a mode of analysis of broad trans-disciplinary application.[1]

Originally confined largely to the influence of a single variable (e.g.,

Reprinted with kind permission from *Academy of Management Proceedings,* 27th Annual Meeting, Washington, D.C., December 27–29, 1967 (1968), pp.66–84.

temperature) on the organism, biological ecology has broadened to multi-variate study of such encompassing phenomena as the functioning of communities of populations and the succession of one population by another. Adaptation tends to be viewed as a one-way proposition, the organism being conditioned by the environment. Even biological ecology will include analysis of two-way impact, however, as the environment itself will change as the more hospitable parts of it are occupied or consumed and as the output of the organism will constantly make the environment more or less hospitable to it and to other organisms. Indeed, the dynamic impact of population on environment holds the key to succession. Yet we rarely see plants or animals actively moulding their own environment. In biology the dramas of ecology are acted out in an objective, fateful, largely nonconscious process.

While research on human organization may derive considerable inspiration from plant and animal ecology, there are important distinctions to be made. Humans have long-term objectives, and they have a certain amount of foresight (as well as hindsight). They can plan for and administer change. Man and the organizations he creates are to a certain extent the masters of their own destiny. To some degree we may shape our own environment, and are not merely shaped by it. This is most clearly evident in the case of such powerful entities as national governments or large corporations, but it is actually characteristic of all human organizations. Indeed, by a physical move or a transmutation of purpose it is frequently possible for an organization to make a complete switch from one environment to another. E. P. Odum reflects that "plants 'stay put' and respond to environmental conditions by growth and structural changes rather than by behavior changes, as do animals."[2] It is proper to add here that human organizations typically are free to change *either* structure *or* behavior *or*, indeed, *both*.

The fact that in the environment of human organization constraints are less immediate, the range of discretion is greater, and the alternative means to reach given ends are more numerous than in biological settings is of tremendous significance. It provides the explanation for two vital phenomena, both rather shabbily treated in received social science theory. The first is the emergence of a multiple goal structure in every organization once its immediate survival seems assured. The second is the viable coexistence of different organization structures and strategies of interaction in the same general environment.

It is hoped that what has just been said brings out the fact that organizational ecology cannot possibly be viewed as an offshoot of environmental determinism trite and simple. While the approach is definitely environmental, the focus is on interaction. We do not, and verily we need not, take sides in the perennial argument concerning the existence of a free will—whether at the individual or organizational level. Indeed, we can even dispense with the notion that organizations have a will at all, although it is convenient to impute organizational objectives. On the other hand, it *is* true that the perspective of ecology is inherently holistic, viewing the organization-environment constellation essentially as an open system including a large set of interconnected subsystems. This *Gestalt* model of sets of interacting variables has methodological consequences. While confining a particular inquiry to a single dependent and a single independent variable may often be legitimate (at this stage even indispensable), it is not to be expected that a finite number of such studies will give us the total picture. The impact of a given independent variable may differ drastically from one context to the next, depending on the relative strength of certain other independent variables in the several contexts. Higher temperature may be endured by many more organisms if moisture is plentiful than if it is not; given an organization of a certain size specialization can be carried much further with good internal communications than in a unit of the same size with poor communications, and so on. Yet, while we should be properly skeptical of the "limiting factor" concept in older ecology literature, we may frequently say that "whenever a factor approaches a minimum, its relative effect becomes very great."[3] Meanwhile, great strides are being made in the development of statistical methodology for the study of many variables simultaneously, and we may also be able to simulate entire systems rather successfully without knowing in infinite detail the real-life role of each variable employed in the simulation model.

A key concept in ecology is viability—the ability to survive. Explicitly or implicitly, this is assumed to be the low-key, minimum "aspiration level" of organisms as well as organizations. This is closely analogous to the emphasis in systems analysis on the notion of homeostatic mechanisms. The ecological view is clearly functionalistic in the general sense that it postulates that a minimum degree of functional fit between organization and environment is necessary for sustained viability. On the other hand, the concern is not with the kind of static equilibrium which is an element of certain types of functionalistic thought. Even while equilibrating forces are at work, the situation (the relative position of organization and environment) is being redefined. We are dealing with a dynamic equilibrium never adequately defined and certainly never fully attained. It would not be worth our while to engage in hot pursuit of such an elusive phenomenon. Fortunately our concern is with the interaction of sets of variables which seem important as determinants of the nature of the organization as a component part of an ecosystem, not with the kind of equilibrium which might eventually result under unrealistic *ceteris paribus* conditions.

Some functionalist thinking has been criticized as being normative in general and conservative in particular ("what is, is good").[4] The foregoing discussion should make clear, however, that organizational ecology is no more inherently normative than other approaches to organization theory

—indeed, the opposite might well be true. Focusing on viability ecology is existentialist rather than conservative. Like the computer makers in the last decade the ecologist frequently has reason to reflect: "If it works, it is obsolete." In a volatile environment what is viable today may well be untenable tomorrow.

Given the fact that one rarely encounters a steady-state ecosystem we could hardly ever expect to find a perfect functional fit between organization and environment. Generally speaking, there are at least half a dozen good reasons why several different organization structures and ecological interaction patterns may be expected to coexist in the "same" environment:[5]

First, different organizations working in a given environment will frequently recognize different performance areas (such as growth, profitability, employee morale, customer satisfaction) or, at least, will place a different relative emphasis on these several areas;

Second, no two organizations are apt to experience identical degrees of uncertainty or, at least, to cope with that uncertainty in the same manner;

Third, the interaction process is often complicated, and cause-effect relationships diluted, by the fact that the impact of a given variable or constellation of variables is subject to differing degrees of time lag;

Fourth, the existence of varying degrees of slack in different organizations, and the fact that some organizations are more concerned about building "buffering" and "leveling" defenses against environmental surprise or volatility than others;[6]

Fifth, different organizations have different resource configurations (access to capital, skilled employees, consumer goodwill, etc.);

Sixth, substitution and complementarity among variables (e.g., between personal selling effort and advertising in the marketing mix of a firm or between intensive and extensive care in a hospital) often give rise to a number of combinations which may have an equivalent impact on interaction;

Seventh, the environment is actually never exactly "the same" for any two organizations—if only because organization *A* is part of the environment of organization *B* and vice versa. This generally results in different organizations occupying partially unique, partially overlapping niches ("markets within the market") in the environment. Indeed, "nichemanship" frequently represents a conscious policy of survival by differentiation.

Despite the bewildering multitude of co-existing ecological relationships there is every reason to believe that we shall be able to discern some patterned variations. It is on this basic premise that we are proceeding here. Before going further it should be emphasized that this essay is in the nature of a working paper; the notions expressed are preliminary and hopefully will be restated in more digested form at a future date. In the meantime other variations on the ecological theme in organization theory are likely to emerge.

The Community of Interest Groups and the Task Environment

Being circumspect indeed in scope the ecological point of view in organization theory may be articulated in many different ways. In tune with some strands of pluralist thought we have found it instructive to look upon the organization as a political community of internal and external interest groups as an initial frame of reference in the process of conceptualization.[7] While any organization could be chosen, we find it convenient to use the corporation for purposes of illustration. It involves no great effort to define the principal member interests participating in this community: consumers, management and other employees, stockholders and other creditors, suppliers, distributors and dealers, competitiors, the plant community and, increasingly, the public at large—plus, of course, government. The government actually plays at least a threefold part in the context: as ultimate overlord (in that the firm exists only at the government's pleasure and in that the government writes a goodly proportion of the rules of the game), as tax collector, and as final arbiter in case conflicts between the other interests cannot be resolved except by recourse to higher authority than management. In addition, the government in a given instance may be a consumer, creditor, supplier, stockholder, or even competitor.

Each interest group is at once a contributor (time, money, component parts, etc.) and a claimant (of money, goods or services, ego-gratification, etc.) in regard to the resources of the firm. This is tantamount to saying that the interests of the group are in part identical with, in part different from (at times even antithetical to) those of the firm.

In such a system, what is the emerging role of management? The answer to this question is important, as it will provide the basis for our later discussion of the objectives of organizations. The answer lies in the motivation of management as an interest group: management has an expansionist bias. Expansion makes for an orderly promotion system, and it builds power and prestige for all.[8] Expansion is also the process by which *change* can be absorbed in the least disruptive fashion. Even at this preliminary stage we may conclude that *survival and growth of the organization itself tends to become the minimal ambition, the core objective of most organizations.* Management performs its role by striving to achieve a working balance, through time, of claims and contributions among the other participating interests. This involves activating and sustaining their desire to cooperate in the corporate nexus while at the same time preventing any one interest group from gaining supremacy. It would be false to infer that the role of management in this view is reduced to that of a claims adjuster. In any typical situation there is plenty of room for leadership and managerial discretion in the harnessing of interacting groups for the pursuit of objectives often but vaguely held in common.

In addition to sustaining the organization the interest groups constitute a critical subset of the task environment. We define as the *task environment* that part of the total setting with which the organization is transacting and in which it is competing. Conceptually not free from objection, this definition seems operationally workable. It will be seen that even beyond the task environment there are environmental factors and phenomena which may affect the organization (and be affected by it).[9] Clearly, the environment is a continuum in which relevance is a matter of degree.[10] This is not very disturbing at a stage when we are still trying to identify the *major* influences at work.

Similarly, ecological analysis will frequently present the researcher with the problem of defining what is the *relevant organization* to be studied. With surprisingly few exceptions this question has been neglected in the past—and yet it is of considerable importance. If we wish to study the effects of different types of faculty structure in a curriculum planning and course scheduling context the students may logically be looked upon as part of the environment. But if we are interested in the relations between a state university and the legislature it is probably more reasonable to include the students as part of the university organization. Where the organization ends and the environment begins on the continuum comprising both will depend on what aspect of interaction is being analyzed in a given case. In many instances the decision of what to include and what to exclude is likely not to be especially critical. Indeed, insistence on a clearcut borderline may sometimes obscure rather than clarify.

Each interest group, whether internal or external, represents a "slice" of the task environment which we shall call a *market*. Banks and stockholders represent the credit market, employees the labor market, consumers the market in which the principal offering (hospital care, religious services, automobile) of the organization produces the revenue on which the survival of the organization ultimately depends. Generally, markets overlap at least to some extent; Ford workers are also auto consumers.[11] We may note that different parts of the total organization will interact with different markets. Marketing men deal with customers, finance men with creditors, personnel men with the labor market, and so on. Under the impact of growing professionalization of management, the heads of such areas as marketing, finance and personnel in a firm tend to become as much representatives of the interest groups to which they correspond in relation to the corporation as they represent it in relation to these groups. This is another example of the plasticity of organizational borderlines.

If we divide the environment into "slices" from a functional point of view we may also speak of different "layers" of environment from the viewpoint of structure. Again the analogy with biology is instructive.

Biologists, quite appropriately, speak of "levels of organization"[12] in nature, covering an entire spectrum: atom, molecule, cell, organ, individual, population, the community of interacting populations, the ecosystem comprising the community with its living and non-living environment. Theoretically the spectrum of levels can be extended indefinitely in both directions. In organizational ecology it seems appropriate to distinguish at least the following levels:

> organization
> auto-setting
> task environment
> macroenvironment
> extra-environment

    relevant environment
    or habitat

Organization is a generic concept comprising species as divergent as the neighborhood bridge club to the United States government or the United Nations. From the viewpoint of proximity the first layer of the environment encountered is frequently the *auto-setting,* i.e., the broader organization of which the unit under study is a semi-autonomous part.[13] The auto-setting comprises that highly relevant part of the environment of the Chevrolet Division (or the English Department) which is represented by all the other divisions of GM (departments of the university) as well as the corporate headquarters of the concern (the university President's office). The *task environment* was defined above as that part of the total setting with which the organization is transacting and in which it is competing.[14] The *macroenvironment* includes such factors as the general social, economic, political, and technological climate in which the organization finds itself operating. Taken together, the auto-setting, the task environment and the macroenvironment constitute the *revelant environment* or *habitat.*[15] The *extra-environment,* finally, refers to those aspects of the total environment of negligible or zero relevance to the organization. Little would be gained by attempting more precise definitions in this context: "from the standpoint of interdependence, interrelations and survival, there can be no sharp break anywhere along the line."[16] Figure 14–1 gives a graphic interpretation of our discussion of functional slices and structural layers in the form of an "ecological grid."

The organization functions (and corresponding "slices" of the total environment) listed in figure 14–1 relate most immediately to a business organization and are, of course, tritely conventional. The diagram is intended to be illustrative only. A taxonomy which would encompass almost any organization includes the functions of input, throughput, output and maintenance. Perhaps management should be added as a separate function, in tune with Fayol and many others. As usual in conceptualization, generic abstraction has to be weighed against specific application. We will

Layers of	Organization Functions				
Environment	Marketing	Production	Finance	Personnel	Etc.
Auto-setting					
Task environment					
Macroenvironment					
Extra-environment					

Figure 14–1
An Ecological Grid

know we have a complete grid at a time when it can be demonstrated that all determinants of interaction between organization and environment can find a home therein.

From the viewpoint of interaction between the organization and its habitat it is pertinent to observe that the factors encountered at each layer of the environment may be divided into parameters and variables. While there is no hard and fast borderline, parameters may be viewed as factors which the organization must regard as given at least in the short run, while variables are factors which may be changed or influenced by the organization, at least in the short run. Generally speaking, the proportion of givens increases as one proceeds from the inner to the outer layers of the environment, while for manipulables the relationships is reversed.

We shall apply the term *ecosystem* to the system comprising the organization and the relevant environment. Occasionally it is also convenient to use the term ecosystem even though only a part of the relevant environment (such as the consumer market) is included in the analysis, as in the next section of this paper. While the term has a specific connotation in biology, as previously indicated, a generic usage is more appropriate in organization ecology. Here it is natural to speak of ecosystems of lower and higher order. A higher-order system may embrace a lower one, but the latter would hardly ever be merely a small-scale projection of the former. The relevant environment of the Housewares Division of the General Electric Company is presumably part of the relevant environment of GE as a whole—but the relevant environment of the corporation as a whole also includes such entire industries as atomics, computers, lamps, major appliances, etc. We conclude that while frequently findings at any one ecosystem level will aid in the study of another level they will never completely explain the phenomena occurring at that level.[17]

A diversified organization may be active in any number of ecosystems of widely different characteristics even though at the same basic level in the hierarchy of systems. The one-hundred-odd product departments constituting the key profit-centers in the General Electric organization represent as many ecosystems. An internationally diversified organization such as the Red Cross or Nestlé Alimentana is a part of a different ecosystem in each national culture within which it operates. Several attempts at identifying and classifying variables of major differential impact on organizations working in different national cultures have been made. Naturally focused on the macroenvironment and its influence on the organization this literature obviously represents an ecological point of view, although it is not generally couched in such terms.[18]

The prolegomenon of this section was a model of the organization as a community of interest groups. This model will be revoked in our analysis of the dynamics of objectives below. However, in our own experience the interest-group model has great limitations from the point of view of empirical research, unless it proceeds at an exceedingly general level.[19] The intervening conceptualization of a transacting ecosystem will make use of variables which seem to lend themselves more readily to operationalization.

The Transacting Ecosystem

In common with biological organisms every human being and every organization is dependent on its environment for survival. Neither nature nor human civilization in the end is an eleemosynary institution. No one is self-sufficient. The interdependence of the organization and its setting stems from the incessant drive towards specialization, or division of labor (or nichemanship, if you please) as the prime means of survival in a world characterized by an all prevailing relative scarcity of resources. In effect, what happens in the process of interaction is that the organization is obtaining the support of the environment by disposing of some of its differential advantage—or conversely, procuring resources from other organizations where they enjoy a differential advantage. The process of exchange is manifested by *transactions*.[20]

In viewing the organization as a community of interest groups we defined the task environment as a set of input and output markets in which the organization must transact. For long-term survival the *customer market* is of paramount significance, as in the end satisfying customer needs is the *only* viable reason for organizational existence. As for simplicity's sake we shall have to confine our treatment here to the market environment, we shall choose the customer market. The fact that it may be difficult to identify who the customers are of some organizations (especially certain governmental and voluntary types) is recognized, but will be of little concern at this general level of discussion.[21] We shall feel free to apply the term ecosystem to the customer market ecology of the organization.

THE MODEL

A model of a transacting ecosystem represented by an organization and its customer market is displayed in figure 14–2. To simplify the representation of interaction between the organization and its environment, we have depicted the two as entirely distinct. Actually, the organization is totally immersed in the environment and, as we have seen, it is frequently difficult to distinguish the borderlines between them. The model admittedly represents a high level of abstraction. It can easily be extended (or even further contracted) in various ways. It is not difficult, for instance, to nominate twice as many variables signifying organizational characteristics, interaction strategies, environmental features as well as objectives and performance criteria. The variables most relevant in any given set will differ from one ecosystem to the next, although those included here have been chosen on the grounds of presumed broad-band applicability. On the other hand it is believed that the nomination of four *sets* of interacting variables is somewhat more definite and somewhat more complete.

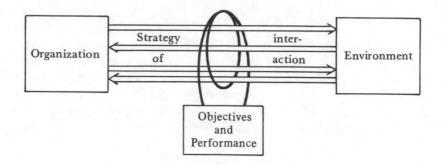

Figure 14–2
Model of Transacting Ecosystem

An action system based on four interdependent sets of variables is envisaged. A sample of variables in each category might include:

Organization Structure	*Interaction Strategy*	*Market Environment*
Size	Product	Size
Centralization	Intelligence and	Geographical dispersion
Diversification	promotion	Competition
Integration	Channel	Diversity of customer
Flexibility	Price	needs
Structuring by area,	Post-transaction service	Customer power
products, function,	Trust	Volatility
clients		Stage in life cycle

Objectives and Resultant Performance Criteria

Survival	Profitability	Customer
Growth	Sales volume	satisfaction
		Productivity

THE SETS OF VARIABLES

Under the heading of *organization* we are primarily concerned with structural variables.[22] Some of these are the same as in the mainstream of organization and management literature. "Flexibility" is intended to refer to both assignment of personnel and commitment of other resources (fixed vs variable costs, etc.). In addition, a few variables ordinarily associated with economics rather than organizational theory should be included here, notably the degree of (vertical) integration and (horizontal) diversification of activities.

The catalogue of *interaction strategy* variables is admittedly highly tentative. In its present state it is largely a representation of variables emphasized in marketing theory. Doubtless useful supplements may be found elsewhere, although it should not be forgotten that marketing more than any other is the science of transactions. Self-evidently "product" is synonymous with service in many firms and in most nonprofit organizations. If promotion is taken to mean outbound communication about the offering of the organization, intelligence is the feedback of reactions to it from the environment and of competitive data. Indeed, in a customer-oriented organization the initial flow of communication can be expected to be inward-bound intelligence. "Channel" refers to the strategy of distributing the product—the type of outlet and the spatial and temporal availability of the product which follows from the use of that type of channel. Under "channel" we may also subsume exclusive dealing arrangements of various types, as they directly govern availability. A "captive" sales and distribution organization in a firm is as much a channel as a conventional wholesaler-retailer setup.[23] Normally, nonprofit organizations work with channels, too; thus the PTA tends to be a channel of the local school, and the county agents constitute a channel for the dissemination of government agricultural consulting service. Whether or not a formal channel is used, to be able to transact every organization faces the necessity of making its offering at a certain place and time. "Trust" has been included in view of its importance as a prerequisite to transactions in many markets (political vote-getting, medical service, industrial purchasing), It is true, of course, that some organizations (as, indeed, some customers) secure a differential advantage by being unreliable—thereby escaping the costs involved in building trustworthiness—even if this type of advantage tends to be rather short-term.

Of characteristics of the *environment*, "size" may be measured in such terms as industry sales volume or total number of clients. For "geographical dispersion" of the clientele a variety of measures are available. The intensity of "competition" is *not* to be measured in the number and size distribution of competing institutions as much as in terms of volatility of market shares, the turnover of competitors, the extent of brand-switching among customers, etc. It hardly needs saying that competition affects government bureaus, religious groups, etc. as well as business firms. While admittedly there is no standard operational measure for "diversity of customer needs" it usually does not present great difficulty to rank environments on this criterion in any given comparative study.

"Customer power" may be conceived as a function of the share of the organization taken by a single customer or group of customers acting in unison. Of course, organizations also wield power over their clienteles: even the most "voluntary" organization derives a modicum of power from its prestige, its appeal to the conscience, etc. Similarly, the corner druggist derives a certain amount of bargaining power from his convenient location. The negative power of customers—their relative ability to withdraw patronage from the organization—is also important. In the end, it is probably the relative bargaining power of the organization and its clientele which is significant as a determinant of interaction patterns.

Environmental "volatility"—quantitative fluctuations and qualitative changes in the nature of demand—is also assumed to constitute a strong influence on interaction and on the organization. "Volatility" should be distinguished from the stage of the "life cycle" in which the environment finds itself, and the type of cycle it is following in terms of steepness, duration, etc.

The set of factors labeled *objectives and performance* will be discussed in the next section of this paper.

Again, it must be emphasized that while we do believe that the general approach outlined here is of considerable merit, no claim is made that the selection of individual variables included within the organization, environment, interaction, and objectives-performance sets will necessarily prove to be the most relevant or forceful in terms of further exploration.

EFFECTS IN SEARCH OF CAUSES

Managerial decision-making as well as scientific inquiry presupposes the existence of at least one independent variable, the action of which affects at least one dependent variable. Even the schematic model of an ecosystem presented here is quite powerful as a generator of hypotheses. For example, relating environment to organization we might postulate that increased geographical dispersion is associated with decreased centralization. Relating environment to strategy, we might assume that the greater the diversity of customer needs, the greater the degree of product differentiation. Or, relating environment to objectives, we might hypothesize that greater customer power is reflected in greater emphasis on customer satisfaction.

To complicate matters, we must assume mutual interaction between all four sets of variables with a cacophony of causal arrows. To depict such interdependence between the sets we may take organization structure and strategy. It is frequently said that "structure follows strategy."[24] And, indeed, the initial structure had better reflect the strategies to be pursued and functions to be performed. In such a situation it may even be natural to say that structure itself may constitute part of strategy.[25] However, as soon as a structure is in place its very nature will in large part determine the range of strategies which can be exploited, at least in the near term. As organizational shake-up tends to be painful, most managements prefer to vary strategies in order to accommodate (or exploit) changes in the environment. Only when the limits of strategy change compatible with the extant structure have been reached, will structure typically be reformed.

A further complication stems from interaction *within* each set of variables. Within organizations, for example, it is often held that size and centralization tend to be inversely related. Among objectives profitability and sales volume often evidence high collinearity. Looking at the strategy variables, marketing men are apt to emphasize the holistic effect: any marketing strategy worth its salt is something more than a marketing mix, that is, it represents a whole that is greater than an odd conglomerate of so many parts of product, price, promotion, etc. Indeed, this qualitative element of integration often seems to be of pivotal significance to the effectiveness of strategy. To some extent this type of problem may be alleviated by factorial-type analysis, but in the long run it will be handled more effectively once we are able to classify overall strategies more meaningfully than at present. Until then we must re-emphasize the legitimacy of research on the effects of individual variables, such as price or advertising, and combinations thereof. Plant ecologists frequently study the effects of climate and soil conditions, taken separately, on plant populations, even though it is clear that there is considerable interaction among climate and soil variables themselves.

Hypotheses about interaction within a given set of variables may be labeled unilateral and propositions concerning interaction between variables from two sets may be termed bilateral. Trilateral hypotheses will present a challenge of a higher order to researchers. Instead of merely saying "the greater customer power, the greater centralization" in the bilateral vein, a trilateral hypothesis would predict that "if customer power is great, centralization of authority will tend to promote profitability (sales volume, viability)." Another illustration of a trilateral proposition: "If in a geographically dispersed environment the product offered customers is a homogeneous one, the organization is more likely to be structured by area than by function or clientele."

The progressive verification and refinement of hypotheses in organizational ecology will require both cross-sectional studies embracing ecosystems of many different types and longitudinal studies of single systems. The former type of study has the disadvantage of tending to be static, but it may represent the quickest way of establishing what variables are relevant within the different sets. Being dynamic, the latter type of study may be indispensable to the tracing of the direction of causal arrows, thus going beyond the observation that interaction exists. One would hope that in the extension of time the structure of ecomodels will be refined sufficiently to warrant the resource input necessary for research at once longitudinal and cross-sectional.

The Dynamics of Objectives

The origins and dynamics of organizational objectives will be discussed against the background of the simple model given in figure 14–3. It is essentially a subset of figure 14–2. In the present context we prefer to use the term "mission" as embodying the objectives and performance as well as the underlying concept—the "domain"—of the organization.

In this view, the mission of the organization is initially determined by

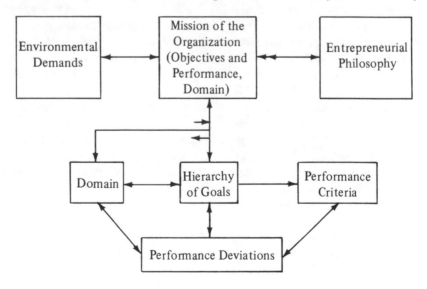

Figure 14–3
The Dynamics of Objectives

environmental demands and entrepreneurial philosophy. As the organization is established the mission is continuously redefined under the impact of interaction between organization and environment. As the mission of the organization gradually becomes institutionalized in the eyes of the interest groups constituting the environment and in the minds of the entrepreneurial spirits at the helm of the organization, the mission begins to change their expectations. Despite this mutual interdependence of the mission and these external and internal interest groups, it seems most realistic to view the mission rather as a passive derivative than as an active agent.[26]

Entrepreneurial philosophy is clearly an important determinant of the mission of the organization, yet it is probably true to say that an indispensable element of a viable entrepreneurial philosophy is a reasonably clear view of environmental demands, and what can be done to satisfy them. Indeed, it may well be that the most successful entrepreneurs are those more adept at crystallizing environmental demands. Furthermore, there is considerable evidence that in selecting successors for top executive positions organizations tend to pick men believed capable of handling the particular type of problem facing the organization at the time. Frequently these problems stem from an imbalance in the relationship of the organization and one or several interest groups in its environment. In comparison with the chief executive, environmental demands have received too little attention in the literature on organizational objectives.

To push the discussion of the mission of the organization a step further, it is necessary to define the notion of "domain." The domain represents the extent of the organization along each of five vital dimensions:

> area (geographical)
> product (service, output)
> functions performed (modus operandi)
> clientele
> time

The reader will find that every organization has a characteristic domain in terms of these dimensions.[27] If we think of the universe as an entity extending to the upper limit of all these dimensions, it becomes natural to view the domain as the *niche* which the organization has carved (or thinks it has carved) out of the total environment. "The establishment of domain cannot be an arbitrary, unilateral action. Only if the organization's claims to domain are recognized by those who can provide the necessary support, by the task environment, can a domain be operational."[28] The (initial) domain of the organization is often at least vaguely expressed in its charter or by-laws.

Generally speaking, however, the domain is not a sufficient expression of the mission of the organization. The domain defines the dimensions of the operation but says little about its expected goals or actual performance (results). We do not feel any obligation to go into the metaphysics of whether organizations can have goals, as long as it is operationally readily established that organizations do set explicit or implicit targets for themselves and frequently take considerable pains to gauge their actual performance vs the planned targets. At the current level of discussion the metaphysical issue seems irrelevant. For reasons indicated earlier (based on management's motivations as an interest group) survival and growth tend to be ultimate objectives for most organizations. Again, these objectives are so broad as to be of little interest as guides to the day-to-day activities of any given organization.

To reach further it is necessary to recognize that every organization operates with a diversified goal structure. As figure 14–3 suggests, the organization has a hierarchy of goals. The general nature of these goals is specified by environmental demands, i.e., by the interest groups upon whom the organization is dependent for continued existence. The specific targets within these goal areas at any given time are also governed by the environment to a large extent, but they are further defined by entrepreneurial philosophy and *perception* of the environment and by the capacities of the organization suggested by its domain. As indicated by figure 14–2, these targets may be in the areas of profitability, sales volume (or market share), customer satisfaction, and productivity (of labor, capital, or any other resource utilized by the organization).[29] In some cases the list of primary goals is considerably longer, and may include employee satisfaction, product leadership, and so on. The point to be emphasized is rather that organizations have multiple goals, in part overlapping and in part mutually conflicting. As Herbert A. Simon and others have pointed out, the set of primary goals tends to be spelled out into second, third, etc. order goals in a pyramid of ends and means.[30] No claim is made that the set of primary goals is identical for all organizations (short of survival and, possibly, growth).

Indeed, the relative emphasis on various elements in the mix of objectives typically changes from time to time *within* any given organization. As an employee of the General Electric Company the writer had reason to observe how the relative emphasis would change from market share in one year to profitability in another, and to product innovation in a third. Anyone who has served as a member of the academic community for the last ten years or more is aware of the increasing prominence of research in most universities, a prominence gained at the relative cost of instructional and public service objectives. The mix also seems to change with the life cycle of the market in which the organization operates. Finally, we have the well-known phenomenon labeled displacement of goals: as the organization realizes an important objective it tends to redefine its mission, acting under the imperative of survival. As polio vaccines were developed, the March of Dimes focused its attention on birth defects. As the members of trade unions in some West European countries obtained what they felt were acceptable standards of well-being and job security, the membership became lethargic. Union leaders responded by shifting the attention to co-determination as a presumed means of promoting the interests of employees—and assuring the survival of unions.

To know whether it is "on target" the organization develops performance criteria and performance measurement systems. In principle, performance criteria for the organization may be logically deduced from its objectives. In practice, to find valid and reliable yardsticks is troublesome indeed. To the extent that the performance criteria do not adequately reflect the nature or relative prominence of each objective, their very existence tends to generate dysfunctional behavior on the part of employees, as demonstrated by Blau and others.[31]

We are now ready to close the loop indicated by the feedback mechanism in figure 14–3. The performance criteria provide the organization with a yardstick with which to measure actual performance deviations from the planned performance implied by the hierarchy of goals. These deviations (positive or negative) will tend to trigger equilibrating changes of two kinds, frequently occurring simultaneously. The first type is a change in behavior on the part of the members of the organization, while the second is a change in aspiration levels among the interest groups exercising a specifying influence on the goals of the organization. The result is a new set of performance levels and/or a new set of goal priorities. While ability to meet environmental demands will ultimately determine the fate of the organization, there is generally much room for entrepreneurial initiative and stimulation in the dynamic process of establishing and reformulating objectives.

It may be observed, finally, that the ecologist may hold the key to the seemingly endless debate about the "social responsibility of the businessman." The rapid rise of not-for-tangible-profit considerations in the last twenty years is largely due to inexorable pressures from interest groups in the environment. In other words, such concerns are increasingly tied in with long-term viability. While it is not necessary to invoke some kind of new Spirit of Altruism, we are naturally not denying that executives, like other humans, may be motivated by compassion and a desire to promote social welfare. Beyond meeting the minimal claims imposed upon them by goal-specifying groups in various performance areas, successful organizations have varying discretionary powers to allocate their surplus resources to these performance areas or to additional causes. In what direction—and how far—they should move would seem to be eminently a policy matter.

The Organization and its Market

In the preceding section the mission of the organization was viewed as dependent primarily on environmental factors, but also on entrepreneurial philosophy (itself in part environmentally conditioned). This was a case of essentially unidirectional causation. To illustrate bilateral interaction between sets of variables in our basic model (figure 14-2), one should preferably focus on the relationship between organization structure and interaction strategy or between interaction strategy and market environment.[32] From the viewpoint of organization theory proper it seems more urgent, however, to outline the relationship between organization structure and market environment. The direction of influence in this case is primarily from market environment to organization structure. The influence of the organization on the environment penetrates via strategy, with organization structure playing mainly a supportive role.[33]

One does not have to go far to find tangible evidence of organizational adjustment to the market environment. The reductions in staff with which many firms meet a business recession furnish a crude example. The size of the organization tends to increase as the clientele grows larger; the post office in a town of 10,000 inhabitants will have several more employees than the office in a community of a thousand souls. As firms engage in international business operations they typically tend to structure by area at a fairly high level of the organization. Where the diversity of customer needs exceeds the range of outputs of the organization, it can accommodate by subcontracting part of the job to other organizations, and so on.

The illustrative sample of variables included in the organization structure and market environment sets in figure 14-2 may be used to formulate a variety of tentative hypotheses concerning environmental conditioning of organization structures. A set of hypotheses of this type is exemplified by figure 14-4. It should be emphasized that each of these hypotheses is surrounded by a great *ceteris paribus caveat*. The set has been selected to include all organizational and environmental variables identified in figure 14-2 and all of the propositions would seem to have at least some common-sense foundation. A word of comment about the several hypotheses may be in order.

Hypothesis 1 seems legitimate in view of the post office example cited above. On a common-sense basis it seems reasonable that a larger market provides more room for the organization to grow, and to prevail upon economies of scale, than a smaller one. Again, the fact that competition may grow even faster than the market suggests the importance of the *ceteris paribus* proviso.

Hypothesis 2 finds support in the territorial organization of the Boy Scouts of America as well as most retail chains.

Hypothesis 3 is supported by the common-sense argument that decen-

Figure 14–4
Illustrative Hypotheses of Environmental and Organizational Variables

1. The greater the size of the environment, the larger the size of the organization.
2. The greater geographical dispersion of the clientele, the stronger the tendency to organize by area.
3. The greater geographical dispersion, the greater the degree of decentralization of the organization.
4. The greater the intensity of competition, the greater the degree of decentralization.
5. The greater the diversity of customer needs, the greater diversification of the organization.
6. The greater the relative power of customers, the stronger the tendency to organize by clientele (rather than area, function, etc.).
7. The greater customer power, the greater the degree of centralization.
8. The greater environmental volatility, the more flexible the organization.
9. The greater volatility, the more decentralization.
10. The later the stage in the market life cycle, the stronger the tendency towards vertical integration in the organization.

tralization in terms of delegation of decision-making authority permits maximal accommodation to local customer needs. This hypothesis seems reasonable especially when customer needs evidence strong local variations.

Hypothesis 4 is perhaps the most controversial among those stated. Some writers claim that greater competition calls forth greater centralization. It may well be that the influence of competition is curvilinear. Where there is very little competition other variables are probably of greater importance in affecting the locus of decision-making authority. Beyond a certain threshold competition will encourage decentralization, but only as long as the viability of the organization is not an issue. When competition reaches such an intensity as to threaten survival, organizations may well resort to greater centralization.

Hypothesis 5 seems intuitively reasonable, whether one has diverse functions or diverse products in mind. The greater demand among appliance customers for service, parts, and technical advice has forced both manufacturers and their local representatives to adopt new organizational arrangements to handle these functions. Consumers at shopping centers evidence a manifest or latent demand for a wide variety of goods. This has led to "scrambled merchandising"—the tendency of supermarkets, drugstores, and other outlets to diversify their assortment far beyond their traditional confines.

Hypothesis 6 finds empirical support in the electrical manufacturing industry. The power of the public utility customers looms large in General

Electric and Westinghouse. While the marketing functions of these electrical giants have gone through many a transformation, a specially designated organization has always catered to the utility industry. While presumably a great deal larger than that of the utilities, the power of family consumers is diffused. The electrical manufacturers tend to handle customer distribution by product lines or by territory rather than by consumer category.

Hypothesis 7 is at least tangentially supported by the fact that many otherwise decentralized marketing organizations insist on centralized handling of so-called national accounts. Additional tangential support is found in the "hot line" for direct contact between the chief executives of the United States and the Soviet Union.

Hypothesis 8 is supported by innumerable accounts of events on battlefields around the world. In the heat of battle, neatly defined organizational lines, formal ranks, and functional assignments are frequently drastically rearranged, or at times abandoned outright in the interest of survival.

Hypothesis 9 finds at least a measure of support in W. R. Dill's study of environment as an influence on managerial autonomy in two Norwegian firms.[34] Dill found that the key men in the firm operating in the more volatile environment "perceived for themselves a greater degree of autonomy" than the key men in the firm operating in a traditionally more stable environment.

Hypothesis 10 is supported by evidence from a number of major appliance markets which have reached the maturity phase (e.g., refrigerators, washing machines). In these markets manufacturers have tended to integrate forwards as regards service and physical distribution, occasionally even establishing their own captive sales organization. Conversely, large-scale retailers in these markets tend to integrate backwards towards manufacturing or, at least, towards the marketing of their own private brands.

It should again be emphasized that throughout this section we have had in mind primarily that part of the organization which engages in direct interaction with the consumer market environment.

Organizational Ecology: A Trial Balance

That organizations and environments interact cannot be doubted. Isolated and, on the whole, surprisingly modest attempts in various disciplines to explain such interaction have not been strikingly successful. We think the ecological approach to organization study has promise for three main reasons. Ecological analysis has been applied in biology and in urban studies to situations in many respects analogous to that of the organization in its setting. Biologists and students of "human ecology" are sufficiently encouraged by past results to continue the exploration of this avenue.

The ecological viewpoint has the merit that it is inherently applicable to any and all types of organizations. Its applicability is not limited to any given level of organization. Thus, it may be extended to embrace what Wroe Alderson termed behavior systems, comprising the entire chain of inter-linked organizations from mine to consumer, and the relations between parallel systems. Biologists have made observations concerning food chains and dominant species in plant and animal communities, insights which may prove quite helpful in the analysis of manufacturer-distributor interaction in vertical channel systems, federal-state relations in public administration, etc.

Ecology is inherently trans-disciplinary and suggestive of a multi-disciplinary synthesis in organization theory. Specialization is presumably a virtue in organization study as well as of organization itself. But without integrative themes such as that provided by ecology, we are running the risk of getting few of the benefits of specialization and many of the disadvantages of fragmentation. Tendencies in this direction are observable in all the social sciences. Indeed, this is only natural, in view of the fact that organization theory itself cuts across traditional disciplines.

It is important to emphasize, however, that ecologic organization theory should not be expected to yield a recipe for the "one best" organization (or interaction strategy, or set of objectives) in any given environmental context. In the introductory section of this paper half a dozen reasons were given for what might be called "environmental relativism." Aspirations must be set at a fairly modest level of probabilistic prediction. One may envisage that some day we will be able to make statements of this type: "Given certain environmental conditions—and holding other factors constant (such as objectives and strategy)—an organization of type A will be more viable than one of type B, which in turn will be more viable than one of type C. Organizations of types D and E would probably not survive in the long run under the environmental conditions postulated."

There are several other limitations of the ecological approach in organization theory. While holistic, it cannot pretend to be universal in the sense of including "everything" about organizations and their environments. Ecology is riddled with assumptions of all other things being equal. Even establishing the interface between organization and environment is sometimes a difficult problem, not made any easier by the rich opportunities available to contract out various functions to other organizations or by the recent trend towards diversification noticeable in both the business and "multiversity" communities, a development which constantly brings the organization (or parts thereof) into contact with new environments.

Another difficulty is caused by *time*. The very concept of interaction is dynamic. So is the notion of the market life cycle as well as the idea of time lags as modulating the effect of most variables. But it must be admitted that the ecological approach in and of itself has little to say about the specifics of time or timing in organization-environment relations. Yet the influence of these factors is likely to be crucial to the efficacy of strategy and, indeed, to organizational survival. It is possible that longitudinal studies of eco-systems and research on market life cycles will help us come to grips with the dynamics of interaction.

One problem which at first sight seems formidable indeed is quasi-methodological in nature, namely, to find suitable empirical yardsticks for ecosystem variables. While not for a moment wishing to belittle the issues involved, one may be fairly optimistic about the ability of organization ecologists to find suitable operational measures. It is true that there are no self-evident or universally accepted measures for almost any of the vari-ables which we have named by way of example. But for most of them, operational substitutes and proxies have been used in many studies which were not ecological in character. Behavioral science has several useful measures of "size" and "centralization" in organizations, economics of "price," "competition," and "productivity." Geographers and location theorists have widely-used measures of "spatial dispersion," and so on. Admittedly, the problem of standardization remains, but this question organization ecology has in common with most established approaches to research on organizations. Indeed, it may well be that ecologists will be able to render a valuable contribution to such related approaches by push-ing further the development of standard measures and by assisting in the identification of suitable settings for their use. More importantly, however, it is hoped that this paper makes legitimate the prediction that in moving towards a science of organization one of our central concerns will be the organization-environment interaction process and its determinants.

NOTES AND REFERENCES

1. The first paragraph from Thorelli, Hans B., "Ecology in Marketing," *Southern Journal of Business,* October, 1967, pp.19–25 (originally in Kelley, Eugene, and William Lazer, *Managerial Marketing: Perspectives and View-points,* Third Edition (Homewood, Ill.: R. D. Irwin, Inc., 1967). While hope-fully going beyond the author's previous writings in the field, this essay draws freely on the article cited and the following items: "The Political Economy of the Firm—Basis for a New Theory of Competition?", paper delivered at the annual meeting of the Schweizerische Gesellschaft für Volkswirtschaft und Statistik, St. Gallen, May, 1965, and printed in *Schweizerische Zeitschrift für Volkswirtschaft und Statistik,* Vol. 101, 1965, pp.248–62; "The Multi-National Corporation As a Change Agent," *Southern Journal of Business,* July, 1966, pp.1–11; "Political Science and Marketing," in *Theory in Marketing,* Cox, Reavis, Wroe Alderson, and S. J. Shapiro, editors (Second series, prepared under the auspices of American Marketing Association; Homewood, Ill.: R. D. Irwin, Inc., 1964) pp.125–139. To avoid tedious repetition, no further ref-erence will be made to these articles.

2. Odum, Eugene P., *Fundamentals of Ecology* (Philadelphia: W. B. Saunders, 1959) p.147. A further reason why organization theorists should not uncritically adopt the entire apparatus of biological ecology (while in many respects we are likely to push considerably beyond it) is that in biology ecological inquiry is still a highly developmental area. Terminology is by no means unambiguous (e.g., population density, succession) and some older notions in the field are now quite controversial (climax community, limiting factor).

As might be expected, biological ecologists have found it natural to make use of concepts commonly found in organization literature. Thus Clarke speaks of "division of labor," "leadership," and "coordination" among certain groups of animals. Clarke, George L., *Elements of Ecology* (New York: Wiley, 1954).

3. Spurr, Stephen H., *Forest Ecology* (New York: Ronald, 1964), p.13.

4. Martindale, Don, editor, *Functionalism in the Social Sciences* (Philadelphia: American Academy of Political and Social Science, 1965), *passim*.

5. Using E. P. Odum's terminology we might say that the organization and the environment often have broad mutual *tolerance limits*.

6. Thompson, James D., *Organizations in Action* (New York: McGraw-Hill, 1967), pp.20–23.

7. At this very general level of discussion there appears to be little need to take sides in the classical controversy among political scientists concerning the meaning of "interest."

8. The question whether it is financial rewards, a desire for power or personal acclaim or prestige, or sheer pride in professional workmanship that primarily motivates managers need not be resolved for purposes of the present discussion, as each and all of these incentives will tend to call forth a substantial measure of identification with the progress of the institution by which the manager is employed.

9. The question is whether it is the environment as perceived by the actors in the situation or as it "actually" manifests itself by objective measurement that counts. Most likely, people's perception of the facts counts most heavily in the short run, while in the long run no one can "fly in the face of the (real) facts." Note, however, that in the meantime our misconceptions of the facts may have caused us to act in ways which will result in a set of "real" facts somewhat different from that which would have resulted if our action had been based on perfect perception of the environment and our own situation in it.

10. Note, too, that *potential* influence and potential interaction may be as relevant as actual, as witnessed by the prominent place of potential competition in the past eighty years of antitrust discussion in the United States.

11. Ultimately, organizational ecology should take into account the interaction between these various input and output markets (e.g., in the form of commercial reciprocity), although this level of sophistication seems a bit distant at this time.

12. Odum, *op. cit.*, p.5.

13. While it might be more convenient to say "the intra-organizational environment," this would really be a contradiction in terms.

300 ORGANIZATION & INTERORGANIZATION SSP

14. In a study of inter-divisional transactions in a corporation or of the scramble among divisions (bureaus) for a greater share of total corporate (governmental) resources, the auto-setting becomes an integrated part of the task environment.

15. In biology the term habitat is generally restricted to the physical location at which the organism, population, or community is domiciled.

16. Odum, *op. cit.*, p.6.

17. Cf. Odum, *op. cit.*, p.7.

18. See, for example, Farmer, Richard N., and Barry M. Richman, *Comparative Management and Economic Progress* (Homewood, Ill.: Richard D. Irwin, 1965), especially Chapter 3. Cf. Udy, Stanley H., Jr., *Organization of Work—A Comparative Analysis of Production among Nonindustrial Peoples* (New Haven: HRAF Press, 1959) and Riggs, F. W., *The Ecology of Public Administration* (Bombay: Asia Publishing House, 1961).

19. Cf. Herring, E. Pendleton, *Public Administration and the Public Interest* (New York: McGraw-Hill, 1936), Palamountain, Joseph C., *The Politics of Distribution* (Cambridge: Harvard University Press, 1955).

20. An ecological approach of promise focuses on the process of environmental interaction by analyzing the determinants of when, and on what terms, transactions will take place.

21. Even in the case of the neighborhood boy scout league it is far from clear whether the prime clientele is the boys or their parents, who get relieved of some chores and pay the bills. Admittedly, identifying the customer, in the sense of the final decision-maker in the buying process, will also involve problems from time to time in a business situation.

22. As long as we are only in the takeoff stage of organizational ecology, behavioral variables on the inside of the organization may perhaps be disregarded except insofar as they are reflected in structure or in organization-environment interaction (which, of course, includes external aspects of organization behavior). That it would be fairly simple to include interpersonal behavior inside the organization in our basic ecological model is suggested by Stogdill, Ralph, "Basic Concepts for a Theory of Organization," *Management Science,* June. 1967, pp.B666–B676.

23. From an *institutional* point of view, independent channels are part of the market environment.

24. Chandler, A. D., Jr., *Strategy and Structure—Chapters in the History of the Industrial Enterprise* (Cambridge: M.I.T. Press, 1962), p.14.

25. As many writers have observed there are also trade-off relationships between structure and strategy. To increase sales we can cut price but we may alternatively increase our promotional effort by expanding our sales organization.

26. This is suggested by the double arrows emanating from environmental demands and entrepreneurial philosophy in fig. 14–3.

27. Cf. Thorelli, H. B., and R. L. Graves, *International Operations Simulation, With Comments on Design and Use of Management Games* (New York: Free Press-Macmillan, 1964), p.35f.

28. Thompson, *op. cit.*, p.28. While Thompson's notion of domain is narrower than ours, the quoted passage applies with equal force here. We may

note in passing that one of the variables in the organization structure set (fig. 14–2) reflects the fact that the organization will tend to emphasize at least one of the dimensions of its domain in its structure.

29. While these terms are broadly suggestive of business organizations, analogous goals are encountered in non-business contexts.

30. In the classical economic theory of the firm, profit maximization is a superordinate goal in relation to which any others are secondary or incidental. From the viewpoint of ecological pluralism there is no reason to ascribe such preeminence to any single objective (unless it be one whose preeminence seems legitimate to all of the more powerful interest groups), except possibly survival. As we have said elsewhere, the modern corporation is not in business to earn profits, but it earns profits to stay in business.

31. Blau, P. M., *The Dynamics of Bureaucracy* (Chicago: University of Chicago Press, 1955). In such instances the one-way arrow between "hierarchy of goals" and "performance criteria" in fig. 14–3 should be made two-way.

32. Using a less explicit hypothesis structure than that developed in this section, the author analyzed one important type of interaction process between market environment and interaction strategy, in Thorelli, H. B., "Marketing Strategy Over the Market Life Cycle," *Bulletin of the Bureau of Market Research* (Pretoria: University of South Africa, Fall, 1967).

33. Henry Ford reshaped the auto market by means of the model T, which was a strategic concept. The organization of the Ford Motor Company was in turn adapted to the mass distribution and production strategy.

34. Dill, W. R., "Environment as an Influence on Managerial Autonomy," *Administrative Science Quarterly* (1957–58), pp.409–443.

SELECT BIBLIOGRAPHY

In general, books or articles referred to in individual essays of this volume are not again listed here. In the case of standard reference works in the ssp area there is inevitably some duplication.

Adams, Walter, ed. *The Structure of American Industry.* Revised edition, New York: The Macmillan Co., 1976.

Ansoff, H. Igor, ed. *Business Strategy.* Baltimore and Harmondsworth, England: Penguin Books, 1969.

Ansoff, H. Igor. *Corporate Strategy.* New York: McGraw-Hill, 1965.

Bain, Joe S. *Industrial Organization.* Second edition. New York: Wiley, 1968.

Baumol, William J. *Business Behavior, Value and Growth.* Revised edition, New York: Harcourt, Brace & World, 1967.

Berg, Norman. "Strategic Planning in Conglomerate Companies," *Harvard Business Review,* May–June 1965, pp.79–92.

Berle, Adolf A., and Means, Gardiner C. *The Modern Corporation and Private Property.* Revised edition, New York: Harcourt, Brace & World, 1967.

Blau, Peter M. *The Dynamics of Bureaucracy.* Revised edition, Chicago: University of Chicago Press, 1963.

Boston Consulting Group, Inc. *Perspectives on Experience.* Boston: Boston Consulting Group, 1970.

Bucklin, Louis P., ed. *Vertical Marketing Systems.* Glenview, Ill.: Scott, Foresman & Co., 1970.

Burns, Tom, and Stalker, Gerald. *The Management of Innovation.* London: Tavistock, 1961.

Buzzell, Robert D.; Salmon, W. J.; and Vancil, R. F. *Product Profitability Measurement and Merchandising Decisions.* Boston: Graduate School of Business Administration, Harvard University, 1965.

Chamberlain, Neil W. *Enterprise and Environment.* New York: McGraw-Hill, 1968.

Chandler, Alfred D., Jr. *Strategy and Structure.* Garden City, N.Y.: Doubleday, 1966.

Channon, Derek F. *The Strategy and Structure of British Enterprise.* Boston: Graduate School of Business Administration, Harvard University, 1973.

Chevalier, Michel. "The Strategy Spectre Behind Your Market Share," *European Business,* No. 34, Summer 1972, pp.63–72.

Child, John. "Managerial and Organizational Factors Associated with Company Performance. Part II. A Contingency Analysis," *Journal of Management Studies,* Vol. 12, February 1975, pp.12–27.

Child, John. "Organizational Structure, Environment and Performance: The Role of Strategic Choice," *Sociology,* Vol. 6, 1972, pp.1–22.

Clark, John Maurice. *Studies in the Economics of Overhead Costs.* Chicago: University of Chicago Press, 1947.

Collins, Norman R., and Preston, Lee E. *Concentration and Price-Cost Margins in Manufacturing Industries*. Berkeley: University of California Press, 1968.

Cyert, Richard M., and March, J. G. *A Behavioral Theory of the Firm*. Englewood Cliffs, N.J.: Prentice-Hall, 1963.

Dahmen, Erik. *Entrepreneurial Activity and the Development of Swedish Industry, 1919–1939*. Publ. for the American Economic Association, Homewood, Ill.: Irwin, 1970.

Dalton, Melville. *Men Who Manage*. New York: Wiley, 1959.

Dean, Joel. *Managerial Economics*. New York: Prentice-Hall, 1964.

Douglas, Edna. *Economics of Marketing*. New York: Harper & Row, 1975.

Duer, Beverley C. *Classifying Businesses by Sensitivity of Return on Investment to Profit Influences*. Technical Report on PIMS, MSI No. 75–108. Cambridge, Mass.: Marketing Science Institute, 1975.

Duncan, Robert B. "Characteristics of Organizational Environments and Perceived Environmental Uncertainty," *Administrative Science Quarterly*, Vol. 17, 1972, pp.313–27.

Dyas, G. P., and Thanheiser, H. T. *The Emerging European Enterprise—Strategy and Structure in French and German Industry*. New York: Macmillan, 1976.

Edwards, Corwin D. *Maintaining Competition*. New York: McGraw-Hill, 1964.

Emery, Fred E., and Trist, Eric L. "The Causal Texture of Organizational Environments," *Human Relations*, Vol. 18, 1965, pp.21–32.

Fog, Bjarke. *Industrial Pricing Policies*. Amsterdam: North-Holland, 1960.

Grossack, Irvin M., and Martin, David D. *Managerial Economics: Microtheory and the Firm's Decisions*. Boston: Little, Brown & Co., 1973.

Gulick, Luther, and Urwick, Lyndal, eds. *Papers on the Science of Administration*. New York: Institute of Public Administration, 1937.

Hall, Richard H. *Organizations: Structure and Process*. Englewood Cliffs, N.J.: Prentice-Hall, 1972.

Heflebower, Richard B. "Full Costs, Cost Changes, and Prices." In National Bureau of Economic Research, *Business Concentration and Price Policy*. Princeton: Princeton University Press, 1955.

Hofer, Charles W. "Toward a Contingency Theory of Business Strategy," *Academy of Management Journal*, Vol. 18, December 1975, pp.784–810.

Kaplan, A. D. H.; Dirlam, J. G.; and Lanzillotti, R. F. *Pricing in Big Business: A Case Approach*. Washington: Brookings, 1958.

Kaysen, Carl, and Turner, Donald F. *Antitrust Policy*. Cambridge, Mass.: Harvard University Press, 1959.

Kotler, Philip. *Marketing Management*. Third edition, Englewood Cliffs, N.J.: Prentice-Hall, 1976.

Lawrence, Paul R., and Lorsch, Jay W. *Organization and Environment*. Homewood, Ill.: Irwin, 1969.

Leavitt, Harold J.; Pinfield, L.; and Webb, E. *Organizations of the Future; Interaction with the External Environment*. New York: Praeger, 1974.

Levins, Richard. *Evolution in Changing Environments*. Princeton: Princeton University Press, 1968.

March, James G. *Handbook of Organizations.* Chicago: Rand McNally & Co., 1965.

March, James G., and Simon, Herbert A. *Organizations.* New York: Wiley, 1958.

Markham, Jessie W., and Papanek, G. F. *Industrial Organization and Economic Development: Essays in Honor of Edward S. Mason.* New York: Houghton Mifflin, 1970.

Miles, R. E.; Snow, C. C.; and Pfeffer, J. "Organization-Environment: Concepts and Issues," *Industrial Relations,* Vol. 13, October 1974, pp.244–64.

Negandhi, Anant R., ed. *Modern Organizational Theory.* Kent, Ohio: Kent State University, 1973.

Odum, Eugene P. *Fundamentals of Ecology.* Philadelphia: W. B. Saunders, 1959.

Penrose, Edith T. *The Theory of Growth of the Firm.* Oxford: Blackwell, 1959.

Perrow, Charles. "The Analysis of Goals in Complex Organizations," *American Sociological Review,* Vol. 26, No. 6, December 1961, pp.854–66.

Phillips, Almarin. *Market Structure, Organization and Performance.* Cambridge, Mass.: Harvard University Press, 1962.

Porter, Michael E. "Retailer Power, Manufacturer Strategy and Performance in Consumer Goods Industries." Doctoral Dissertation, Graduate School of Business Administration, Harvard University, 1973.

Profit Impact of Market Strategy (PIMS), see Duer, Beverley C., and Schoeffler, Sidney.

Pugh, Derek S., et al. "The Context of Organization Structures," *Administrative Science Quarterly,* Vol. 14, March 1969, pp.91–114.

Rhenman, Eric. *Organization Theory for Long-Range Planning.* New York: Wiley, 1972.

Rice, A. Kenneth. *The Enterprise and Its Environment.* London: Tavistock, 1963.

Rumelt, Richard P. *Strategy, Structure and Economic Performance.* Boston: Graduate School of Business Administration, Harvard University, 1974.

Scherer, F. M. *Industrial Market Structure and Economic Performance.* Chicago: Rand McNally, 1970.

Schoeffler, Sidney, and Nowill, Paul. *How to Revive the Golden Goose.* Working Paper on PIMS, Cambridge, Mass.: Marketing Science Institute, 1974.

Schollhammer, Hans. "Organization Structures of Multinational Corporations," *Academy of Management Journal,* Vol. 14, 1971, pp.345–65.

Schumpeter, Joseph A. *Capitalism, Socialism, and Democracy.* New York: Harper, 1942.

Scott, Bruce R. "The Industrial State: Old Myths and New Realities," *Harvard Business Review,* Vol. 51, No. 2, March–April 1973, pp.133–48.

Simon, Sanford R. *Managing Marketing Profitability.* New York: American Marketing Association, 1969.

Solomons, David. *Divisional Performance: Measurement and Control.* New York: Financial Executives Research Foundation, 1965.

Starbuck, William H. *Organizations and Their Environments.* Berlin: International Institute of Management, 1973. (Also in Dunnette, M. D., ed.

Handbook of Industrial and Organizational Psychology. Chicago: Rand McNally, 1973.)

Starbuck, William H., ed. *The Handbook of Organizational Design.* Three volumes, Amsterdam: Elsevier Scientific Publishing Co., 1977 and 1978.

Stigler, George J. *The Organization of Industry.* Homewood, Ill.: Irwin, 1968.

Thompson, James D., ed. *Approaches to Organizational Design.* Pittsburgh: University of Pittsburgh Press, 1966.

Thompson, James D. *Organizations in Action.* New York: McGraw-Hill, 1967.

Thorelli, Hans B., ed. *International Marketing Strategy.* Baltimore and Harmondsworth, England: Penguin Books, 1973.

Thorelli, Hans B. "Market Strategy Over the Market Life Cycle," *Bulletin of the Bureau of Market Research,* University of South Africa, September 1967, pp.10–22.

Udy, Stanley H., Jr. *Organization of Work: A Comparative Analysis of Production among Nonindustrial Peoples.* New Haven, Conn.: HRAF Press, 1959.

U.S. National Commission on Food Marketing. *Special Studies in Food Marketing.* Ten volumes, Washington: Government Printing Office, 1966.

U.S. Temporary National Economic Committee. *Monographs and Hearings.* Thirty volumes, Washington: Government Printing Office, 1939–41.

Van Horne, James C. *Financial Management and Policy.* Second edition, Englewood Cliffs, N.J.: Prentice-Hall, 1971.

Vernon, John M. *Market Structure and Industrial Performance: A Review of Statistical Findings.* Boston: Allyn and Bacon, 1972.

Wilcox, Clair, and Shepherd, William G. *Public Policies Toward Business.* Fifth edition, Homewood, Ill.: Irwin, 1975.

Williamson, Oliver E. *Corporate Control and Business Behavior: An Inquiry into the Effects of Organizational Form on Enterprise Behavior.* Englewood Cliffs, N.J.: Prentice-Hall, 1970.

Woodward, Joan. *Industrial Organization: Theory and Practice.* London: Oxford University Press, 1965.

H. Igor Ansoff, Justin Potter Professor of Management, Graduate School of Management, Vanderbilt University, Nashville, Tennessee

Johan Arndt, Professor of Business Administration and Chairman, Department of Marketing, Norwegian School of Economics and Business Administration, Bergen

Frank M. Bass, Loeb Distinguished Professor of Management, Krannert Graduate School of Industrial Administration, Purdue University, Lafayette, Indiana

Albert D. Bates, Assistant Professor of Marketing, Graduate School of Business Administration, University of Colorado, Boulder

Louis P. Bucklin, Professor of Business Administration and Director, Ph.D. Program, Graduate School of Business Administration, University of California, Berkeley

Willard H. Burnap, Vice-Chairman and Director, Continental Oil Company, Houston, Texas

Robert D. Buzzell, Professor of Business Administration and Chairman, Marketing Area, Graduate School of Business Administration, Harvard University

Phillippe J. Cattin, Visiting Assistant Professor of Marketing, School of Business Administration, Univerity of California, Berkeley

William E. Cox, Jr., Professor of Marketing and Management and Head of Marketing, School of Management, Case Western Reserve University, Cleveland, Ohio

Paul W. Farris, Assistant Professor of Marketing, Graduate School of Business Administration, Harvard University

Paul J. Gordon, Professor of Management, Graduate School of Business, Indiana University, Bloomington

Bo L. T. Hedberg, Associate Professor of Business Administration, School of Business Administration, University of Gothenburg, Sweden

E. W. Kelley, President and Chief Executive Officer, Fairmont Foods Company, New York and Houston, Texas

Bert C. McCammon, Jr., Professor of Business Administration, College of Business Administration, University of Oklahoma, Norman

Joseph C. Miller, Associate Professor of Marketing, Graduate School of Business, Indiana University, Bloomington

James M. Patterson, Professor of Marketing and Chairman, Marketing Department, Graduate School of Business, Indiana University, Bloomington

Johannes M. Pennings, Assistant Professor of Industrial Administration and Sociology, Graduate School of Industrial Administration, Carnegie-Mellon University, Pittsburgh, Pennsylvania

Lee E. Preston, Melvin H. Baker Professor of American Enterprise and Chairman, Department of Environmental Analysis and Policy, School of Management, State University of New York at Buffalo as well as Director, Center for Policy Studies of the University

F. M. Scherer, Professor of Economics, Northwestern University, Evanston, Illinois (at time of conference: Director, Bureau of Economics, Federal Trade Commission, Washington, D.C.)

Sidney Schoeffler, Ph.D., Director, PIMS Program and Executive Secretary, Strategic Planning Institute, Cambridge, Massachusetts

William H. Starbuck, Helfaer Professor of Business Administration, Graduate School of Business, University of Wisconsin-Milwaukee

Hans B. Thorelli, E. W. Kelley Professor of Business Administration, Graduate School of Business, Indiana University, Bloomington

Dick R. Wittink, Assistant Professor of Business Administration, Graduate School of Business, Stanford University, Stanford, California

INDEX

In many essays an index word may be found on several consecutive or intermittent pages. In such cases, the index generally cites only the first of these pages.